THE COMPLETE BOOK OF

CHRIS BENTLEY

CARLTON BOOKS

The author would like to acknowledge the invaluable assistance provided by the following people:
Gerry Anderson, Mary Anderson, Nick Austin, Peter Bailey, Bob Bell, Ed Bishop, Stephen Brown,
Ian Boyce, Terry Curtis, Len Davies, Andrew Dawson, Leo Eaton, Gary Files, Andrew Frampton,
Martin Gainsford, Cy Grant, Barlie Kidwell, Chris King, Jan King, David Lane,
Lesley Levene, David McLaughlin, Francis Matthews, Elizabeth Morgan, John Needham,
Mike Noble, Alan Perry, Andrew Pixley, Russell Porter, Robin Quinn, Mel Rowlands,
Lorna Russell, Alan Shubrook, Lynn Simpson, Penny Simpson, Jeff Smart,
Charles Tingwell, Mike Trim, Ken Turner, Rowena White, John Wilkinson,
Nick Williams, Keith Wilson, Jaz Wiseman, Peter Wragg, Carol Wright
and, above all, my mother Joan Bentley.
Without their help, this book would not have been possible.

This book is dedicated to everyone at Century 21 who was involved in bringing
CAPTAIN SCARLET AND THE MYSTERONS to the screen.

FANDERSON is the Official Appreciation Society for the film and television productions
of Gerry Anderson. For further information and a membership application form, please write
(enclosing a stamped self-addressed envelope) to:
FANDERSON, P.O. Box 10, Bradford, West Yorkshire BD10 0YE
or visit the Fanderson website at www.fanderson.org.uk

This is a Carlton book

Published by Carlton Books Limited 2001
20 Mortimer Street
London W1N 7RD

A CIP catalogue for this book is available from the British Library

ISBN 1 84222 405 0

Project Editor: Lesley Levene
Design: Advantage
Production: Janette Davis

CONTENTS

FOREWORD

Many people describe the CAPTAIN SCARLET series as dark. When it was made in 1967 a dark series was the last thing I intended to achieve, but in retrospect I can understand how the show turned out that way. You see, CAPTAIN SCARLET is about a war – a very unusual war, but a war none the less.

During our preparation for the production of the series there was speculation about the possibility of life existing on Mars. Dark lines across the planet's surface were thought by some to be canals made by intelligent beings. Now, of course, we know it is unlikely that the Red Planet can support any form of life – that is, 'life as we know it'.

'Life as we know it' is a much used science-fiction term and I remember thinking that if we turned it round into 'life as we *don't* know it', this could become the embryo of a new series format. It was this notion that triggered the idea of the Mysterons being an intelligent life form on Mars. So far so good, but why couldn't we see these aliens and their cities through our telescopes? Because they were invisible, of course.

In order to make the stories exciting, I decided that the Mysterons should attack Earth. But why would they do that? Bit by bit, it was all coming together.

A paramilitary force would have to be formed to defend Earth against alien incursion. An unusual name for the hero would be Captain Scarlet. Yes, Captain Scarlet, that sounded good to me. Other people in this organization could also have colours for names, and it followed, of course, that if you put all the colours of the spectrum together you got white. The boss man would be a colonel, Colonel White, and Spectrum would be the ideal name for the organization.

All that remained now was to trigger an invasion of Earth by the Mysterons. So, in the first episode, Spectrum would send a reconnaissance unit to Mars to investigate the mystery of radio signals coming from there. The Mysterons wanted to greet their visitors from Earth, but they were misunderstood by Spectrum, who opened fire on their city. The Mysterons swore they would take revenge for what they saw as an unprovoked attack and so began a war of nerves, making this the most unusual war story of all time…

And yes…CAPTAIN SCARLET is a dark series!

The Complete Book of CAPTAIN SCARLET has been written by Chris Bentley. Chris is the chairman of Fanderson, the Gerry Anderson appreciation society, and one of the country's foremost experts on CAPTAIN SCARLET.

If you enjoy CAPTAIN SCARLET, I'm sure you will enjoy this book. And if you enjoy this book, you will enjoy the television series all the more.

Spectrum is Green!

Gerry Anderson MBE
24 May 2001

MT1. <u>C.U. CAPTAIN SCARLET</u>

We are looking at him through a glass panel, on which is etched a printed circuit in silver and gold. The set-up symbolizes a mechanical man. He is rigid, without a trace of movement.

Over the shot is SUPERIMPOSED 'STARRING CAPTAIN SCARLET'.

After a moment, a projected title slides across his face, following its contours. It reads – 'THE MYSTERONS'.

MYSTERON (V.O.): (Radio Treatment) This is the voice of the Mysterons.

STACCATO CUT TO:

MT2. <u>INT. COCKPIT. ANGEL 1 (JET AIRCRAFT)</u>

C.U. DESTINY ANGEL: she is wearing flying helmet and suit. She looks thoughtfully into camera. The projected title 'THE MYSTERONS' slides over her helmet, following its contours.

SUPERIMPOSED CAPTION – 'AND DESTINY ANGEL'.

MYSTERON (V.O.): (Radio Treatment) We know that you can hear us, Earthmen.

STACCATO CUT TO:

MT3. <u>INT. SPECTRUM CONTROL (CLOUD BASE)</u>

M.S. COLONEL WHITE (LT. GREEN to one side in the background): through a loudspeaker voice in the foreground we hear the voice of the MYSTERON. The projected image of the title 'THE MYSTERONS' slides across his desk in the foreground.

SUPERIMPOSED CAPTION – 'COLONEL WHITE' (70%) 'LT. GREEN' (30%).

MYSTERON (V.O.): We are transmitting on all your radio and television frequencies.

STACCATO CUT TO:

MT4. <u>INT. AMBER ROOM</u>

Four shot: RHAPSODY, HARMONY, MELODY and SYMPHONY ANGEL. They are in relaxed positions. In the centre of the room on a table is a Zenith type transistor radio.

CAPTION OVER – 'AND INTRODUCING – RHAPSODY, HARMONY, MELODY and SYMPHONY ANGEL'.

The projected image of the title 'THE MYSTERONS' slides across the floor of the room.

MYSTERON (V.O.): Our first act of retaliation will be to assassinate your World President.

STACCATO CUT TO:

MT5. <u>M.S. WORLD PRESIDENT</u>

He is sitting at an imposing ornate desk.

CAPTION OVER – 'GUEST STAR PATRICK MCGOOHAN in the role of World President'.

CAPTION FADES OUT as projected image of 'THE MYSTERONS' title slides on to his face and stops there, thus marking this week's victim. Camera zooms in to C.U.

MYSTERON (V.O.): I repeat – our first act of retaliation will be to assassinate your World President.

STACCATO CUT TO:

MT6. <u>L.S. CAPTAIN BLACK</u>

He is standing in front of a wrought-iron gate – mist is swirling at his feet. Through a grey haze in the background and through the gate we can see one or two distant gravestones.

CAPTION OVER – 'MYSTERON AGENT – CAPTAIN BLACK'.

There is a terrifying chord on the music. In time with the same drumbeats that accompany the staccato cuts, we now cut beat by beat into a series of ever-closer shots until the screen is filled with CAPTAIN BLACK's black uniform and is therefore black.

Main Title Sequence from 'The Mysterons',
a television pilot script by Gerry and Sylvia Anderson,
August 1966

THE MAKING OF
CAPTAIN SCARLET
AND THE MYSTERONS

BEFORE CAPTAIN SCARLET

During the long, hot summer of 1966, it seemed that nothing could go wrong for the AP Films marionation mini-Hollywood established by producer Gerry Anderson on the Slough Trading Estate. The first twenty-six-episode season of the company's television series THUNDERBIRDS had completed its initial broadcast on ATV Midlands at the end of March and proved immensely popular with both children and adults. A repeat run of the series was scheduled to begin screening at the end of September, building up to the cinema opening of the first THUNDERBIRDS feature film, *Thunderbirds Are Go* (1966), in time for Christmas.

Merchandisers were lining up for licences to produce THUNDERBIRDS-related toys, games and books to have them ready in time for the 'THUNDERBIRDS Christmas' and, in recognition of THUNDERBIRDS' financial and artistic success, Gerry Anderson was awarded the silver medal for 'Outstanding Artistic Achievement' by the Royal Television Society. Further recognition for his contributions to television came when he was also made an Honorary Fellow of the British Kinematograph Sound and Television Society.

So it was that, with everything set to continue filming a second season of THUNDERBIRDS episodes for the next ten months, the AP Films team was dealt a savage blow when Anderson was called to a meeting with ITC financier Lew Grade.

'All our planning was geared towards a second series of THUNDERBIRDS and that it would continue for a long time,' remembers Anderson. 'It was only when I went to see Lew Grade during filming of those last six episodes that he shook me by saying that he really wanted

International Rescue come to the aid of the personnel of the drilling rig Seascape in the second-season THUNDERBIRDS episode **Atlantic Inferno.**

something else. This came as a serious blow to the organization. I was absolutely shattered. At that time, we had two studios, a weekly comic, a record company and a whole merchandising operation. We had just opened an office in Hong Kong and ordered a million pounds' worth of machine tools, all based on the success of THUNDERBIRDS – and the series was cancelled. When the trade heard that we were not going to be making any more THUNDERBIRDS, people started cancelling orders and the whole thing went down the drain.

'What happened was that Lew couldn't get a sale for the series in America. I have never been involved in the sale of the programmes and, therefore, I don't know the whole story, but Lew went to America and came back with two of the three networks having made an offer for it. When he got back to London Airport, he was tannoyed and when he went to the telephone it was the other network saying that they wanted to bid for it as well. Unfortunately, the deal fell through and I can only speculate why: whether Lew asked too much or whether the network had second thoughts, I don't know the reason. But when that one network dropped out of the bidding, panic set in with the other two and they began asking, "I wonder why they've dropped out?" and so on. It was tragic. We couldn't get an American sale with THUNDERBIRDS, so it was cancelled and we had to do something new.'

That 'something new' was CAPTAIN SCARLET AND THE MYSTERONS.

AP Films had been formed some ten years beforehand, early in 1957, by twenty-eight-year-old film editor Gerry Anderson and his business partner, cameraman Arthur Provis. For Anderson, this was the realization of a long-held dream to form his own film production company making major motion pictures, but fate played a surprising trick on the young film-maker – one that was totally unforeseen but was to ensure his recognition as one of the British film industry's most innovative film and television producers into the next century.

Born in Hampstead, north London, on Sunday 14 April 1929, Gerry Anderson was educated at Willesden County secondary school, but left at the age of fourteen to study architecture at the local polytechnic. He soon realized that being an architect was not what he had originally imagined it would be – more technical drawing and calculating stresses than letting his imagination run free – although he did find that he had a genuine aptitude for decorative plastering, fashioning cornices and ornamental figures. He had also developed a keen interest in pursuing a career in the film industry and set his heart on a job producing mouldings for film sets. These ambitions flew out of the window when he discovered that he was allergic to the lime in the plaster and developed dermatitis which took the skin off both arms up to his elbows.

Still keen on finding work in the film industry, he managed to arrange a meeting with film executive Sidney Bernstein, who told him that if he came back in six months, he would find him a placement with a camera crew to set him on the road to becoming a cameraman. Anderson decided that, in the interim, he would apply for work in a photographic studio, which would give him experience with cameras and lighting. He was offered a job in a photographic portrait gallery in Regent Street but felt that his time there was being wasted, developing passport photos in the gallery's darkroom. He moved to another gallery in Oxford Street, where he was set the task of dry-mounting photographs, but he found this even more boring than his previous job and spent his evenings writing numerous letters to film production companies in search of any employment that might be available.

Eventually, Anderson was offered a placement as a trainee with the Colonial Film Unit, a branch of the Ministry of Information that made newsreels and short educational films. Here, he gained an insight into every aspect of film production, but found that he had a considerable talent as an editor, and it was in this capacity that he was able to get work at Gainsborough

GERRY ANDERSON SCREENOGRAPHY
FILM

THE WICKED LADY (1946)
Assistant Editor, US-release version
CARAVAN (1946)
Assistant Editor
JASSY (1947)
Assistant Editor
SNOWBOUND (1948)
First Assistant Editor
SO LONG AT THE FAIR (1950)
First Assistant Editor
THE CLOUDED YELLOW (1950)
Dubbing Editor
NEVER TAKE NO FOR AN ANSWER (1952)
Assembly Cutter and Dubbing Editor
SOUTH OF ALGIERS (1952)
Assembly Cutter
APPOINTMENT IN LONDON (1953)
Assembly Cutter and Dubbing Editor
THEY WHO DARE (1953)
Dubbing Editor
ABDULLA THE GREAT (1954)
Dubbing Editor
A PRIZE OF GOLD (1955)
Dubbing Editor
FURTHER UP THE CREEK (1958)
Dubbing Editor
CROSSROADS TO CRIME (1960)
Producer
THUNDERBIRDS ARE GO (1966)
Executive Producer and Screenplay
THUNDERBIRD 6 (1967)
Executive Producer and Screenplay
DOPPELGÄNGER (1968)
Producer and Screenplay
CROSSPLOT (1969)
Producer – Visual Effects Sequences

SUPERCAR, the Mercury-manned star vehicle of the first Gerry Anderson Supermarionation series made for Lew Grade's ATV and its international distribution arm ITC.

Pictures, one of the country's leading independent film-makers, at their studios in Lime Grove, London.

His first job on arriving at Gainsborough was to assist in re-editing *The Wicked Lady* (1945) for its American release. The highest-earning British movie of 1946, it was considered too erotic for American audiences, so Anderson was involved in cutting certain scenes in different ways and inserting newly shot footage with higher necklines in order to tone down the shots of Margaret Lockwood's heaving beauty-spotted bosom. This American version of the film was released in the US on 21 December 1946.

Anderson's first full motion picture debut was as assistant editor for director Arthur Crabtree and producer Harold Huth on *Caravan* (1946), a period romantic drama starring Stewart Granger and Jean Kent. He then went on to work on *Jassy* (1947) and *Snowbound* (1948) before he was called up for National Service in the RAF. Posted to RAF Manston in Kent as a radio telephone operator for air traffic control, he ended his service as a direction finder on an airfield. He resumed his film career in 1949 at Pinewood Studios with work as assistant editor on the Dirk Bogarde film *So Long at the Fair* (1950) and as dubbing editor on the Ralph Thomas thriller *The Clouded Yellow* (1950). He was then invited to assist editor Peter Graham Scott at the Cinecitta Studios in Italy, cutting the co-Italian production *Never Take No for an Answer* (1951), a film adaptation of Paul Gallico's book *The Small Miracle*. Dogged by a resentful French crew and lab technicians who were suffering from tuberculosis, Scott and Anderson found the experience a nightmare, but the picture was nominated for the 1951 Best Film award by the British Film Academy.

More work followed at Elstree Studios on Jack Lee's *South of Algiers* (1952, released in the US as *The Golden Mask*), before Anderson moved to Shepperton Studios to work on a pair of Dirk Bogarde Second World War dramas, *Appointment in London* (1952) and *They Who Dare* (1953), and Mark Robson's crime adventure *A Prize of Gold* (1955). He was then invited to join an independent television production company, Polytechnic Films, based at Taplow near Slough. It was here that Anderson made his directorial debut on an unbroadcast documentary television series called YOU'VE NEVER SEEN THIS, and established a good working relationship with the documentary's cameraman, Arthur Provis. When Polytechnic went into liquidation early in 1957, Anderson and Provis decided to pool their resources and form their own production company. They were joined by three other former members of the Polytechnic staff, designers Reg Hill and John Read, and secretary Sylvia Thamm – later to become Sylvia Anderson when she and Gerry married in November 1960.

Based at Islet Park on the banks of the Thames in Maidenhead, the company was named AP Films after the initials of the two partners, but very little production work came their way and Anderson was forced to take on freelance directorial assignments for television. After six months in business, the company was on the verge of bankruptcy when the partners were approached by Associated-Rediffusion executive Suzanne Warner and children's author Roberta Leigh to produce a puppet series, THE ADVENTURES OF TWIZZLE, for the newly formed Independent TeleVision. Desperate for the work, Anderson and Provis jumped at the contract, resolving to make the best puppet shows they could and hoping to prove that they could make even better live-action features given the chance. Fifty-two episodes of TWIZZLE were filmed between August 1957 and January 1958 on a budget of £23,000.

Roberta Leigh was delighted with the work on TWIZZLE and her company, Pelham Films Ltd, commissioned the production of five pilot episodes for a second series, TORCHY THE BATTERY BOY, and then a further twenty-one episodes to complete an initial series of twenty-six at an all-inclusive cost of £27,000. With the budget more than doubled for the production of each episode, Anderson and Provis were able to considerably upgrade the construction of the puppets and the sets.

Filming on TORCHY THE BATTERY BOY lasted from October 1958 to April 1959, by which time

Roberta Leigh had made it clear that she wanted AP Films to make an additional twenty-six episode series. However, the partners had already decided to branch out and produce their own children's puppet series, FOUR FEATHER FALLS. They had secretly carried out design and construction work on the new puppets, fearing that Leigh might cancel their contract and withhold payment on the completed episodes if she were to get wind of their plans. The terms of the contract between Pelham Films and AP Films gave Roberta Leigh sole ownership of TORCHY THE BATTERY BOY and all the component elements used to make it, so the two companies parted amicably and Roberta Leigh took the puppets and sets to Associated British Pathé, who made the second series with director Vivian Milroy.

FOUR FEATHER FALLS was a fantasy Western series which pioneered the use of a more sophisticated style of puppetry as Anderson and his team began to experiment with electronics to match dialogue to the puppets' mouth movements. The fibreglass head of each puppet was fitted with a solenoid connected to special tungsten wires on which the puppet was strung. Pulses could then be fed down the wires from a tape recorder running pre-recorded dialogue, and these pulses would trigger the solenoid to operate the puppet's mouth perfectly in sync. This was the basis of the technique which eventually became known as Supermarionation.

A pilot episode of FOUR FEATHER FALLS was made at Islet Park in April 1959, but at this point Anderson and Provis parted company, disagreeing over the steps that Anderson was taking to expand the business. Anderson successfully sold FOUR FEATHER FALLS to Granada Television and in June 1959 AP Films moved into new, larger premises in Ipswich Road on the Slough Trading Estate to make a further thirty-eight episodes. Filmed between June 1959 and April 1960, FOUR FEATHER FALLS proved to be very popular, so Anderson forged ahead with plans for a new series, SUPERCAR, but Granada declined to finance the show and APF was left on the verge of bankruptcy once again.

Looking for work, Anderson approached Anglo Amalgamated, who gave him £16,000 to produce and direct a feature film, *Crossroads to Crime* (1960), a live-action thriller shot in five weeks on location in and around Slough and Maidenhead. Despite everyone's best efforts, the film was not well received by the financiers, Stuart Levy and Nat Cohen, and Anderson was not invited to make any further features for them.

Then a chance call to an old friend, Frank Sherwin Green, at Beaconsfield Studios led Anderson to a meeting with Lew Grade, head of ATV and its international distribution arm, ITC. Grade was so impressed with the AP Films set-up and Reg Hill's promotional brochure for SUPERCAR that he agreed to put up the money for a full series of twenty-six episodes, at a cost of

GERRY ANDERSON
SCREENOGRAPHY
TELEVISION

YOU'VE NEVER SEEN THIS (1956)
Director

MARTIN KANE, PRIVATE INVESTIGATOR (1957) Director

THE ADVENTURES OF TWIZZLE (1957–8)
Director

TORCHY THE BATTERY BOY (1958–9)
Director

FOUR FEATHER FALLS (1959–0)
Producer and Director

SUPERCAR (1960–61)
Producer and Writer

FIREBALL XL5 (1961–3)
Producer, Director and Writer

STINGRAY (1963–4)
Producer and Writer

THUNDERBIRDS (1964–6)
Producer and Writer

CAPTAIN SCARLET AND THE MYSTERONS (1967) Executive Producer, Format and Writer

JOE 90 (1967–8)
Format and Writer

THE SECRET SERVICE (1968–9)
Format and Writer

UFO (1969–70)
Executive Producer, Director, Format and Writer

THE PROTECTORS (1971–2)
Producer

THE INVESTIGATOR (1972)
Producer and Director

SPACE: 1999 (1973–6)
Executive Producer and Creator

THE DAY AFTER TOMORROW (1975)
Producer

TERRAHAWKS (1983–4)
Producer and Writer

SPACE POLICE (1986)
Producer, Creator and Writer

DICK SPANNER (1986–7)
Producer

SPACE PRECINCT (1994–5)
Producer and Creator

LAVENDER CASTLE (1997–8)
Producer and Writer

Professor Rudolph Popkiss and Dr Horatio Beaker, creators of Supercar, with their young friend Jimmy Gibson in SUPERCAR.

Left to right: Fireball XL5, flagship of the World Space Patrol fleet (FIREBALL XL5); Fireball crew members Captain Steve Zodiac and Dr Venus (FIREBALL XL5); atomic-powered super-submarine Stingray, pride of the World Aquanaut Security Patrol (STINGRAY).

£2,000 each. This was Anderson's first foray into science fiction and followed the adventures of pilot Mike Mercury and the crew of an amazing land, sea and air vehicle based at a secret laboratory in Nevada. Filming began at the start of September 1960 with a shooting schedule of two weeks per episode, so it was a full year before all twenty-six episodes were completed.

Delighted with the strength of overseas sales, Grade commissioned a second season of thirteen SUPERCAR episodes and filming began again early in October 1961. Realizing that they needed to drastically reduce the time it was taking to complete each episode, Anderson and Hill devised a rotational filming schedule which enabled two separate camera crews to share the limited studio space and film two different episodes simultaneously. In this way, two episodes could be completed every fortnight, enabling all thirteen episodes to be filmed in just over three months.

SUPERCAR was a massive success for ITC in America, so when Anderson offered to produce a new Supermarionation series, Grade didn't have to think twice about commissioning it. Entitled FIREBALL XL5, this new series charted the interplanetary adventures of Colonel Steve Zodiac and the crew of a World Space Patrol spacecraft exploring Sector 25 of the galaxy in the year 2063. ITC sold the thirty-nine-episode series to NBC in America and it became the first British television series to be networked on American television. Grade was so pleased with the series' performance both at home and abroad that he bought AP Films for £3 million on the understanding that Anderson would continue to run the company.

Grade also invested £75,000 to move the company into larger, custom-built premises in Stirling Road, half a mile away on the other side of the Slough Trading Estate. Here, Reg Hill supervised the construction of three shooting stages, two for puppet filming and the other for special effects. Although small in comparison with live-action film studios such as those at Pinewood and Shepperton, the new AP Films Studios were ideal for Anderson's brand of film-making and became the company's home for the next eight years. The site incorporated production offices, a property department, a preview theatre and twelve cutting rooms, with additional offices for the art department in Edinburgh Avenue, just around the corner from Stirling Road.

All this activity was in anticipation of production on the company's first colour series, STINGRAY. Although several other British television series had already been filmed in colour, most notably the ITC series THE ADVENTURES OF SIR LANCELOT (1956) and MAN OF THE WORLD (1962), STINGRAY became the first British children's television series to be given the colour treatment. Essentially reworking the format of FIREBALL XL5 by relocating the heroes under the sea, STINGRAY followed Captain Troy Tempest and the crew of the World Aquanaut Security Patrol super-submarine Stingray, patrolling the world's oceans in the year 2064, battling with hostile under-sea races and combating the evil plans of Titan, Lord of the under-sea kingdom of Titanica. Massively successful in Britain, the thirty-nine-episode series also netted over £3 million in overseas sales when the programme was syndicated in America.

Neither Grade nor Anderson was content just to rest on his laurels and both men were determined that the next Supermarionation production would be even bigger. Originally planned as a twenty-five-minute programme (as SUPERCAR, FIREBALL XL5 and STINGRAY had been), the first season of THUNDERBIRDS ended up as a series of twenty-six fifty-minute instalments when Grade decided to increase the budget to £40,000 per episode. His intention was to sell the series as a prime-time family entertainment show for transmission in an early-evening time-slot, where much of the series' potential audience would consist of adults as well as children.

Set in the year 2065, THUNDERBIRDS told of a secret organization, International Rescue, formed by millionaire ex-astronaut Jeff Tracy to carry out rescue operations using a variety of incredible vehicles and equipment in situations where conventional equipment had proved useless. Acting in secrecy and operating from a luxurious island base somewhere in the Pacific Ocean, the members of International Rescue would be ever on the alert, with a vast manned space satellite monitoring radio messages for any situations that might require their very special talents and machinery.

Even with two puppet units filming separate episodes simultaneously and three model units shooting the spectacular visual effects sequences, principal photography on THUNDERBIRDS lasted for nearly eighteen months. It was the most complex and expensive production that AP Films had so far undertaken, but everyone agreed that the results were worth it. Public response to the series was phenomenal. The programme netted ITC over £350,000 in advance sales to overseas markets before it had even been screened, and it was seen in some thirty different countries, ranging from Ghana to Holland, from Saudi Arabia to Japan. AP Films' licensing subsidiary, AP Merchandising, issued around 120 licences for THUNDERBIRDS toys, which sold in their millions in the early part of 1966.

A second series was commissioned, to be filmed alongside a £250,000 feature film, *Thunderbirds Are Go* (1966), and nearly six months of principal photography began on both in March 1966. Everything was going smoothly and Gerry Anderson had no inkling of the bombshell that Lew Grade was about to drop on him when he attended one of their regular meetings in July 1966.

'I could see THUNDERBIRDS continuing for a very long time and I was full of ideas for the new episodes, so I was very shaken when Lew opened the discussion by telling me, "I think it's time we made a new show." It came as a serious blow to our organization, but the fact was that I had largely assumed that we would be going on with THUNDERBIRDS. I still believe that we should have done, but it's all too easy in a situation like that to assume things. Lew obviously had his eye on selling our programmes abroad, particularly in America, and he felt that he could sell a new Supermarionation series much more easily than going back with THUNDERBIRDS again.

'Of course, I wasn't really prepared for this. On the earlier shows, as we came towards the end of each series, I expected that we would move on to new things and I tended to think in advance, aiming for continuity of employment for everyone at the studios. But I hadn't seen this one coming and it pulled the rug out from under me.'

As filming was completed on *Thunderbirds Are Go*, the production team at AP Films became resigned to the fact that THUNDERBIRDS' life as a television series had come to an end with the sixth episode of the second season. It was time to move on to start work on the company's next television production, which, it was hoped, would prove to be even bigger and better than THUNDERBIRDS.

In its hangar at Tracy Island, Thunderbird 2 is prepared for another dangerous rescue mission (THUNDERBIRDS).

Captain Scarlet, Captain Blue and Lieutenant Green on the Moonmobile set during filming of Lunarville 7.

PRE-PRODUCTION

The technicians in the puppet workshops at Slough had not been idle during the filming of THUNDERBIRDS' second season and the feature film, and had continued to work on refining and developing the technology of Supermarionation. The puppets on all of the previous series had been constructed with heads that were disproportionately large to the bodies in order to accommodate the solenoids that controlled the puppets' mouth movements. In order to give the puppets correct human proportions, the bodies would have to be scaled up to such a size that the complete puppet would become too heavy for the puppeteers to control from above. The puppet sets would also have to be scaled up to match, necessitating higher gantries for the puppet operators and larger stages, none of which was economically possible at the AP Films Studios.

Then puppet sculptors John Brown and Terry Curtis hit upon the solution. They discovered that it was possible to relocate the solenoids from the head to the chest of the puppet, the movements of the solenoids being transmitted through the puppet's neck by thin metal wire to activate the mouth movement in the head. This development meant that the size of the head could be reduced for the first time to be correctly proportional to the body, resulting in the next generation of Supermarionation puppets, more believable, easier to model and easier to dress.

Terry Curtis recalls, 'John Brown and I kind of instigated the move towards the more realistic-style characters. As I understood it, Gerry always wanted to get into live-action and either couldn't afford it or wasn't really encouraged to do it by Lew Grade, so he was keen to make things as lifelike as possible. John Brown made the very first realistic one as a test to show Gerry that it could be done. It wasn't supposed to be any particular character, but it was a male puppet which looked a bit sort of James Bond-ish. Gerry loved it.'

Not everyone was enamoured of the new style of puppet, though. Director David Lane remembers, 'In all honesty, I didn't like the more realistic-style puppets. I thought that they were wonderful pieces of sculpting and, technically, all the gear being shrunk down to fit better was a marvellous achievement, but I think it was a mistake. I was called into Gerry's office one day and he told me to sit down because he had something to show me. John Brown came in with this box – it was like a little coffin. He opened this box and it was as if there was a little dead person in there. It looked a bit like James Bond, but because it was perfect in all its proportions it just looked odd...to me anyway.'

Anderson, however, was delighted with the prototype and now saw the opportunity to start using the new realistic puppets. Having already established the disproportionate characters, it would not have been possible to introduce the new type of puppet as long as THUNDERBIRDS was still in production, but now that THUNDERBIRDS had been cancelled by Lew Grade, the creation of a new series was the ideal opportunity to begin using the more advanced marionettes. With his wife, Sylvia, Anderson began to develop a new series concept specifically for the correctly proportioned style of puppet, turning for inspiration to a live-action series idea that had previously been rejected by Lew Grade.

'I was practically paranoiac when it came to thinking of new concepts and trying to do things differently,' remembers Anderson. 'One idea I had pitched to Lew was for a live-action show, a really knockout American police story over sixty-five episodes. I told Lew that we could get a big name American artist to star, and then at about episode twenty-seven have a massive gunfight. The viewers would expect anyone to be killed except the hero, but guess what happens? The hero is killed stone dead. Then in the next episode we would bring in another international star as the new boy and he slowly comes to prove himself. It would do away with the theory that the star of a show can never be killed. The audience would be on the edge of their seats for the rest of the series, because just maybe the new hero would get killed too.'

While the practice of killing off a series' leading character is more acceptable to audiences

'If you take the whole history of my career you go from papier-mâché puppets to mouth movement and eye movement to very nearly invisible control wires – and the whole time it was me trying to make puppet films look like real films. CAPTAIN SCARLET was that much closer.

'I still wonder about the wisdom of our decision to change the puppets. The heads were reduced in size to make them in proportion with the rest of their bodies, but the problem was that exact and precise movements became even more vital than ever and that caused us terrible difficulties. After creating Snow White in perfect human form, Walt Disney said that he'd never repeat that mistake, and I still have doubts about whether or not we did the right thing.'

GERRY ANDERSON

and network executives today, the concept was anathema to Grade in 1966. 'He told me, "You need your head examined! You must be mad to suggest such a thing. You can't build a top-rating show with a huge audience and then kill off the lead." At the time, I thought that he had a point, but I believe that if we'd been daring enough to do it, it might have made television history.'

The idea was still floating around in Anderson's mind when he was thinking about ideas for the follow-up to THUNDERBIRDS and hit upon the idea of developing a character who could be killed off in the very first episode, but then somehow come back to life, perhaps re-created as a robot or an android. What if, he thought, there was something about this character that meant he could actually be killed off in every single episode and then resurrected, as good as new, in time for next week's show?

Initially intending the new series to be entitled 'The Mysterons', Anderson developed the concept of an alien race of sentient computers housed in a city complex on Mars, beings with fantastic powers and the ability to reverse matter, reconstructing inanimate objects and creating duplicates of dead humans which act under their control. In an unusual twist to what might otherwise have become a standard 'Earth versus the Martians' scenario, war is initiated by people from Earth when they mistake a sensor device for weaponry and destroy the complex. Taking revenge for this unwarranted act of aggression, the Mysterons vow to destroy all life on Earth.

In the pilot script written by Gerry and Sylvia Anderson, it is the year 2068 and peace on Earth is maintained by Spectrum, a super-efficient security organization manned by agents recruited from the various established World Government services, each assigned a colour codename to protect their true identities. When a Spectrum exploration team, led by Captain Black, provokes the conflict with the Mysterons, Spectrum's personnel and facilities are mobilized to combat the alien offensive. One of the first casualties is Spectrum's top agent, Captain Scarlet, killed and then re-created in the service of the Mysterons, but their hold over him is broken after he falls 800 feet from a sky park during a showdown with Captain Blue. Using a specially designed computer, Spectrum restore the original Captain Scarlet's memories, personality and loyalties, but the new Scarlet retains the Mysteron ability to survive injuries that would prove fatal to any other man. Captain Scarlet has become Spectrum's greatest weapon in an unceasing war against the menace from Mars.

Tim Cooksey (in foreground) and Terry Curtis making revamp puppet heads in the puppet workshop.

The puppet cast of CAPTAIN SCARLET AND THE MYSTERONS *on the Cloudbase Conference Room set during filming of* **Flight to Atlantica.**

One important aspect of the Andersons' original concept of Captain Scarlet hinted that the character was no longer truly flesh and blood but a 'mechanical man' of sorts, albeit one that was indistinguishable from the original. Detailing his initial ideas for the series' end titles, Anderson wrote, 'These will comprise still shots of Captain Scarlet in association with computers, printed circuits and electrodes, thus conveying the premise that Captain Scarlet is a mechanical man.'

Armed with this pilot script, John Brown's team of puppet sculptors set to work creating the cast of the fourteen main characters who would be seen in the series on a regular basis. Mary Turner, a puppeteer who had worked on the Anderson productions since TORCHY THE BATTERY BOY and had previously created Lady Penelope and Brains for THUNDERBIRDS, sculpted Captain Scarlet. Terry Curtis made Captain Blue, his Spectrum colleagues Captain Grey, Captain Ochre and Captain Magenta, as well as the female pilot Destiny

'The CAPTAIN SCARLET puppets were not built to walk. They were too heavy and were not weighted properly anyway. The only strings went to the puppet's head and occasionally one would be put on each hand to that they could move their arms, but there were no strings on the legs.

'It is virtually impossible to get a string puppet to walk convincingly on film unless it is a very caricatured puppet. In CAPTAIN SCARLET, if a puppet had to move off-screen, it was done in a head-and-shoulders shot — the floor puppeteer would hold the legs of the puppet and then move the puppet physically out of shot at the right time, trying to make the body and shoulders move as if the puppet were walking. In CAPTAIN SCARLET, or any of the Supermarionation programmes after, you never once saw the legs actually moving.'

JAN KING

Captain Scarlet and Captain Blue report to Colonel White.

Angel. Tim Cooksey created Spectrum commander-in-chief Colonel White and his communications officer, Lieutenant Green. Captain Black and the four other Angel pilots, Symphony, Harmony, Rhapsody and Melody, were made by puppeteer Christine Glanville, who had been involved with the Anderson programmes right from the start with THE ADVENTURES OF TWIZZLE and had previously created Scott Tracy and Alan Tracy for THUNDERBIRDS. John Brown himself created Dr Fawn.

Each main character's head would be originally sculpted in clay or Plasticine, roughly painted and wigged and then screen-tested for approval by the producers before being made permanent. A silicone rubber mould would be taken from the clay sculpture and this would then be laminated with layers of Bondaglass, a fibreglass cloth and polyester resin, similar to that used to make custom-car bodies. Completely dry within an hour, the beige-coloured fibreglass head shell could then be removed from the mould, sanded down, and fitted with flexible leather mouth parts and eyeballs mounted on a rocker mechanism. A track rod for the eye movement would then be inserted into the head shell before it was finally painted and wigged with mohair. Female characters were fitted with wigs made from real human hair by a specialist company, Wig Creations.

Continuing a successful technique that had been pioneered on STINGRAY, each character was given four or five different interchangeable heads which could be altered between takes to simulate changes of expression. In addition to the 'normal'-expression head, there would be a smiling head, a frowning head, and a special 'blinking' head in which the eye movement was engineered to go up and down (enabling the puppet to blink or fall unconscious) rather than from side to side. The puppets also required a duplicate 'normal' head, as one was needed for each of the two puppet units.

Terry Curtis recalls the process of creating one of the main characters. 'You'd probably take around two weeks building up the general image of the character in Plasticine. Then, when it was agreed that it looked all right, a mould would be taken in silicone rubber and from that you'd take the fibreglass head. Then you would generally make four different versions of the same head: one smiler, one frowner, one normal and maybe a blinker. You'd use the original head and take a cast and work on it to create the different expressions. The painting had to be done very carefully. The eyelashes had to be just right, and the lower lashes too, because they were generally painted on by hand. These faces all had to match each other as they were meant to be the same character.

'I was quite intimidated by the change to the SCARLET-style puppets because they had no caricatured features, so you couldn't afford to do an exaggerated nose or forehead or anything like that. They all had to be just perfect. Everything had to be in proportion and, although the puppets were the same size as the THUNDERBIRDS ones, the features were smaller, so we found it a little more difficult to get it right. It didn't take us long to get it worked out, but for a while it was a bit of a problem. 'You found yourself being very critical. The changes of expression on those puppets had to be perfect and in no way exaggerated like the old ones were. I remember when Tim Cooksey did Colonel White, he had a lot of trouble doing different expressions as the face was just so realistic. I had a similar problem with Captain Blue. I remember I did a Blue smiler head and people could hardly tell the difference between that and the normal one. The mouth only turned up at the corners a little and his eyebrows were slightly different too, but it was really pretty close to the normal face.'

Curtis tells how the puppet sculptors often turned to real-life faces for inspiration. 'I was a big James Bond fan and I tended to base a lot of my puppets on Sean Connery. Zero X Captain Paul Travers in *Thunderbirds Are Go* was probably my best version of Connery, but Captain Grey in SCARLET was Connery too. I think that some of the other sculptors thought that Connery lookalikes were all I could do! Of course, being a Bond fan, when it came to Destiny Angel, I based her on Ursula Andress.

'The other thing I did was to base characters on myself. I would often use a mirror to see how a certain expression looks and so quite often a character would take on some of my own facial traits. Captain Blue was a kind of version of myself. When we were developing the new style of puppets, I created this character that was sort of based on me. He had brown hair brushed into a quiff like the THUNDERBIRDS characters. Well, Sylvia came into the workshop one day and said, "We've got this actor doing the voice of Captain Blue and I want you to make the puppet look like him, but I want him blond." Off she went and left us with a picture of Ed Bishop. Anyway, this character that I had already done looked really good as a sort of handsome lead character, so I just put a blond wig on him and brushed the hair forward. John Brown said that he liked how it looked and so that was Captain Blue. Years later, I met Ed Bishop, who said to me, "Oh, you know that Captain Blue was actually sculpted to look like me?" and I said, "Sorry, mate, he wasn't. I know, because I'm the guy who made it."

Captain Scarlet and Captain Blue in the Cloudbase Officers' Lounge with Lieutenant Green, Symphony and Melody.

'Tim Cooksey based Lieutenant Green on Cy Grant, who did the voice for the character in the show itself. He did a really nice job and Green was a very nice character. We had never really done black characters before SCARLET, but we wanted them to look like real coloured people and I think Tim pulled it off. Melody Angel was pretty much like all the other Angels, just painted brown, but Green was very well done and Tim took a long time getting him right. I remember he had a bit of a problem getting the hair right, but ended up using a special mohair which we could wind around a hot piece of metal. It would come out curly and when you stuck it on and trimmed it down it gave you a pretty realistic hairstyle which worked quite nicely.'

Following the appearance of puppet versions of pop stars Cliff Richard and The Shadows in *Thunderbirds Are Go*, Anderson was keen to expand upon the use of puppet replicas of celebrities in CAPTAIN SCARLET. One of his earliest ideas for the series was that each episode would feature a leading guest character voiced by an internationally renowned actor, whose face would be replicated in miniature on the puppet character. In the series' pilot script, Anderson specified that an artist such as Patrick McGoohan, then known for his role as John Drake in ITC's DANGER MAN series, would voice the World President with a puppet version of McGoohan appearing as the World President on screen. Other actors considered for such roles in CAPTAIN SCARLET included THE SAINT star Roger Moore, Efrem Zimbalist Jr from 77 SUNSET STRIP and THE F.B.I., Robert Horton from WAGON TRAIN and A MAN CALLED SHENANDOAH, comedy actor Peter Sellers and film actors Robert Taylor and Dirk Bogarde. Sadly, this idea was abandoned as it would place an unnecessary strain on the budget.

A further innovation in the Supermarionation technique that came into effect for the first time on CAPTAIN SCARLET was the creation of a repertory cast of revamp puppets. These were puppets that would appear as one-off guest characters on an episode-by-episode basis, or as background characters in crowd scenes. On the previous Supermarionation series, it was an unusual occurrence if a supporting character such as this appeared in more than one episode, as Terry Curtis explains.

'On THUNDERBIRDS, the revamp heads, the ones we used over and over, were all sculpted in Plasticine over a vacuum-formed plastic head which was a shell of a head, like a skull, I suppose. You would then build up the character's face with Plasticine and fit all of the technical stuff, the eyes and the lip-sync mechanism, into the head to see that it all worked and lined up. Then in would go a leather lower-lip piece and you would sculpt on top of that. Once a character was completed, you'd give it a screen test and when you were happy that it looked OK, you'd paint over the Plasticine, put on a wig and then do all the finishing touches to make it perfect. We generally wouldn't make more than one head for a revamp character, so we'd look

'The earlier programmes were done more cheaply and guest characters were reused or had the heads remoulded. By the time I was directing, the money was there to keep the characters and use them as a repertory company. I would sometimes read a script and think, "That one with the craggy face and grey hair from that episode I did the other week would be good in this part."

'One of the problems was that we had two episodes being filmed at the same time. I might go over to the puppet store and think to myself that I'd grab a certain one for a scene, only to find that Alan Perry had already got him for the episode that he was doing that week. Another time, I might have said to Christine, "I liked that blond-haired, good-looking one we used the other day. Is it available?" and I would be told, "Yes, but he's got black hair, a flat nose and glasses now."'

KEN TURNER

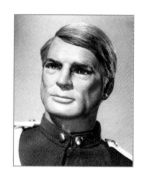

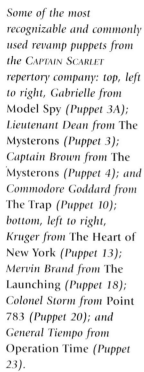

Some of the most recognizable and commonly used revamp puppets from the CAPTAIN SCARLET repertory company: top, left to right, Gabrielle from Model Spy (Puppet 3A); Lieutenant Dean from The Mysterons (Puppet 3); Captain Brown from The Mysterons (Puppet 4); and Commodore Goddard from The Trap (Puppet 10); bottom, left to right, Kruger from The Heart of New York (Puppet 13); Mervin Brand from The Launching (Puppet 18); Colonel Storm from Point 783 (Puppet 20); and General Tiempo from Operation Time (Puppet 23).

through the script to see what expression the character would mostly have and that is what we gave them.' Unfortunately, this type of revamp puppet had its drawbacks. 'Virtually every day, the puppets would be sent back to be repaired. I used to wonder what they actually did with the things on the set, because they'd often come back in a right state. Because the revamps' faces were Plasticine, the noses would get sliced off by the wires, or the puppet would have fallen over and the whole face would have been squashed. They looked absolutely terrible, and we'd have about an hour to do something about it.'

For CAPTAIN SCARLET, Gerry Anderson decided to create a complete repertory company of more than fifty revamp puppets with permanent heads made to the standard of the main character puppets. Representing a wide variety of facial types and hair colouring, across a range of age groups, each revamp puppet was numbered and photographed as it was completed. The photos were then filed in a volume that could be used as a casting directory of sorts by the directors, enabling them to select the puppets they wanted to play the additional characters for each new episode. The variety of faces could be expanded with the addition of moustaches and beards, as well as changes to hairstyles and hair colours.

Curtis remembers, 'I liked doing the different guest characters because it was good fun creating them or working on characters we already had to make them look the part. We would add little goatee beards and things like that, paint them brown and add glasses. I remember we did love moustaches. The director would say, "We need something for the next episode. He has to be a military type. Can you sort something out?" We would sit there and listen and look as if we were planning to create something spectacular, and then after the director left we'd pick a character and say, "Stick a moustache on him – he'll do!"'

The heads were fitted to hollow fibreglass bodies made by Ernest 'Plugg' Shutt. These were constructed with legs made from heavy resin which helped to anchor the puppets to the studio floor during filming. Measurements were taken of the physical proportions of members of the puppet workshop and these were scaled down to determine the correct proportions for making the puppets' bodies in three different styles: a 24-inch-high 'tall male', the equivalent of a man 6 feet 1 (Scarlet, Blue, Colonel White); a 23-inch-high 'average male', representing a man 5 feet 10 (Black, Green), and a 20-inch-high 'small female' for the Angels and other female characters. Even with these three standard bodies, the heights of the characters could be varied by cutting the legs off at the thighs and trimming them down or packing them with extra resin before sticking them back on. 'Wired up' with a maximum of seven special steel wires drawn from tungsten at a diameter of 0.005 inches by P. Ormiston and Sons Ltd, the puppets would be tested from the 12-feet-high puppet gantry before being passed to Iris Richens's wardrobe department for dressing.

As on the previous Supermarionation series, Sylvia Anderson supervised the design of all the

clothes for the main characters herself, taking into account the conflict between design and the practical requirements of the puppet operators. Just as there were duplicates of each main puppet character, each costume had to be duplicated to dress them. Iris Richens and her staff of miniature dressmakers avoided man-made fibres in the creation of the costumes, using only silk, cotton or wool, which allowed the puppets freedom of movement in a way that nylon and polyester did not.

When it came to the design of the Spectrum uniforms to be worn by Captain Scarlet and the other officers, Sylvia was heavily influenced by the fashion designs of Pierre Cardin, in particular the Cosmos space-age outfit he created for his 1966 Cosmonaut collection. Unveiled to the public for the first time in September 1966, the Cosmos outfit incorporated a sleeveless, collarless jacket falling to the hip, fastened with an off-centre big ring zip running full-length vertically. Belted at the waist, with a big ring zip-fastening breast pocket and epaulettes, the Cosmos jacket was seen worn with a black polo-neck shirt and black trousers. It was available in a range of unpatterned bright colours – white, scarlet, green, blue and so on.

For the Spectrum uniform, designer Keith Wilson adapted the Cosmos jacket by cutting it short at waist level, lowering the breast pocket to rib level and thickening the ridged collar. The shoulders were brought out to points and mounted with tubular epaulettes. This jacket was then worn over a dark grey polo-neck shirt with matching trousers and colour-coordinated boots. The uniform was completed with a colour-coordinated cap and finished with Spectrum emblems designed by Tony Dunsterville.

The alteration of the proportions of the puppets made the design of the puppet sets significantly easier for art director Bob Bell and his art department team at their office in Edinburgh Avenue, around the corner from the Century 21 Studios in Stirling Road. On all of the previous Supermarionation series, Bell's biggest problem had been reconciling the differing proportions of the puppets' heads, hands and bodies within their surroundings: matching furniture that suited the puppets' bodies with tableware that suited their hands, for example. With Captain Scarlet, the production design team could concentrate on creating a series of stunningly futuristic miniature settings without being handicapped by the variance of scales, as everything could simply be scaled down uniformly at one-third full size.

For the first time on the Supermarionation productions, the design team was split between aesthetic design and technical design. Aesthetic design involved settings such as offices, living rooms and conference rooms, as well as any exterior sets, such as forest clearings and roadsides. Technical design incorporated sets of a purely technical nature, such as flight cockpits and computer control rooms, as well as computer consoles and instrumentation that occasionally featured in the aesthetic sets.

As he needed to concentrate on the production design for a second Thunderbirds feature film, *Thunderbird 6* (1967), which was to be filmed at the Century 21 Studios in tandem with Captain Scarlet, Bell delegated the aesthetic design work to Keith Wilson and the technical design to John Lageu, a former engineering draughtsman in the aerospace industry. Between them, Wilson and Lageu were responsible for the look of all the interiors in Captain Scarlet, while art director Grenville Nott was responsible for translating their designs into physical three-dimensional sets.

The first sets to be designed were the Cloudbase interiors, the series' permanent sets that would be seen in virtually every episode. Foremost among these was the Cloudbase Control Room, described in Scene 26 of the pilot script as follows:

The control room comprises the usual array of instrumentation with one notable difference – there are no control consoles as we know them. Instead, we find the Controller, Lieutenant Green, a man in his early twenties, and assistant to the Commander-in-Chief of the Spectrum Organization, sitting behind an entirely new type of console. It is a long sheet of glass approximately 2′6″ in height and approximately 15′ in length. It stands on its edge and runs parallel to the ground supported at intervals by stainless-steel legs. The whole area of the glass is etched in silver and gold and is, in fact, a printed circuit. Along the bottom of the glass are the normal controls, switches, flashing lights and so on.

All these components are of slender and futuristic design. Lieutenant Green's chair is mechanically propelled, and slides up and down the length of the console, thus enabling

The Cosmos jacket by Pierre Cardin from his 1966 Cosmonaut collection – the inspiration for the Spectrum uniform in CAPTAIN SCARLET.

'The shoulder lights on the Spectrum uniform had wires going through the puppet's body and down the trouser leg. A battery would be connected when the lights needed to operate.

'The cap microphone worked by air through a small connection at the back of the cap. A rubber bulb and tube were joined to this and when the bulb was squeezed, the microphone dropped down. The camera angle always hid the rubber tube from view.'

JAN KING

The Cloudbase Control Room set, designed by Keith Wilson and John Lageu.

Rhapsody and Symphony in the Cloudbase Amber Room set designed, by Keith Wilson.

him to reach any of the many controls. The control room is divided into two – in the second half the floor is raised, thus giving it a split level. On the higher level and seated with his back to Lieutenant Green we see Colonel White, Commander-in-Chief of Spectrum. He faces into a semicircular modern desk and when in this position is facing a giant illuminated chart which occupies the whole of the wall.

Wilson's design for this, the largest of the regular puppet sets, was remarkably faithful to Anderson's vision, extrapolating from the idea of the glass sheet computer to dress the set with curving panels of green Perspex. To this, Lageu added Colonel White's circular control desk and Lieutenant Green's computer console, while Nott developed a 15-foot moving walkway which ran the length of the computer. This walkway consisted of an endless belt looped on rollers beneath the set driven by an electric motor which was capable of providing different speeds while remaining entirely free of vibration, so as not to effect any puppet characters seen standing on it.

Wilson and Lageu went on to design the five other permanent sets – the Angels' Amber Room, the Cloudbase Conference Room, the Spectrum Sick Bay, the Officers' Lounge and the Spectrum Pursuit Vehicle interior – before turning their attention to the additional sets that would be required for the first episode: the interior of the Mysteron complex, the cockpit of the Martian Exploration Vehicle, the foyer of the Maximum Security Building, the World President's Security Suite and various exterior sets of the London Car-Vu.

In the visual effects department, supervising visual effects director Derek Meddings and his visual effects designer Mike Trim created the Spectrum Cloudbase Headquarters and a range of aircraft and ground vehicles that would be seen in the series on a regular basis. Trim had joined the model workshop early in the production of THUNDERBIRDS and was initially set to work dirtying down the completed models and running repairs on models that got damaged during filming. During the course of production, however, he started to design many of the subsidiary rescue vehicles used by International Rescue. Meddings was so pleased with his work that he reorganized the visual effects department for CAPTAIN SCARLET, giving Trim the opportunity to design several of the main vehicles.

Now that the puppets themselves were more realistic, Meddings and Trim were aware that the futuristic world that they created for CAPTAIN SCARLET on the model stages had to become more believable too. The more outrageous designs of some of the THUNDERBIRDS vehicles, for example, would now look out of place, so all of the Spectrum vehicles had to be designed with the appearance of genuine functionality. Meddings himself designed Cloudbase, creating a giant platform with jet engines, as described in Scene 24 of the Andersons' pilot script:

Close up on the word 'SPECTRUM': it is painted on the side of Spectrum's aerial launch platform, call sign 'Cloud Base'. The camera zooms back to extreme long shot and we find that we are looking at something quite new. It is, as its name implies, an aerial launch platform, a large structure with a deck similar to an aircraft carrier, on which is a control room with large glass windows. On the main superstructure below, a number of smaller windows indicate that there are living quarters in this vast complex. The structure remains airborne by virtue of a number of powerful jet engines that are pointing downwards and are obviously powered by atomic energy. Thus the principle is that of an aircraft carrier which is suspended in the sky at approximately 40,000 feet in a stationary position using the mechanical principle of one of the new Hoverjets. We note that on its deck are only three aircraft. Their small wing area indicates their high potential speed and their cockpits capable of carrying only one person indicate that they are strike aircraft. They are parked at one end in a 'V'-shaped formation.

The Cloudbase miniature on the visual effects soundstage.

From Meddings's design, the model workshop constructed a huge Cloudbase miniature over 6 feet long which was so heavy that it could not be suspended on thin wires and had to be supported by a metal pole.

In addition, Meddings designed the Spectrum Angel Interceptor strike aircraft and the Spectrum Pursuit Vehicle. For the Angel, Meddings developed a sleek delta-wing jet with downward-pointing wingtips fitted with landing skids, but the Spectrum Pursuit Vehicle was much more difficult to visualize from its description in the pilot script:

The Vehicle has no windscreen on the front since the driver sits backwards and steers the vehicle by watching a television picture of the forward view. The principle of the vehicle is that it is driven by a lightweight power unit. This can be lifted out from its housing easily by one man. Its power source, which drives a shaft, can be used to power the vehicle or, alternatively, a one-man helicopter; a seagoing dinghy; a one man hovercraft; a drill; a winch; and a multitude of other devices yet to be invented.

The back of the vehicle is lined with drawers and cupboards which contain all the components necessary to assemble the devices just described. It is, of course, a high-speed vehicle and bullet-proof. Needless to say it carries radio, radar, food supplies and ammunition.

The Spectrum logo designed by Tony Dunsterville, as seen on all Spectrum uniforms, vehicles and installations.

With very little to go on in terms of the look of the SPV, Meddings designed a steel blue tank-type vehicle which ran on a combination of large and small wheels but was also fitted with rear-mounted caterpillar tracks. He added a shock-absorbent battering ram to the nose and then finished the vehicle with air vents in place of windows. The result was the series' most popular vehicle and a rival to Thunderbird 2 as Supermarionation's most recognizable icon. Under the supervision of Ray Brown, the model department constructed a range of SPV models from 1/48 to 1/12 scale, carved from hardwood or balsa with rubber or nylon wheels, the largest SPV model being 24 inches long.

The Cloudbase miniature is prepared for filming on the visual effects soundstage.

An SPV model races across the Hotspot bridge model set during filming of the visual effects for Noose of Ice.

Angel Interceptors designed by Derek Meddings lined up on the Cloudbase flight deck model set.

Meddings left Mike Trim to design the other Spectrum vehicles – the Spectrum Saloon Car, Spectrum Passenger Jet, Spectrum Helicopter and Maximum Security Vehicle – as well as the futuristic buildings that would be seen prominently in the pilot episode, the Maximum Security Building and the London Car-Vu. Later, with Meddings needing to concentrate on the visual effects for *Thunderbird 6*, the design of the twenty-first-century model world of CAPTAIN SCARLET was entrusted entirely to Trim.

He remembers that this occasionally brought him into conflict with the art department. 'One of the major problems for me as a designer on CAPTAIN SCARLET and the later Gerry Anderson series was to ensure that what we created for the special effects matched what was being constructed by the art department on the puppet side. In an ideal world, we would have found ourselves several weeks ahead of them and therefore their large-scale sections and sets would have had to follow our designs for the complete craft or vehicle. However, in reality, they were often in front of us and when I started to design a model, I would find myself trying to work around an existing puppet set.

'Although the liaison between the two departments was usually good, coordinating model designs with the puppet interiors always created horrendous problems. For the most part, these were caused by the fact that the art department worked mainly with flat sheet material – thin marine ply, hardboard, clear plastic sheeting and so on – all of which could be bent in only one direction. Therefore, their ability to create sections of cars or aircraft with sleek compound curves was almost non-existent. The sharp angles and smooth flowing shapes that we liked to use in the model department were virtually impossible for them to achieve. So it was not unknown for us to end up with a fairly sleek and futuristic-looking model that suddenly, and sometimes violently, changed character in order to match their set. The cockpit of the Magnacopter in the CAPTAIN SCARLET episode *The Trap* is a classic example of a set that doesn't fit in with the rest of my design.

'Of course, sometimes the boot would be on the other foot, especially at the start of the series, and I was very aware of just how easy it was for me to produce some streamlined design, compared to the struggle the art department would have trying to match it. But, as you can probably imagine, despite this apparent understanding of each other's problems, the air was often fairly blue on both sides of the divide.'

Throughout November and December 1966, the members of the puppet workshop, art department and visual effects department laboured to prepare all the necessary elements to enable filming to begin on the first episode of the new series early in the new year. The various developments in Supermarionation for CAPTAIN SCARLET AND THE MYSTERONS represented the biggest advance in the techniques used on the Anderson productions since the creation of the synchronized puppet mouth movement six years earlier. As a reflection of this great leap forward, the company directors decided that it was time to finally discard the old AP Films name for the film and television production arm of the business in favour of one that more accurately reflected the studio's output: Century 21 Productions. The company name was formally changed on Saturday 3 December 1966.

THE VOICE ARTISTS

Before a single frame of film could be shot on the puppet stages, the dialogue of the puppet characters had to be recorded and edited so that it could be played back during filming to generate synchronized puppet mouth movement. From their experiences with the previous Supermarionation productions, Gerry and Sylvia Anderson knew that the kind of actors and actresses they required needed to be able to perform convincing accents from both sides of the Atlantic in a variety of different vocal styles. With such a versatile cast, it would be possible to record all of the different voices for the entire series with just twelve actors.

Taking their cue from the new style of puppets and the greater realism of the fictional world that they were creating, the Andersons decided that they would not rely so much on the repertory of character performers that they had established with FIREBALL XL5, STINGRAY and THUNDERBIRDS, and instead sought actors whose voices had a more natural sound. For the first time, they also felt confident that sales of the programme in the United States would not be adversely affected if the leading characters spoke with English rather than American accents (by 1967, English accents had become more acceptable to American audiences with the success of television series such as THE SAINT, DANGER MAN and THE AVENGERS).

So it was that British character actor Francis Matthews was cast in the lead role of Captain Scarlet. Born in York on 2 September 1931, Matthews was educated at St Michael's Jesuit College, Leeds. He began his career in the theatre at the age of seventeen as an assistant stage manager at Leeds Repertory Theatre and made his stage debut playing a schoolboy in a production of Emlyn Williams's *The Corn is Green*. After National Service in the Royal Navy, he returned to repertory theatre in Oxford and Bromley and went on to appear as Ranjit Kasel in George Cukor's *Bhowani Junction* (1956).

A string of film roles followed, including *Small Hotel* (1957), *The Mark of the Hawk* (1957), Hammer's *The Revenge of Frankenstein* (1958), *The Hellfire Club* (1960), *The Treasure of Monte Cristo* (1961), *Nine Hours to Rama* (1963) and *Murder Ahoy* (1964), in addition to starring roles in the sitcoms GOLDEN GIRL and A LITTLE BIG BUSINESS and guest appearances in THE ADVENTURES OF ROBIN HOOD (*The Little People* and *The Minstrel*), O.S.S. (*Operation Powder Puff*), INTERPOL CALLING (*White Blackmail*), THE SAINT (*The Noble Sportsman*) and HANCOCK (*The Writer*).

Just prior to being selected for CAPTAIN SCARLET, Matthews had been seen in two further Hammer films, *Dracula – Prince of Darkness* (1965) and *Rasputin, the Mad Monk* (1965), and as a comic foil for Morecambe and Wise in *The Intelligence Men* (1965) and *That Riviera Touch* (1966). He was also seen in an episode of THE AVENGERS (*The Thirteenth Hole*) and then appeared alongside THUNDERBIRDS voice artist Peter Dyneley (Jeff Tracy) in another episode of THE SAINT, *To Kill a Saint*.

Matthews remembers how he first became involved with CAPTAIN SCARLET. 'It started with a phone call asking if I could do various voices for THUNDERBIRDS, which I could have done but I wasn't very interested. My agent's enthusiasm for me earning money changed that decision when CAPTAIN SCARLET was being planned. I got the part because Gerry had heard my Cary Grant impression on Pete Murray's *Open House* radio programme and simply wanted that sound. He just telephoned me out of the blue and asked if I would be interested in voicing Captain Scarlet using the Cary Grant style of voice. I was a huge fan of Cary Grant and I always believed that he was hugely underrated as an actor. Some of his performances were astonishing.

'At the time of CAPTAIN SCARLET, I had just completed work on a new TV series, MY MAN JOE, and I was in Manchester appearing in Noël Coward's *Present Laughter*. To voice the Anderson series I had to fly down from there to Denham very early in the morning and then fly back in the evening. We did them very much like radio plays and the recording sessions were fun. Gerry was lovely, although he wasn't around much during the voice recordings. Sylvia seemed to be more in charge of that. It was a lovely gang – Ed Bishop, Donald Gray and the others – and the best part of it all was the Guinness and lunches in the local pub every day.

'I did not think about my character at all. Since I could not see what was going on just talking into a mike, and the stories without pictures were almost totally unintelligible, I simply tried to sound authoritative! I never saw the puppets or models while we were doing it, but when we finished it all, Gerry took us to the studios to see some of the filming. We saw the

Francis Matthews.

'I have two sons and at the time one was three and the other four. When the series was ready, the producers asked if we would take our boys to the studios to watch the first episode, because they wanted to see how they would react. So we went to the studio, we were given a very nice lunch and then they showed the episode. Well, the moment we heard, "This is the voice of the Mysterons," my eldest son ran screaming from the room, but my other son just sat there riveted. The producer said, "Oh, my God, what have we done? I hope all the children aren't going to be screaming from the living room!" It was all quite funny.'

FRANCIS MATTHEWS

Ed Bishop as Commander Ed Straker in the UFO episode Timelash.

'I don't see a lot of Francis Matthews these days, but we meet up occasionally when we record the voices for the CAPTAIN SCARLET *characters in commercials and things like that. His hair is snow white, we both wear glasses, and it's so funny to see these two old guys getting their scripts out and there I am saying, "S.I.G., Captain Scarlet," to this white-haired old guy with glasses!'*

ED BISHOP

Captain Blue.

model shots and the miniature street scenes and it was all quite fascinating.'

After CAPTAIN SCARLET, Matthews went on to star in the BBC's PAUL TEMPLE detective series, an episode of OUT OF THE UNKNOWN (*The Yellow Pill*) and the feature films *Taste of Excitement* (1969) and *Crossplot* (1969). Later, he starred in a string of BBC series, TRINITY TALES, DON'T FORGET TO WRITE!, A ROOF OVER MY HEAD, TEARS BEFORE BEDTIME and BRAT FARRAR. More recently he has appeared in episodes of TAGGART (*Fatal Inheritance*) and JONATHAN CREEK (*Black Canary*).

Captain Scarlet's partner Captain Blue was voiced by American actor Ed Bishop. Born George Victor Bishop on 11 June 1932 in Brooklyn, New York, he was educated at Peekskill High School and, briefly, Courtland State Teachers' College. After National Service in the US Army, he studied drama at Boston University and was awarded a Fulbright grant to continue his studies at the London Academy of Music and Dramatic Art. After completing his LAMDA training, Bishop stayed on in London when he found himself cast in a number of television and theatre productions: an episode of Granada Television's DRAMA 61 (*Edge of Truth*), *Look Homeward Angel* at the Pembroke Theatre, Croydon, and a West End production of *Bye Bye Birdie*.

Bishop made his feature-film debut with a minor role in Stanley Kubrick's *Lolita* (1961), closely followed by another small part in *The War Lover* (1962) with Steve McQueen. He was much in demand in the theatre during the mid-1960s with roles in productions of *Little Mary Sunshine*, *The Rehearsal* and *Man and Superman*, but he was also seen in the films *The Mouse on the Moon* (1963) and *The Bedford Incident* (1965), and on television, guesting in episodes of THE SAINT (*The Revolution Racket, The Saint Steps In, The Saint Bids Diamonds* and *The Man Who Liked Lions*), COURT MARTIAL (*Shadow of a Man*) and THE BARON (*Storm Warning – Part 2: The Island*).

Bishop has fond recollections of his work on CAPTAIN SCARLET. 'CAPTAIN SCARLET will always hold a place in my memories as a wonderful project to have worked on. We worked two days a month at the Anvil Studios in Denham, and we took all day to do four episodes. We would do two episodes in the morning, have lunch, and then do two episodes in the afternoon. The pace was leisurely and there was no pressure on us from Gerry to "get it in the can quickly".

'It was an interesting composition of actors and we all got along with each other very well. After a while we would get to argue about our characters and say, "I would never say that!" We'd be told, "Relax, fellas, they're only puppets. Don't get carried away here."

'The one thing I particularly liked about CAPTAIN SCARLET, as with all of Gerry's productions, was the attention to detail. We would read the scripts and then they would fit the puppets to match our voices, match our inflections. If you read a line in a certain way and it sounded interesting, they would adjust the puppets to match. How they did it, I don't know, because I was never very aware of the technical side of the thing, but they would make the puppet reflect that certain inflection of voice. That was an example of technology assisting acting, the interpretation of the text and script.

'Every actor received the same fee per episode – £15 15s – so there was never any tension over money. It didn't matter whether you played the lead or just came on and said one tiny little part, every actor got the same money. While I was working on CAPTAIN SCARLET, I was enjoying a huge personal success in Joan Littlewood's production of *MacBird* at the Theatre Royal, Stratford East. Joan, alas, paid no wages – she had no money! – so I will always be grateful to the CAPTAIN SCARLET project for helping me support my young family at a crucial point in my career.'

For Bishop, CAPTAIN SCARLET was the start of a long and happy working relationship with Gerry Anderson. The following year, he appeared as David Poulson in the feature film *Doppelgänger* (1968) and went on to star as Commander Ed Straker in the 1969 live-action series UFO, the role for which he has probably become best known. He later guested in an episode of Anderson's series THE PROTECTORS (*The First Circle*), narrated THE DAY AFTER TOMORROW (a pilot for a television series that never materialized), voiced one of the puppet characters in a commercial for Jif dessert toppings, and provided the voice-over on a promotional trailer for Anderson's 1994 series SPACE PRECINCT.

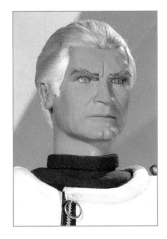

Outside the Anderson camp, Bishop has gone on to have a long and successful career in film, television, theatre and radio. On the big screen he has appeared in more than thirty features, including *You Only Live Twice* (1967), *Battle Beneath the Earth* (1968), *2001: A Space Odyssey* (1968), *Diamonds Are Forever* (1971), *Brass Target* (1978) and *The Lords of Discipline* (1983). On television he has made guest appearances in episodes of MAN IN A SUITCASE (*The Boston Square*), STRANGE REPORT (*Report 5055 Cult 'Murder shrieks out'*), OUT OF THE UNKNOWN (*Beach Head*), the STAR TREK cartoon series (*The Magicks of Megas-Tu*), COLDITZ (*Liberation*), THE PROFESSIONALS (*Long Shot* and *Man Without a Past*), DICK TURPIN (*Dick Turpin's Greatest Adventure*) and THE YOUNG INDIANA JONES CHRONICLES (*The Curse of the Jackal*) among many others. He has appeared in more than thirty stage productions, including *Deathtrap, Feiffer's America, Waiting for Lefty, Death of a Salesman, The Price* and *Broken Glass*, while on radio he is renowned as the definitive Philip Marlowe in a series of BBC adaptations of the novels by Raymond Chandler.

The distinctive tones of Colonel White, the Mysterons and Captain Black were provided by veteran actor Donald Gray. Born Eldred Tilbury on 3 March 1914 at an ostrich farm in Port Beaufort, Cape Province, South Africa, Gray was educated at Marist College, Uitenhage. In 1933, he became the South African winner of Paramount's Search for Beauty contest – the prize was $1,000 and a Hollywood bit-player film contract which saw him appearing in films such as *Come On, Marines* (1934), *Wagon Wheels* (1934), *Here is My Heart* (1934) and *Father Brown Detective* (1935). When his passport expired, he moved to London, where he took roles in *The Belles of St Clements* (1936), *Sword of Honour* (1938), *Murder in the Family* (1938) and *The Four Feathers* (1939).

Colonel White.

Rejected by the British Army because of a duodenal ulcer, he enlisted as a private in the Gordon Highlanders in 1940 and became a lieutenant in the King's Own Scottish Borderers the following year. While on leave he made *We'll Meet Again* (1942), but then lost his left arm to a German anti-tank shell at Caen in 1944. After the war, he joined the BBC's radio repertory company, but left in 1951 to continue his film career with roles in *Saturday Island* (1952), *The Diamond* (1954) and *Burnt Evidence* (1954).

In 1952 Gray became a newsreader for BBC Television, but feeling that he was underworked, he accepted the title role in Edward and Harry Lee Danziger's MARK SABER television series for ITV. The series ran for five years, surviving a title change to SABER OF LONDON and making Gray a household name as the one-armed detective. During the run of MARK SABER, Gray appeared in the feature films *Timeslip* (1955), *Satellite in the Sky* (1956), *The Secret Tent* (1956), *Schemer* (1956) and *Flight from Vienna* (1956), but when the series finished he found himself typecast and could only get work doing narrations and commercials.

Donald Gray.

Captain Black.

Ed Bishop has particularly vivid memories of his CAPTAIN SCARLET co-star. 'Donald was very conservative. I think he played a lot of majors and brigadiers in his career and maybe it got to him, but he was an ultra-conservative guy, politically, and actors are mostly a liberal, radical rabble. We had a black actor in the company, Cy Grant, who was doing the voice of Lieutenant Green. At the time, Rhodesia had just declared unilateral independence and because of apartheid and all the rest it was very, very tense in those days in the 1960s. One day Donald drove up in his car and he had this sticker on it saying "Support Rhodesia", and Cy Grant said, "Hey, Donald, I want to have a word with you about that, man!" He took great exception to Donald's attitude, because most people regarded Rhodesia as a country in which the ruling white minority repressed the black population, so there was a little bit of tension for a while.

'That apart, the recording sessions were friendly and amicable. Donald was a nice man, but he had lost his arm in the war and I think he felt that his career had been curtailed very much because of it. He did SABER OF LONDON, which I saw in the States, and he tended to feel that he had only got that part because the producers thought that a one-armed detective would be a good gimmick. No pun intended, but he seemed to have a kind of chip on his shoulder and maybe that was it.'

After CAPTAIN SCARLET, Gray began to resurrect his career somewhat in the early 1970s with television appearances as Sir John Brinder in the drama serial THE GOLDEN BOWL and guest roles in DOCTOR IN CHARGE (*Brotherly Hate*), DIXON OF DOCK GREEN (*The Hired Man*) and EMMERDALE FARM. His last small-screen appearance was in the BBC's HILL OF THE RED FOX in 1975. He

Cy Grant as Richard Congoto with Roger Moore as Lord Brett Sinclair in THE PERSUADERS! *episode* **Greensleeves.**

Right: Lieutenant Green.

Right: Destiny Angel.

Liz Morgan.

returned to South Africa, where he died of a coronary three years later, aged sixty-four.

The aforementioned Cy Grant was an actor and singer born in British Guiana who made his television debut in a 1952 BBC production MAN FROM THE SUN and his film debut as a Masai chief in Terence Young's *Safari* (1956). He was also seen on television in the late 1950s in NOM DE PLUME, HOME OF THE BRAVE and the series FOR MEMBERS ONLY, while on the big screen he appeared in *Sea Wife* (1957) alongside Joan Collins, Richard Burton and Basil Sydney as one of four wartime ship-wreck survivors, and *Calypso* (1958), an Italian musical documentary film that attempted to cash in on a short-lived calypso craze.

Grant was familiar to Gerry and Sylvia Anderson from his regular appearances singing topical calypsos on the BBC's long-running TONIGHT current affairs programme, and they cast him in CAPTAIN SCARLET as Lieutenant Green. He recalls, 'Lieutenant Green was a black character and for the 1960s this was a very good thing to do. Gerry Anderson should be congratulated for introducing a black character to one of his shows. I was mostly in Cloudbase, but it was a great, fun thing to do. It wasn't a very big part, but I did get my repeat fees – in fact, I've probably earned more from that part than from any other acting part I have ever done!'

After SCARLET, Grant went on to appear in Joseph Mankiewicz's *The Honey Pot* (1967), took a small role as Dr Gordon in Gerry Anderson's *Doppelgänger* (1968) feature film, and starred with Richard Roundtree in the third *Shaft* film, *Shaft in Africa* (1973), playing Emil Ramala. He also guest-starred as Richard Congoto in *Greensleeves*, an episode of THE PERSUADERS!, and made his final film appearance as Ra, leader of a subterranean tribe, in the film adaptation of Edgar Rice Burroughs's *At the Earth's Core* (1976). Grant was last seen on television in 1980 as Hal Mellanby in the BLAKES 7 episode *Aftermath*.

The roles of Destiny, Rhapsody and Harmony Angels were played by Welsh actress Elizabeth Morgan, best known at the time as the presenter of schools programme FINDING OUT. 'I was delighted to do the voices, because we had such fun doing them. We would record every fortnight. Cy Grant and I both lived in Highgate at the time, so he would pick me up at around 7.30 a.m. and we would drive down to the studios to meet up with the rest of the cast. It was a curious place, more like a barn than a studio. We would do some recording and then break for sandwiches and coffee, that sort of thing.

'As an actor, you couldn't just read the script out loud. You had to be aware of the fact that you were recording a voice for puppets that had to be animated afterwards. I completely forgot about this one day while we were recording *Attack on Cloudbase*. It was a moment when Destiny was very worried about Captain Scarlet and she was making impassioned pleas for him. Well, I started to cry, and immediately a voice came down from the recording booth and Reg Hill, who was directing that particular week, said, "No, Liz, love. Do it again, love. Puppets don't cry!"

'I think the selection of the voice artists was done very, very carefully over a number of weeks. I remember going to Gerry Anderson's house in Gerrards Cross at least two or three times to read. They obviously needed to be careful about selection, as we had to do four scripts in one day and there was not a lot of time for direction, so we needed to be able to get on with it. We didn't actually see very much of anything when we were recording, but we all said that we wished that we had seen the puppets before doing the dialogue, as it would have been helpful to have something physical to base the voices on. I knew that Destiny was French and that Rhapsody had to be frightfully "Sloaney", but that was about it. I also did Harmony in the earlier episodes, but later on they brought in a Chinese girl, Lian Shin, to play her.'

After CAPTAIN SCARLET, Liz appeared briefly in the Hammer film *Frankenstein Must Be Destroyed* (1969), starred in THE OLD DEVILS for BBC Wales, appeared as District Nurse Joanna in two seasons of HTV's WE ARE SEVEN, and as Joyce in the LWT sitcom THE TWO OF US. She has also developed a successful writing career, with over two dozen plays for BBC Radio 4 to her name, and both wrote and appeared in the 1994 sitcom pilot SISTERS THREE.

Jeremy Wilkin as Lieutenant Gordon Maxwell in UFO.

British actor Jeremy Wilkin provided the voice for Captain Ochre. Born in Byfleet, Surrey, Wilkin trained as a doctor before switching to the stage and studying at the Royal Academy of Dramatic Art. He emigrated to Canada, settling in Toronto, where he became established as a leading performer, appearing in over 100 television programmes. Returning to London in the mid-1960s, he guested in episodes of COURT MARTIAL and MAN IN A SUITCASE (*Variation on a Million Bucks*), and took the starring role as Drewe Heriot in the ITV science-fiction series UNDERMIND before being cast by Gerry and Sylvia Anderson as the voice of Virgil Tracy in the second season of THUNDERBIRDS and the feature films *Thunderbirds Are Go* and *Thunderbird 6*. It was this role that led directly to CAPTAIN SCARLET.

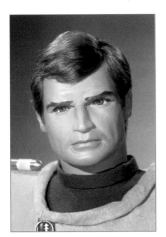

Left: Captain Ochre.

Left: Captain Grey.

Wilkin went on to appear in each of the next five Gerry Anderson productions: he was a Launch Control Technician in *Doppelgänger* (1968), contributed various voices to JOE 90, voiced The Bishop in THE SECRET SERVICE, took the regular role as Lieutenant Gordon Maxwell in UFO and guested as Inspector Lars Bergen in THE PROTECTORS episode *Route 27*. He has since been seen in DOCTOR WHO (*Revenge of the Cybermen*), THE NEW AVENGERS (*House of Cards* and *Medium Rare*), BLAKES 7 (*The Way Back*) and the James Bond film *The Spy Who Loved Me* (1977).

Paul Maxwell as Lieutenant Jim Lewis in the UFO episode Sub-Smash.

Captain Grey was voiced by Paul Maxwell, a Canadian actor who had also previously provided puppet voices for the Andersons, first as Colonel Steve Zodiac in FIREBALL XL5 and then as Captain Paul Travers in *Thunderbirds Are Go* and Captain Ashton in the THUNDERBIRDS episode *Alias Mr. Hackenbacker*. A graduate of Yale School of Drama, Maxwell arrived in England in the late 1950s after an extensive career in Hollywood, with appearances in television series such as ALFRED HITCHCOCK PRESENTS, HIGHWAY PATROL and SEA HUNT to his name. His first British film role was in Spencer Gordon Bennet's *Submarine Seahawk* (1959) and he went on to star in *Shadow of Fear* (1963) and *City of Fear* (1965).

Prior to his SCARLET role, Maxwell had been seen on television in episodes of DANGER MAN (*The Girl Who Liked GIs* and *The Relaxed Informer*), UNDERMIND (*Onset of Fear*) and THE BARON (*Epitaph for a Hero* and *The Man Outside*). Afterwards, he appeared as Steve Tanner in CORONATION STREET and guested in episodes of THE CHAMPIONS (*The Silent Enemy*), RANDALL AND HOPKIRK DECEASED (*The Trouble with Women*), OUT OF THE UNKNOWN (*The Naked Sun*), THE ADVENTURER (*Love Always, Magda*) and RETURN OF THE SAINT (*Tower Bridge is Falling Down*). He was employed by the Andersons one last time when he

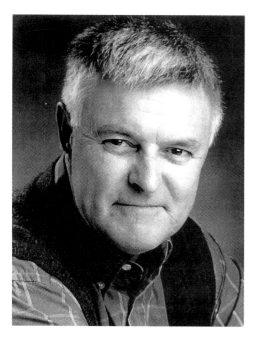

Gary Files.

'I look back on CAPTAIN SCARLET now with a great deal of affection, affection for the people I worked with, for what we did and how we used to meet every fortnight. Sometimes it was a bit cold in the studio but we always had tremendous fun. It was a great experience and one I would repeat gladly at any time. It was innovative and great to be involved with. It brought children and adults alike a great deal of pleasure and if you are a part of that it gets your adrenalin going.'
LIZ MORGAN

Captain Magenta.

made a guest appearance as Lieutenant Jim Lewis in the UFO episode *Sub-Smash*.

From the late 1970s, Maxwell's film career flourished with roles in *The Pink Panther Strikes Again* (1976), *A Bridge Too Far* (1977), *Aliens* (1986) and *Indiana Jones and the Last Crusade* (1989). He was also seen on stage in productions of *On Golden Pond, Death of a Salesman* and *Brighton Beach Memoirs,* and continued working until his death in December 1991.

Australian actor Gary Files was cast as Captain Magenta. The only Australian graduate of the three-year acting course at the National Theatre School of Canada, Files worked for eighteen years in Canada and England with companies as diverse as the Stratford Shakespearian Company in Canada and the Bristol Old Vic Theatre Company in England.

He made his movie debut as a driver in *The Dirty Dozen* (1967) and went on to appear in numerous television roles in both England and Australia, from SOFTLY, SOFTLY, THE SULLIVANS and PRISONER to A COUNTRY PRACTICE, THE FLYING DOCTORS and E.A.R.T.H. FORCE, although he is perhaps best known for his regular role as Tom Ramsey in NEIGHBOURS. More recently, he has been seen in BUTTERFLY ISLAND, THE MAN FROM SNOWY RIVER and PIGS BREAKFAST and the feature films *A Cry in the Dark* (1988) and *Mull* (1989). He has also developed a successful writing and directing career.

During production of CAPTAIN SCARLET, Files voiced various characters for Gerry Anderson's *Thunderbird 6* (1967) feature film and later continued to provide voices for the Supermarionation programmes with numerous guest voices in JOE 90 and Matthew Harding in THE SECRET SERVICE. He also made a brief appearance as Phil Wade in the UFO episode *Identified*. He remembers, 'To begin with, I really had no idea just who or what the Century 21 people and their puppet series were about. It was only after I was one of the team that I realized just what a big success they were, both in England and in the States, and the amazing things that they were doing with their funny puppets out in Slough. I was tremendously grateful for the job at the time, as it supported me and my little family and allowed me to do a lot of unusual work in both TV and theatre that I wouldn't otherwise have been able to do. My residuals from the Century 21 Productions even supported my early efforts in theatre on my return to Canada in 1969.

'In those days, they did everything in style. I remember being flown down for a day's recording from Edinburgh, where I was doing a play in the Festival at the Traverse. They guaranteed to get me back for that night's performance – how they could do that without getting God on their side was beyond me, but I believed them. The flight was impressive enough, and being met at the airport by Gerry's chauffeur holding up a board that read "Mr Files" just blew me away, but then we drove to the session at Denham in Gerry's Rolls-Royce!

'We were shown around the Century 21 Studios at Slough a couple of times, as much to get to see what our characters looked like as to understand the way that they moved them and the constraints involved. For instance, we could never overlap lines. Even if the scene's dynamics called for it – an argument, for example – we just had to "butt up" our cues as closely as we could to each other to get the pace needed. When we saw what the Supermarionation wires were like in the tiny heads of the puppets and how our pre-recorded voices moved their lips, we could see the problem. In shooting a wide shot of, say, several puppets, each puppet's voice had to be clear of the others so that they could throw it to the right one. Overlap and some other puppet's head would have a moving lip as well – not good if the person speaking was one of the women and there was this man's voice coming out of her head!

'We saw the first episode up on the big screen as part of a huge presentation for the Delfonts at the Columbia Theatre in Shaftesbury Avenue. As I said, Gerry did it with style in those days. It tickled us all no end to be attending as "the voices" in a television series for children which was being premiered at one of the major movie houses in the West End!'

Dr Fawn was played by another Australian actor, Charles Tingwell, who had previously provided the voice for Dr Tony Grant in *Thunderbirds Are Go* (1966) and several guest characters in THUNDERBIRDS' second season. Born in a suburb of Sydney on 3 January 1923, Tingwell was a pilot for the Royal Australian Air Force during the Second World War, flying Spitfires and Mosquitoes from a base in Britain. He went back to Australia after the war and began his acting career with roles in *Smithy* (1946), *Always Another Dawn* (1947) and *Bitter Springs* (1950), but returned to the UK in late 1956 to film the studio scenes for *The Shiralee* (1957). He landed the regular role of Alan Dawson in ATV's EMERGENCY WARD 10, and decided to stay on in Britain when he left the series after six years.

Tingwell had a prolific career in British films and television during the 1960s, with appearances in *Tarzan the Magnificent* (1960), *Murder She Said* (1963), *Murder at the Gallop* (1963), *Murder Most Foul* (1964), *Murder Ahoy* (1964), *The Secret of Blood Island* (1965) and *Dracula – Prince of Darkness* (1965), in addition to guest roles in episodes of DANGER MAN (*The Affair at Castelvara*), THE AVENGERS (*The Nutshell* and *Return of the Cybernauts*), ADAM ADAMANT LIVES! (*The Sweet Smell of Disaster*) and OUT OF THE UNKNOWN (*The Counterfeit Man*, *Lambda 1* and *Immortality Inc.*).

He remembers how he first became involved with the Anderson productions. 'I had known an actor called Ray Barrett for a very long time and he arrived in London about two or three years after me. I recommended him to the producer of EMERGENCY WARD 10 and he was given a part as the second Australian character in the show. Later, Ray had been doing a lot of work for the Andersons on STINGRAY and THUNDERBIRDS and he repaid me for my earlier recommendation by putting a good word in for me with Gerry and Sylvia. They were apparently on the lookout for Canadian and Australian radio actors to do the puppet voices and he told them that I was a very experienced radio actor from Sydney.

Charles Tingwell as Captain Beaver James in the UFO episode Mindbender.

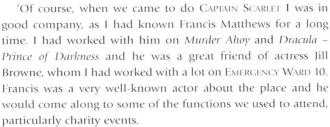

'Of course, when we came to do CAPTAIN SCARLET I was in good company, as I had known Francis Matthews for a long time. I had worked with him on *Murder Ahoy* and *Dracula – Prince of Darkness* and he was a great friend of actress Jill Browne, whom I had worked with a lot on EMERGENCY WARD 10. Francis was a very well-known actor about the place and he would come along to some of the functions we used to attend, particularly charity events.

'At the time, I was heavily involved with the theatre and so I was quite often away on tour. This meant that I was only able to appear in the first twelve episodes of CAPTAIN SCARLET – it was simply a question of not always being available at the right time. It would have been nice to have done more, especially as I keep getting residual payments for the episodes that I did.'

Left: Dr Fawn.

After SCARLET, Tingwell was employed by the Andersons one more time as Captain Beaver James in the UFO episode *Mindbender*. Following a regular role as Mr Bennett in CATWEAZLE, Tingwell returned to Australia, where he has enjoyed a prolific career over the last three decades. For three years he starred as Inspector Reg Lawson in the long-running Australian series HOMICIDE, and then appeared in guest roles in CERTAIN WOMEN, PRISONER and NEIGHBOURS. He has also made big-screen appearances in films such as *Summerfield* (1977), *Breaker Morant* (1980), *A Cry in the Dark* (1988) and *The Castle* (1997), among numerous others.

David Healy as SHADO technician Joe Franklin in the UFO episode Ordeal.

Additional character voices in CAPTAIN SCARLET were provided by American actor David Healy. Born in New York on 15 May 1931, Healy read drama at Southern Methodist University in Dallas. He joined the US Air Force and was stationed in Britain during the Second World War, where he became an entertainments officer. Leaving the military in 1964, he moved to London, where he soon found work in the theatre, appearing in West End productions of *Deathtrap* and *On the Twentieth Century*. Prior to joining the SCARLET cast, he was seen in episodes of THE BARON (*Storm Warning – Part 2: The Island*) and THE SAINT (*Simon and Delilah*), and made his feature film debut in *Be My Guest* (1965).

Liz Morgan remembers, 'David Healy was a great character and always provided us with lots of laughs. He was a lovely colleague, sympathetic, gentle and always ready with a joke. It was the height of the Vietnam War when we were recording CAPTAIN SCARLET and David had been going through a bad

A sound engineer and director Ken Turner in the director's booth during filming of an episode of CAPTAIN SCARLET AND THE MYSTERONS.

'We never imagined that people would still be talking about CAPTAIN SCARLET over thirty years later, let alone still buying the merchandise surrounding the show. As soon as I tell someone that I did voices on CAPTAIN SCARLET, it becomes all they want to know! You'd be surprised at how many people you meet in this profession - directors, actors, you name it - who, as soon as they find out about SCARLET, want to sit and chat about it.'

LIZ MORGAN

period of no work, as we all do from time to time. On one memorable recording session, he bowled in grinning broadly. He told us that he had at last heard from his agent that he had been offered a tour in a Shakespeare play. It was good money and would be going on for several months. I remember congratulating him, "That's great, David. Wonderful news and not before time!" He smiled back and said, "Yep, I asked that old son of a bitch where the tour was and d'you know what he said? 'No problem, David. Saigon's a great place!'" He curled up into howls of laughter and so did we all.'

The same year, Healy joined the Royal Shakespeare Company to appear in Jules Feiffer's *Little Murders* and went on to work with the RSC in numerous other productions. He still found time to voice characters in the subsequent Supermarionation programmes, appearing as WIN chief Shane Weston in JOE 90 and various guest character roles in THE SECRET SERVICE. He later made a guest appearance as SHADO technician Joe Franklin in the UFO episode *Ordeal*, and voiced the character of Armand Loyster in *Protect and Survive*, an episode of Anderson's 1994 series SPACE PRECINCT.

Healy's other television work included episodes of DEPARTMENT S (*Soup of the Day*), RANDALL AND HOPKIRK DECEASED (*Murder Ain't What It Used to Be*), STRANGE REPORT (*Report 3906 Cover Girls 'Last year's model'*), THE PERSUADERS! (*Element of Risk*), JASON KING (*Flamingos Only Fly on Tuesdays*) and RETURN OF THE SAINT (*The Arrangement*). He also appeared on American television in episodes of HARRY O, CHARLIE'S ANGELS (*Target: Angels*), VEGA$ (*Judgment Pronounced*) and DALLAS, and was seen in the feature films *You Only Live Twice* (1967), *Patton* (1970), *Diamonds Are Forever* (1971), *Stardust* (1974), *Supergirl* (1984) and *Haunted Honeymoon* (1986). But it was on the musical stage that Healy came into his own, with numerous roles in productions such as *Songbook, Guys and Dolls* and *Follies*. He died in London in October 1995, aged sixty-four.

Other roles in CAPTAIN SCARLET were played by Janna Hill, Martin King and Sylvia Anderson herself, who took the part of Southern belle Melody Angel. Canadian actor Shane Rimmer, who had previously voiced Thunderbird 1 pilot Scott Tracy in THUNDERBIRDS, made occasional uncredited vocal appearances in subsidiary roles.

The pre-recording of the dialogue for each episode of CAPTAIN SCARLET AND THE MYSTERONS took place at the Anvil Films Recording Studio in Denham, under the supervision of Anvil Films' Douglas Hurring. Recording sessions were scheduled for Sundays, with the cast performing as many as four half-hour episodes in a single day. Producer Reg Hill and Gerry or Sylvia Anderson would often oversee the recording sessions to ensure that the scripts were being interpreted correctly and performed in a way that would not cause problems for the puppeteers during filming.

Once the dialogue had been recorded, it had to be edited to remove any extraneous noise, such as the actors turning the pages of their scripts, and to insert retakes to cover mistakes. The dialogue track would be cut down to a suitable length for filming and returned to the Century 21 studios on ¼-inch master sound tape. A special duplicate of this tape would then be played back during filming, and through a resistance-capacity network pulses would be taken off the tape to operate the solenoids in the bodies of each puppet figure, controlling the lip mechanism so that the lip moved in perfect synchronization with the recorded sound.

Since the original development of the Supermarionation lip-sync system, sound engineer Maurice Askew had furthered the development of a retention scheme, adding more realism to the puppets' lip movements by means of an additional resistance-capacity network fed off the tape's sensitivity level, so that the lower-lip solenoid opened only a little way for the narrow sounds (such as 'he' and 'me') but much wider for the long-sustained vowels (like 'oh' and 'ah').

With the dialogue recorded and edited for the first episode, everything was finally in place for filming on CAPTAIN SCARLET AND THE MYSTERONS to begin on the puppet stages at the Century 21 Studios on Monday 2 January 1967.

PRODUCTION

Despite the poor showing at the box office when *Thunderbirds Are Go* went on general release in the UK in December 1966, executives at United Artists, the distributors of the film, had already decided that they wanted Gerry Anderson to make a second THUNDERBIRDS feature film. Budgeted at £300,000, *Thunderbird 6* was scheduled to begin shooting at the Century 21 Studios on 1 May 1966, exactly half-way through the planned production schedule for CAPTAIN SCARLET AND THE MYSTERONS. Already fully committed to having thirty-two episodes of CAPTAIN SCARLET ready for transmission by the autumn of 1967, the Andersons, Reg Hill and John Read realized that, in order to cope with the increasing level of production at the studios, they would have to promote some of the experienced junior technicians and take on a significant number of new employees to fill their shoes.

The Mysteron complex model on the visual effects soundstage.

Tony Barwick was appointed as script editor of the new series. He had joined AP Films early in 1965 to help THUNDERBIRDS script editor Alan Pattillo to double the length of existing half-hour scripts in the wake of Lew Grade's eleventh-hour decision that the series' episodes would become an hour long. He had gone on to write two complete episodes of THUNDERBIRDS' second season, *Lord Parker's 'Oliday* and *Ricochet*, and on the strength of this work he was invited to become a full-time Century 21 employee.

As script editor on CAPTAIN SCARLET, Barwick was responsible for commissioning scripts from new writers and often found himself completely rewriting episodes, for which he received no credit. His first job, however, was to write the scripts for the three episodes that would follow Gerry and Sylvia Anderson's pilot into production, *Winged Assassin*, *Big Ben Strikes Again* and *Manhunt*. He went on to pen a further fifteen episodes, his scripts invariably characterized by new developments in the war with the Mysterons, or new revelations about the main characters and the set-up of the Spectrum organization.

In an interview completed in 1986, Barwick spoke about his approach to writing CAPTAIN SCARLET. 'The big decision to switch the size of the puppets' heads and make them more realistic obviously had to be reflected in the storylines of the series. Unlike Gerry's previous series, there wasn't much humour in CAPTAIN SCARLET and I think that the whole thing was geared around making people almost forget that they were watching puppets. It was pretty hard-nosed stuff.

Tony Barwick.

'I saw the format of SCARLET as almost a variation of International Rescue. The characters are all stuck up on an aircraft carrier in space, Cloudbase, so that's like Tracy Island. The central characters are a team of heroes who are ready to go in and get people out of trouble (albeit a different kind of trouble from what was usually on hand in THUNDERBIRDS) and, in the same way as THUNDERBIRDS had the Hood, the mysterious heavy who's lurking around in the background, CAPTAIN SCARLET had Captain Black and the Mysterons. I think it was really quite formalized writing. You have your hero figure, Captain Scarlet, and then you have your coloured guy, Lieutenant Green. Then you've got Colonel White, who's the head guy, the commander, very authoritative. Captain Blue's the foil, the nice guy, and then the girls, the Angels, are from all sorts of backgrounds: one's Oriental, one's English, one's American, and so on. It was all for the American market and to that extent there was no deep characterization. They all balanced one against the other.'

A primary area for concern was finding new directors to handle CAPTAIN SCARLET. Of the directors who had previously helmed the episodes of THUNDERBIRDS, Alan Pattillo and David Elliott had left the company to pursue their careers elsewhere, while David Lane would be fully occupied for much

Director Ken Turner positions the Captain Scarlet puppet for a scene in Noose of Ice.

A floor puppeteer and an art department member prepare the hunting lodge set for a scene in Spectrum Strikes Back.

of SCARLET's principal photography planning and directing *Thunderbird 6*, leaving only Desmond Saunders and Brian Burgess.

Alan Perry had joined AP Films as a clapper loader on SUPERCAR and became a camera operator on STINGRAY and THUNDERBIRDS. 'Even on those earlier shows, I was never just a cameraman. I was always somebody who got involved with the cutting and I tried to research into the script and give as much help as I possibly could from my side. Whether I shone or whatever way it went, I was picked out and when we came to CAPTAIN SCARLET, Gerry Anderson said, "Right, fancy having a go at one?" And I did, but it was awfully frightening for a young man to take on all that responsibility. Suddenly, you weren't part of the crew – everyone was looking to you for direction.

'When I saw my first episode at the end, there was a great feeling of, "Yeah, I made that!" There were quite a few of those episodes that I made .and I enjoyed doing that. Even now when I see them, they bring up the old hairs on the back of the neck. That's nice, the feeling that you've achieved something which is there for keeps.'

Ken Turner started out as an art assistant, working for Bob Bell and Keith Wilson on THUNDERBIRDS. Recognized as someone with a particular talent for organization, Turner was invited to join David Lane on *Thunderbirds Are Go* as his assistant director and this led directly to his appointment as one of the main unit directors on CAPTAIN SCARLET.

He recalls, 'I think that David Lane was integral in my landing the SCARLET job. I was ecstatic to be asked to do it, but I was very apprehensive at first. I would get old THUNDERBIRDS scripts and take them home and try to break them down into shots and see if I was doing it as it should be done. I would ask Alan Pattillo for advice on this side of things and he was marvellous. He was a script editor and director on THUNDERBIRDS and really knew what was required on this type of programme. Fortunately, I didn't need to go through too many scripts before he said to me that I was doing all right and breaking it all down in the way that he would have, which was a great relief.'

Other directors with prior experience in filmed television were drafted in from outside the Century 21 Studios. Veteran film-maker Robert Lynn had entered the film industry as an assistant director in 1946, with work on films such as *Black Narcissus* (1947), *An Inspector Calls* (1954) and the classic Hammer films *The Abominable Snowman* (1957), *Dracula* (1958) and *The Revenge of Frankenstein* (1958). He made his directorial debut on the TALES FROM DICKENS television series and went on to helm episodes of INTERPOL CALLING, GHOST SQUAD, THE PURSUERS and THE SAINT, before making his film directing debut with *Two Letter Alibi* (1962). Prior to joining the crew of CAPTAIN SCARLET, Lynn had also directed *Dr Crippen* (1962), *Blaze of Glory* (1963), *Mozambique* (1965) and *Spy Against the World* (1966). When he arrived at the Century 21 Studios in January 1967, he was the most respected and experienced film-maker working for the company, even though he had never worked with puppets before.

The other new directors on the series were much less experienced. Twenty-two-year-old Leo Eaton had been working at the Associated British Studios in Borehamwood on the ITC series GIDEON'S WAY and THE BARON, and had become second assistant director on THE SAINT. 'I was good friends with Frank Hollands, who was one of the first assistant directors on THE SAINT, and when he was recruited by Gerry Anderson to become his production manager, Frank suggested that I might like to join him at Century 21, as it would give me a chance to move up to first assistant director. I met Gerry and Sylvia and the other key executives, was hired and left THE SAINT for CAPTAIN SCARLET just before it went into production.

'Coming out of a live-action TV background, where the first assistant director runs the set, my job was to bring a similar discipline to the puppet shows. Although they'd had assistant directors on *Thunderbirds Are Go*, they had been more general assistants to the director. I think part of Gerry's thinking, by bringing in Frank Hollands and live-action assistant directors such as myself and Peter Anderson (who came in at much the same time) was to make the new series run as smoothly as possible. It was my job to run the floor, to make sure work was completed on schedule, that the director had everything that he needed, and to keep him moving fast enough to complete the day's schedule. This is the primary role of a first assistant director, like a sergeant-major in the army, keeping things moving while the director concentrates on the creative job of getting pictures on the screen.

'It was a bit of a strange transition after THE SAINT, as none of the puppet crews were used to this type of assistant director, not even the directors, and I kept on having to say, "'No, don't worry about that. That's what I'm here for." Up through THUNDERBIRDS, they'd had to do everything themselves. By the beginning of CAPTAIN SCARLET, the operation was becoming much more of a factory assembly line and the inclusion of first assistant directors was part of this streamlining operation. As a first assistant director on a normal TV series, one of the major roles is keeping the crew quiet during a take. I remember that soon after my arrival at Century 21, I yelled for quiet and a puppeteer called down from the rail, "Why?" It was an adjustment, for them and for me.

'When I first joined the company, Gerry made it clear that if I worked out successfully, I'd be quickly given the chance to direct. At one point, he had me directing THUNDERBIRDS commercials for Lyons Maid ice lollies. It was then that I really decided that the commercials side of the business wasn't for me, sitting in a conference room with a bunch of highly paid advertising executives as they argued endlessly about the precise angle that Lady Penelope should hold the ice lolly. Since I'd also been doing a lot of writing on my own, I had wanted to write scripts from the start and Tony Barwick said that if I gave him a treatment he liked, he'd let me write the script. I'd been thinking for some time about writing a sci-fi short story about someone releasing poison into a big-city reservoir, so I decided to turn it into a script. *Place of the Angels* was both my first produced script and the first TV show I ever directed.

'From that point on, I was one of Gerry's stable of directors. There was the older, more experienced group, who were already moving up into management, people like Desmond Saunders, Brian Burgess and Dave Lane, all of whom had been with Gerry for some time. And then there were the "young Turks", as we saw ourselves: Ken Turner, Alan Perry, myself and, later on, Peter Anderson. This core group continued with Century 21 right through the later Supermarionation series JOE 90 and THE SECRET SERVICE and then on

'Trying to lose those strings was such a pain. The earlier shows gave you a little more scope, I guess, as the characters were quite obviously puppets. By the time I was directing, the puppets were almost, at a glance, like real people. We couldn't afford to have the slightest hint of a string or a wobbly bit of movement. You were sometimes in a situation where you couldn't do any more to hide the strings and if they still showed up you had to let it go. We spent so long trying to hide them that you'd be doing it all day if you weren't careful, so sometimes you'd just say, "Leave it. We've got to get on with the filming."'

KEN TURNER

Assistance from the visual effects department during filming of a scene in Seek and Destroy.

The set of the World President's office is prepared for a scene in which a Mysteron duplicate of Captain Brown explodes.

'I found that I got the best stuff from the puppets when I tried to make them behave in the most human fashion. If, in doing that, it became "puppet-like", then I'd pull back a little and ask the puppeteer to give me a little less. Automatically, that lessened the movement that we got from the puppets compared to what we'd seen in STINGRAY or THUNDERBIRDS. It wasn't a concerted effort to make the SCARLET puppets stiff and immobile; it just came out of knowing our limitations. The more realistic the puppet, the more realistic the movement had to be. If that meant that a character moved very little and looked realistic, then that is what we had to do.'

KEN TURNER

into the live-action series UFO.'

Arriving at the Century 21 Studios from the bigger live-action studios in Borehamwood, Eaton was particularly struck by the difference in the studio set-up. 'The studio location was a depressing place, set on the Slough Industrial Estate in prefabricated buildings that looked indistinguishable from all the other small factories and businesses in the area. We used to quote Poet Laureate John Betjeman's poem, "Come, friendly bombs, and fall on Slough".

'The Century 21 complex consisted of four buildings at that time. Furthest to the west was the special effects building, where Derek Meddings had three units operating at all times. Next was the building containing the two puppet stages, where I did most of my work. There were always two units operating simultaneously on two different episodes, but during any pause in production, there'd be a lot of visiting backwards and forwards between the two stages. The next building to the east contained the big puppet stage where *Thunderbird 6* was made. This was joined to the other buildings by an open-sided walkway covered with a corrugated-iron roof. All the roofs of all the buildings were corrugated iron and in a heavy rainstorm the drumming could drown out anything said on stage. Coming from Elstree Studios, where a silent sound stage was essential, it used to amaze me how noisy these Century 21 stages were. Also, I don't remember if there was any air-conditioning on the stages, but if there was it never worked very well. In summer they were sweltering, especially under the lights. We'd all strip down as far as was decent and hang outside at every available moment, panting. The puppeteers up on the rail had it even worse, as heat rises.

'The final building held the cutting rooms and other post-production offices, but we had little to do with this area. The directors didn't have much input in the editing, and the 35mm film magazines vanished at the end of the day, although I seem to recall that viewing rushes was a daily activity.'

There were also new recruits to the team of puppeteers under the supervision of Christine Glanville and Mary Turner. Jan King left school at sixteen and walked straight into a job in the puppet workshop. 'I joined the company in October 1966 and started by working in the workshop for about six weeks, putting puppet bodies together and stringing new puppets for CAPTAIN SCARLET. I also did one or two manipulation tests to get the feel of the puppets as they were such a different design to the THUNDERBIRDS puppets. The atmosphere was very friendly and very enthusiastic, because THUNDERBIRDS had been such a success. I was very young at the time and it was like working in a fantasy world.

'My first trial on the floor was on the second episode of CAPTAIN SCARLET, when it took me seventeen takes to turn one puppet's head towards another one, say a line of dialogue and then turn the head back again. We took two weeks, ten working days, to shoot all the puppet shots for each episode, but this would usually go over schedule by one or two days. We would work evenings quite a lot, to make up time, and occasionally Saturdays too.'

Rowena White answered an advertisement in *The Stage* newspaper for a wardrobe assistant. 'Mary Turner wrote back to me enclosing a puppet and asking me to make a shirt and trousers for it, which I did. As a result of this, I went up to Slough for an interview. Mary told me that a vacancy for a floor puppeteer had arisen and asked if I would prefer that. I said, "Yes, please, I would." So in January 1967, I started work on the first episode of CAPTAIN SCARLET as a floor puppeteer.

'To start with, I found it all very strange. I don't know what I'd been expecting – something smaller and more homely, I think, not this vast studio like an aircraft hangar, with a concrete floor, no windows, just skylights, and big double doors at the end which looked out on to a playing field and let the daylight in when they slid back. There was this great high bridge, a control booth where the lip-sync operator and director sat looking at the monitor, lights everywhere, cables all over the place and various young men painting the roller backings and dressing the set. In one corner by the sliding door into the workshop was what was known as the puppet corner – this was the puppeteers' domain. There was a large set of drawers containing everything from a needle to a hammer, some chairs and the puppets hung from a batten on the wall on strings about 12 feet long.

'Everyone was very friendly and I soon became part of the family. I had terrible problems at first with the puffing of the strings with powder paint to get rid of them on camera. I took ages and even then the results weren't good enough. I remember that Alan Perry was the director on that picture and he took over once and did them for me. I was so bad that I nearly lost my job, but then suddenly I got the hang of it and never looked back. The puppeteers themselves were an occasional hazard when you were doing the strings. You would puff the strings and get them just right and then an extra puppeteer would be called on to the set. They would walk across the bridge, knocking the strings, and all the powder paint would fly off so you'd have to do it all over again.

'A floor puppeteer was rather similar to a continuity girl. You have to know little details, such as which hand a puppet was holding something in, or was it looking to the left or right of camera, things like that. Luckily, I had a photographic memory and could remember without writing it all down. Mel Cross was one of the puppeteers and he had been the floor puppeteer immediately before me. He told me, "Even if you're not sure about something, pretend that you are, be positive and they will believe you." It worked and it was good advice, I think.

'I had what was called a puppet box, sort of like a tool box, which I carried around with me. It contained all that was needed to make running repairs on the set: anti-flare and puffer bottles containing the powder paint to spray the strings, scissors, screwdrivers, puppet wire, camera tape, lead pellets, a comb, hairspray, glue, needles and a bottle of carbon tetrachloride. This was needed to clean the puppet's hair when you puffed the strings a little too enthusiastically and a great lump of powder paint, usually black, landed on the puppet's head. The puppeteers relied on camera tape quite a lot, because it could be used to lash a puppet to a block of wood to stop it swaying about in close-up or to stiffen an arm to hold something like a telephone. It was one of our mainstays. We also used to use G-clamps to weight the puppets down and keep them fixed to the floor.'

Each puppet unit would normally include the director, camera crew, an assistant director, lip-sync operator, three set artists for dressing the sets, three electricians, two bridge puppeteers operating the

Puppeteer Christine Glanville positions the game warden puppet for a scene in Spectrum Strikes Back.

Scarlet, Blue and Gabrielle are weighted down with G-clamps and lashed to wood blocks with gaffer tape for a scene in Model Spy.

A puppeteer holds Captain Scarlet's legs in place as he opens fire on Goddard in a scene from **The Trap**.

'Sometimes things got a bit fraught, particularly if a picture was over schedule. On one film that Ken Turner was directing we had a water fight. It started with one of the puffers used for the powder paint being filled with water and squirted at me. It all snowballed until eventually the whole crew was involved. Eventually, Ken got the firehose out and soaked us all. We didn't even think how dangerous it was with all the live cables lying about. It all came to an end when Reg Hill came walking around the corner dressed in a smart pinstriped suit to be confronted with Ken wielding the firehose.'
ROWENA WHITE

Right: A floor puppeteer works the under-control Harmony puppet while at the same time a member of the art department works Harmony's flight controls.

puppets from the gantry, and a floor puppeteer. During filming, the puppets were controlled from a bridge walkway 3 feet wide and 30 feet long, supported some 12 feet above the set on a gantry that could be easily moved about on the smooth concrete floors of the studio. From here, the puppeteers were able to watch their puppets' performances on a 23-inch CCTV monitor which displayed the image seen through the viewfinder of the film camera via an all-transistor Pye Lynx camera that was coupled to it. This image was also displayed on other monitors on the studio floor, in the director's booth and the producers' offices, enabling everyone to see each scene as it was filmed.

In an interview completed in 1992, Christine Glanville recalled some of the problems that the puppeteers encountered when they started to work with the new-style puppets. 'The puppets themselves were very difficult to work with, more so than on the earlier series. We couldn't turn or animate them at all well. If you look at a photograph of the figures on the set, they look very good and you have to look quite closely to see if they are real or not as the proportions are so accurate. But they didn't work like people – they still worked like puppets.

'To get the puppets to turn their heads, more often than not in a close-up, a member of the team would stand just out of shot with their fingers just above the puppet head, twisting the wires to get the head to turn round. To add to the challenge, as the wires were live, the floor puppeteer would have to insulate the head wires with gaffer tape to prevent themselves from being electrocuted! We just couldn't get their heads to turn with that length of string.

'I had this idea of having the puppets worked from beneath the set, like a glove puppet, as there was always the difficulty of hiding a hole in the top of an aircraft canopy from the camera. So I suggested that the puppeteers might work from underneath and the reply came back from the production office, "Don't be ridiculous, it's a silly idea, we've never done it that way before," and so on. In the end, I took a puppet head and staged a crude mock-up, placing it in a cockpit. A camera was turned on in the hope that Gerry would see it on the monitor in his office, which he did. From then on, we used that technique in most of the scenes involving puppets in vehicles and we found that we could get much more interesting angles on the craft.'

Rowena White recalls the under-control puppets, as they came to be known, only too well. 'Part of my job was to work the puppet heads when they were seen in close-up, or to move a puppet along as if it was walking. This involved lying on the set, out of shot, usually in a very uncomfortable position under the hot lights for hours on end. And working the under-control puppets was just as uncomfortable. I can remember spending one whole afternoon down a pit under some staging with a member of the art department. I was working one of

the under-control Angels in the cockpit of her aircraft and he was working some effect in the craft. It was very cold down there and when the tea trolley arrived, the whole crew abandoned us and left us trapped under there!'

As the winter months turned into spring, filming on CAPTAIN SCARLET settled into a routine of sorts. Ken Turner remembers the general day-to-day process of preparing an episode. 'First of all, you were given a script and told, "That's your one." You couldn't pick and choose which scripts you wanted to do. I'd look over the script and try to find time to meet with Christine Glanville, Derek Meddings and usually Bob Bell and Keith Wilson. They were always very busy and I would have to squeeze myself in to their schedules. Sometimes, you would have a chat over a cup of tea in the morning or at lunchtime – whenever you could really. Often I'd meet with Mike Trim if Derek was really up against it. Mike was a fantastic designer and artist, and he could do the storyboards if Derek was tied up with the filming itself.

'Coming from a background in the art department, I would often go through a new script and think that I might have an idea for a set or even a craft, but I knew that Derek and Bob were in charge of some very good people who needed no assistance from me and so, basically, I let them get on with it. Derek, in particular, was overflowing with ideas and he and Mike were two of the most talented and enthusiastic blokes I think I've ever worked with. Sometimes I thought we couldn't keep up with them and their ideas and designs.

'But then that was the nature of the company. Everybody knew that the other departments were top class and that they would be coming up with exciting and interesting things. The main concern for everyone was that the scenes and the models and sets used in them were cost effective. If, for example, Captain Scarlet was to be seen in a vehicle cockpit, we would work out how much of it really needed to be seen and Bob would then tell his boys that only this or that section needed building, as that was all that would be required on camera. The same with Derek. If a rocket was to crash or collide with something, he would decide that only a certain section needed building for that shot, and it saved time and money. That was the beauty of the storyboards and the meetings we had. It enabled us to go into each shot of each programme with a pretty clear idea of what we were going to be doing on the floor each day.

'A good example of that was when we would need to shoot insert shots of real hands holding a gun or picking something up – things that it was impossible to get the puppets to do. When I came to direct on CAPTAIN SCARLET I would go through a script and pick out the scenes that I knew would have to be real-hand shots. Then I made sure that the appropriate people knew that a full-size section of set was needed or a particular piece of Captain Scarlet's uniform was required.

Captain Scarlet, Dr Kurnitz and his receptionist in a scene from Dangerous Rendezvous.

'We picked up loads of little tricks to give the viewer the impression of movement without actually seeing a puppet move. We'd shoot a character just getting up out of a chair, then we'd see another puppet raise his head as if he was looking at the other one, then maybe a shot of a real hand pressing a button which then opens a door. With good editing, all these shots would give the impression of a fluid movement of the character from a chair, across a room and out of a door.'
KEN TURNER

Left: A puppeteer manipulates the Colonel White puppet for a tricky scene in Spectrum Strikes Back.

A model-maker dresses a miniature street set that will be used for scenes in **Big Ben Strikes Again.**

Director Alan Perry wearing a partial Spectrum uniform to play Captain Scarlet in live-action insert footage for **The Trap.**

Quite often, it would be more trouble than it was worth trying to explain to someone else, "I want Scarlet to reach over and pick the bomb up off the floor, but don't do it too roughly." I knew what I wanted and I would more often than not just do it myself. All of the directors did actually. It cut down on time and kept things on schedule. The programmes were expensive to make and if anything could be done to keep the costs down and up to speed, we would do it. It may shatter a few illusions, but quite often in my episodes I was Captain Scarlet, Captain Blue and all the rest of them. I would have sleeves with the Spectrum emblem on them and sometimes we had a sort of bib that looked like the suede tunic. If we could get away with just the sleeves we would. Anything to keep it simple.'

Keeping it simple was also Derek Meddings's philosophy over on the special effects stage, where the majority of CAPTAIN SCARLET's effects involved explosions, collisions and vehicles crashing off mountain roads, usually as the prelude to the Mysterons' latest act of retaliation. Experience on THUNDERBIRDS had taught Meddings and his team that the key to creating convincing destruction in miniature was the correct use of materials. If a model vehicle had to be blown up, it would be pre-scored to break apart in pieces of the right size when the charge inside was detonated. Collapsing buildings would be made in the same way, constructed from sections of wood and polystyrene loosely stuck together and then coated with a thin layer of plaster. To make the destruction of such buildings even more convincing, the model-makers would fit them with miniature rooms built into plastic tool-box drawers, furnished in detail with tiny tables and chairs. This was the case with the impressive 6-foot-tall Maximum Security Building model built for the series' pilot episode *The Mysterons*. Unfortunately, when the explosives were detonated, they created so much dust that all the fine detail was obscured from the camera.

Many of the model sets were made at $1/12$ scale, which enabled the special effects crew to film scenes with a high level of realism, particularly when it came to explosions or scenes of buildings and vehicles on fire. Some of the most spectacular effects in CAPTAIN SCARLET were only possible because the budget enabled the model sequences to be filmed at a much larger scale than before, as seen in sequences such as the oil rig fire in *Fire at Rig 15*, the explosion of the Second National Bank in *The Heart of New York* and the collapse of the Hotspot Tower bridge in *Noose of Ice.*

With Derek Meddings unable to spend as much time supervising the effects on CAPTAIN SCARLET as he would have liked, due to his dual commitments to the *Thunderbird 6*

feature film, model sequences such as these were handled by the two special effects main unit directors Shaun Whittaker-Cooke and Jimmy Elliott, while a third unit, under the supervision of Peter Wragg, handled all the flying sequences. This unit was based in a separate building on the Slough Trading Estate, as space in the studio was at a premium.

Peter Wragg remembers, 'It was basically a flying unit, for all the straight flying shots that didn't require sets and landscapes – the air-to-air flying shots. That was all down to a time-scale in order to get the episodes finished so that they could be dubbed and meet their transmission dates. One effects unit would be working on one episode, another effects unit would be working on another episode and I would be doing straight flying shots for both episodes.

'Flying a model convincingly on wires was a devil of a job. You're standing on the edge of a plank, hovering over the edge of a set, holding something out at arm's length. There was quite a sense of balance that you had to have and it was a case of shifting your weight from one foot to

another without going up and down, while keeping your hand and body on the same plane. If you got a slight twitch in the hand, it was accentuated on the model below, so you got an enormous lurch of the model.'

Filming on *The Mysterons* was completed by mid-January 1967 and the raw 35mm film was passed to Len Walter's editing team in the Century 21 cutting rooms. It was another two months before Walter and Anderson were happy with this all-important first episode and the print could be passed to composer Barry Gray for scoring.

Prior to his first meeting with Gerry Anderson in 1957 on THE ADVENTURES OF TWIZZLE, Lancashire-born Barry Gray had enjoyed a long and happy working relationship with Dame Vera Lynn as her accompanist-arranger, scoring her arrangements for the stage, Decca recordings and radio and television shows. He also maintained a lucrative career as a composer of music

and jingles for many of British television's earliest commercials, for products such as Esso petrol, Typhoo tea and Wall's ice cream. He was introduced to Anderson by Roberta Leigh and the producer was so impressed with Gray's fully orchestrated arrangements of the songs for TWIZZLE that he employed him to score each of his subsequent television and film productions.

Via the Gerry Anderson productions, Barry Gray made an indelible mark on popular culture, producing such magnificent orchestral pieces as the themes to THUNDERBIRDS, JOE 90, THE SECRET SERVICE, UFO and SPACE: 1999, and the scores for *Thunderbird 6* (1967) and *Doppelgänger*

Derek Meddings perches on a ladder to fly an Angel Interceptor model closing in on the tailwing of Major Reeves's jet for a complicated visual effects sequence in Renegade Rocket. *To give the effect of the Angel as seen in Reeves's rear-view mirror, the camera is focused on a mirror positioned in front of a sky backdrop and angled to reflect the model action behind the camera. The completed scene lasts no longer than two seconds in the finished episode.*

Flying unit director Peter Wragg uses a smoke candle to create foreground clouds blown by Alan Berry with a vacuum cleaner for an effects sequence of the Angel Interceptors in flight.

Barry Gray, composer of the themes and incidental music for no fewer than fifteen Gerry Anderson productions.

(1968), as well as a host of memorable theme songs, including 'Four Feather Falls', 'Supercar', 'Fireball' and 'Aqua Marina'. A keen proponent of electronic music, Gray did much to pioneer the use of early synthesizers such as the theremin and the Ondes Martenot (a French instrument which produced sound oscillations controlled from a keyboard) in film and television music. He integrated his very differing musical styles in the scores for the Gerry Anderson productions, often using orchestral pieces for Earth-based scenes and his unique electronic effects to complement scenes set in space.

The sinister alien presence of the Mysterons provided Gray with plenty of opportunity to develop chilling electronic themes for CAPTAIN SCARLET AND THE MYSTERONS. Gray added a Baldwin Electronic Harpsichord to his repertoire and this was used to great effect on the themes for both the opening and secondary title sequences, each of which was punctuated by a seven-beat tom-tom staccato. This staccato was used throughout the episodes of CAPTAIN SCARLET as an effective scene-changing device, with the film edited to alternate between scenes with each drumbeat.

Although today he recognizes that this staccato was an ingeniously simple device which imbued CAPTAIN SCARLET with a unique and highly memorable style of television presentation, Gerry Anderson was furious when he first heard what Gray had composed for the series. 'The titles on the series were always devised by me, not because I was the only person who could do it, but because I believe that only one person can devise a title sequence in terms of concept. When it came to CAPTAIN SCARLET, I was frightened that people would say, "Oh, it's the same old Crash! Bang! Wallop! stuff again," so I made a conscious effort to do something totally different.

'I had a great admiration for Barry Gray and we got on famously, but at times he could also be very irritating to me. He was a highly intelligent person who was steeped in music and a great technician. He deserved ten times the respect that he received. There were occasions, though, when I could not get things across to him and I don't know to this day if he was just playing daft and it was his way of resisting what I wanted him to do. For CAPTAIN SCARLET, I wanted him to create a fanfare that we could cut to, but either he couldn't understand or didn't want to. At the session where the musician played this piece of music for me, I thought, "Is this all he could produce?" but in retrospect it worked quite well.'

The staccato also introduced the series' end title song, 'Captain Scarlet', initially recorded by Gray as an instrumental piece with electronic vocal interruptions. The track was recorded at Gray's own recording studio at his home, Red Gables, in Esher, Surrey, on Sunday 26 February 1967, with Gray himself performing the electro-voice, aided by EMI engineer Charles Gregory and with vocal backing by Fred Datchler, Ken Barrie and Fred Lucas. This version of the theme appeared on the first fourteen episodes of the series, but was then replaced with a version performed by The Spectrum, a five-piece London-based group who had been manufactured by RCA Victor to compete with the success of the American manufactured band The Monkees.

The Spectrum, manufactured and promoted as Britain's answer to The Monkees, performed the end titles song for CAPTAIN SCARLET AND THE MYSTERONS.

The Spectrum comprised Keith Forsey (drums and harmonica), his brother Colin (vocals, rhythm guitar, harmonica and piano), Bill Chambers (organ, piano and guitar), Anthony Judd (bass guitar) and Tony Atkins (lead guitar and banjo). A highly talented and much underrated group of musicians, The Spectrum had scored chart success in Spain with their first single, a recording of The Monkees' hit 'Saturday's Child', released on a double-A-sided record with 'Samantha is Mine'.

During the early summer of 1967, the single was being heavily promoted on Radio 1 in the UK by Tony Blackburn when it was heard by Gerry Anderson's chauffeur. He drew the producer's attention to the coincidence of the group's name being identical to that of the secret organization in his latest series and Anderson immediately decided to sign the group to a £100,000 contract and promote them in tandem with the launch of CAPTAIN SCARLET. Gray rearranged his end titles theme as a song with lyrics for the group to perform, and this new version was recorded on Wednesday 26 July 1967.

While CAPTAIN SCARLET was airing on British television, The Spectrum released a string of singles, following 'Samantha is Mine' with 'Portobello Road', 'Headin' for a Heatwave' and 'London Bridge is Coming Down', often

performing in life-size replicas of the Spectrum uniforms from the series. 'Headin' for a Heatwave' was a number-one hit in Spain and their later recording of The Beatles' 'Ob-La-Di, Ob-La-Da' topped the charts in Germany. The band released numerous other singles over the next two years, including 'Little Red Book', 'Free', 'Glory' and 'I'll Be Gone', as well as an album, *The Light is Dark Enough*.

Feeling that they had been treated badly by their record company, the band split up and went their separate ways in 1970. Keith Forsey later became a major player in the music industry, progressing from being the drummer with Boney M (performing on 'Rasputin', 'Brown Girl in the Ring' and 'Rivers of Babylon', among others) to writer of Irene Cara's 'Flashdance (What a Feeling)' and the Simple Minds hit 'Don't You Forget About Me', before becoming a producer for Billy Idol.

From 16 March to 3 December 1967, Barry Gray composed full incidental scores for eighteen episodes of CAPTAIN SCARLET, recorded at his own studio with an orchestra which varied from four to sixteen performers. Much of this was then used as incidental music for the remaining fourteen episodes by music editor George Randall, who also drew on pieces that Gray had recorded for the earlier Anderson productions, including the main titles track from Anderson's live-action film *Crossroads to Crime* (1960).

By the time that CAPTAIN SCARLET AND THE MYSTERONS made its debut on British television on Friday 29 September 1967, just over twenty episodes had been completed, ready for transmission. Filming on CAPTAIN SCARLET continued until late October 1967 and the final episodes were ready for transmission by the end of the year. By this time, the promotion and merchandising campaign for CAPTAIN SCARLET was in full swing to make Christmas 1967 a 'CAPTAIN SCARLET Christmas', but the film-makers at the Century 21 Studios were already hard at work on the next Supermarionation series, as well as a new live-action project that was to prove the beginning of the end for Gerry Anderson's puppet empire.

'Headin' for a Heatwave', a number-one hit in Spain for The Spectrum.

The crew of CAPTAIN SCARLET AND THE MYSTERONS *with The Spectrum on the puppet soundstage at the Century 21 Studios, autumn 1967.*

THE WORLD OF CAPTAIN SCARLET
AND THE MYSTERONS

DATELINE: 2068 A.D.

The Culver Atomic Centre (Manhunt*)*.

In the world of 2068, incredible advances in biological and technological research have almost entirely freed Earth from the misery of poverty, disease and famine, and the discovery of new sources of food and fuel has eased the difficulties of massive population growth.

At Kufra in North Africa, huge subterranean lakes beneath the Sahara have been tapped to irrigate the desert, while in the Najama valley in the foothills of the Andes, processed sea water from the Pacific Ocean is being used to fertilize hundreds of miles of arid Argentinian wasteland. The development of thermic power has eased the pressure on the planet's depleted resources of fossil fuels and reduced the reliance on potentially dangerous atomic and solar power sources. Instead, the heat at the Earth's core is tapped by a shaft in the Nevada Desert and fed in the form of energy waves to six thermic sub-stations around the world, providing enough power to service the needs of almost every community on the planet.

Medical science has taken great leaps forward with the development of gene replacement, synthetic histogenesis and sonic microsurgery. Recent pioneering work by Dr Theodore Magnus at London Hospital has seen the successful development of a cerebral pulsator which aims to eliminate the risk in brain operations, while at Slaton Hospital Dr Edward Mitchell and Dr Paul Baxter have perfected a recovery unit which maintains a patient in stasis until vital functions can be restored. The Bacteriological Center in Maryland and the Biological Research Centre in Manchester currently lead the field in viral research and the development of airborne anti-pathogens, which are expected to completely eliminate the incidence of fatal infection within a decade.

The viability of off-world colonization has been proved with the founding of a thriving lunar community. In the century since the first manned lunar landings of the 1970s, a programme of lunar colonization has established a series of computer-controlled Lunarville complexes on the Moon, in which some 4,000 men and women now live and work in safety and comfort. The development of water synthesis from the Moon's natural elements has enabled this community to be entirely self-sufficient, opening up tremendous possibilities for the colonization of other planets.

The Lunarville 7 colony on the Moon (Lunarville 7).

Back on Earth, political stability has been achieved by the formation of a World Government, based at the World Government Senate building in Unity City, Bermuda. This body advises on and supervises political administration on a global scale, yet still offers a large measure of autonomy to its member countries. Recognizing a single world leader in World President Younger, the member countries each retain their own elected government bodies, such as the United States Congress under President Roberts, the Congress of Europe supervised by Presidents Henderson, Olafson and Meccini, and the Assembly of the United Asian Republic headed by Director General Xian-Yoh.

Unfortunately, the threat of war persists from a small number of hostile nations not aligned to the World Government, as well as from the under-sea communities and outer space. To protect Earth and the World Government member countries, individual armed forces have been unified as the Earth Forces, administrated from a Supreme Headquarters in New York. This authority, established by the World Government, commands an impressive line of defence, including the World Navy, based at the Atlantica Complex, the World Aquanaut Security Patrol at Marineville, the World Space Patrol at Space City and the World Police at their headquarters in Paris. SHEF (Supreme Headquarters Earth Forces) also encompasses the World Army and the World Army Air Force, sited at strategic bases in every World Government member country.

Just over two years ago, the World Government recognized the need for a global security force that would cut through the legal and diplomatic red tape that hampered other security organizations and take the burden of peace-keeping from the specialized forces. From this radical initial concept, Spectrum was formed, planned from the outset as a super-efficient security organization that answered only to the World President himself. Personnel were recruited from the various established World Government services, each assigned colour codenames to protect their true identities and granted unlimited security access and authority.

A Clam submarine at the World Navy's Atlantica complex (Flight to Atlantica).

With its headquarters on the vast floating aircraft carrier Cloudbase, hovering on the edge of Earth's atmosphere and under the command of Colonel White, Spectrum swiftly became the supreme peace-keeping force, equipped with a fleet of ground vehicles and aircraft specially designed and modified for the organization's very specific requirements. Formally launched on 10 July 2067, Spectrum's operations as a security force were highly effective and the results more than justified the vast expense. In recent months, however, Spectrum's role has dramatically changed to combat an unforeseen new menace to world security.

Earlier in the year, an ill-fated mission to Mars unleashed the power of the Mysterons, the greatest threat the world has ever known. A highly advanced race of people from an unknown galaxy in outer space, the Mysterons had left their own planet to establish a thriving community on Mars some 3,500 years ago. Masters in the art of computer technology, they created a huge computer complex filled with sentient computers programmed to defend their community and retaliate ruthlessly if attacked. The Mysterons lived peacefully on Mars until the early twentieth century, when they suddenly and inexplicably fled the planet, abandoning their complex but leaving behind the sentient computers.

With newly developed ultra-sensitive monitoring equipment installed on Cloudbase, Spectrum detected and monitored a series of extraterrestrial signals apparently originating on Mars and dispatched a Zero X exploration team, under the command of one of Spectrum's leading officers, Captain Black. In the Cranium rock plateau on Mars, Black and his team discovered the Mysteron complex but mistook the friendly intentions of the Mysteron computers for a hostile offensive and opened fire on the alien city, completely destroying it. Using their incredible powers of retro-metabolism, the ability to re-create matter, the Mysteron computers reconstructed the complex and immediately declared war on the people of Earth for their unprovoked attack.

The Mysteron complex on Mars discovered by the crew of Zero X (The Mysterons).

This has taken the form of a war of nerves, with the Mysteron computers issuing cryptic warnings of their next offensive, and then using their amazing powers to influence people, vehicles and inanimate objects in order to carry out their threats. The Mysterons' primary Earth agent is Captain Black, who has been reconstructed from the body of the original Spectrum agent.

The Spectrum organization's personnel and facilities are now mobilized solely to combat the threat of the Mysterons, and leading this fight is one man fate has made indestructible: Captain Scarlet.

THE CHARACTERS

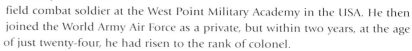

*Right: Scarlet pilots an Angel Interceptor (*Attack on Cloudbase*).*

CAPTAIN SCARLET

Paul Metcalfe was born in Winchester, England, on 17 December 2036. With a father, grandfather and great-grandfather who had all served in the World Army, it was only natural that Metcalfe would follow in their footsteps. Graduating from Winchester University with degrees in technology, the employment of mathematics and history, he trained as a field combat soldier at the West Point Military Academy in the USA. He then joined the World Army Air Force as a private, but within two years, at the age of just twenty-four, he had risen to the rank of colonel.

The selection committee of Spectrum had followed his brilliant career, noting his amazing leadership ability, sense of combat strategy, integrity and dedication to the WAAF. Metcalfe was approached to join Spectrum and accepted the post of agent number one: Captain Scarlet. Following a Mysteron threat to the life of the World President, Metcalfe was killed in a car crash engineered by the Mysterons. Using their power of retro-metabolism, the Mysterons created an indestructible *doppelgänger* of Metcalfe with the original man's character and memories.

However, this *doppelgänger* was freed from the Mysterons' hold after an 800-foot fall from the London Car-Vu and has now become Spectrum's leading agent in the fight against the Mysterons. He retains an incredible ability to survive injuries that would prove fatal to any other man, making a complete recovery within a matter of hours. He can also detect the presence of a Mysteron agent in his immediate vicinity, experiencing nausea if any Mysteron reconstruction is nearby.

On duty, Metcalfe is a highly professional agent and totally reliable, carrying out Colonel White's orders quickly and efficiently. Off duty, however, he changes completely. Full of fun, carefree and bursting with energy, he is very popular with all the Spectrum agents, particularly the Angel pilots, who find him attractive and charming.

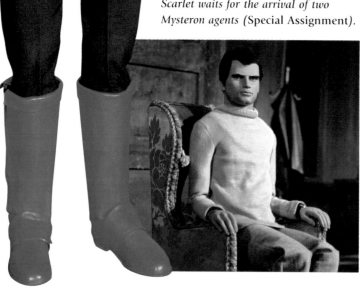

*Scarlet waits for the arrival of two Mysteron agents (*Special Assignment*).*

*Scarlet gains access to a crate containing a core reactor (*Expo 2068*).*

CAPTAIN BLUE

Born in Boston, USA, on 26 August 2035, Adam Svenson is the eldest son of a wealthy financier. Educated at Harvard University after winning a full scholarship in 2051, Svenson attained first-class honours in economics, technology, computer control, applied mathematics and aerodynamics, and seemed destined to follow in his father's footsteps. He surprised his family, however, by enrolling in the World Aeronautic Society, intent upon becoming a test pilot.

Exhibiting outstanding courage and determination, Svenson soon became renowned as a top test pilot, but his superiors recognized qualities in him that made him ideally suited to assignment as an active agent in the WAS security department. With twenty hand-picked men, Svenson was entrusted with the difficult task of weeding out enemy agents who had infiltrated the society.

Although three attempts were made on his life within his first six months on the job, with enthusiasm and ruthlessness he finally succeeded in his aim and expelled all enemy infiltrators and saboteurs from the WAS. This success attracted the attention of the Spectrum selection committee and, given the codename Captain Blue, Svenson was drafted into the organization as one of seven active agents on permanent assignment to Spectrum Cloudbase.

Off duty, Svenson participates in active outdoor pursuits, taking every opportunity to visit the eastern coast of Australia, where he water-skis, surfs and goes deep-sea harpoon-fishing. He also holds the world record for the longest surf-ride, an estimated distance of 5,000 feet recorded at Waikiki Beach, Oahu, in 2064.

COLONEL WHITE

Charles Gray was born in London on 14 July 2017. He studied at King's College, Canterbury, and then graduated from Norwich University with first-class honour degrees in computer control, navigation and technology. On completing his education, he volunteered for active service with the World Navy and rose quickly through the ranks, proving his military capabilities time and time again. Promoted to commander, Gray saw service on destroyers and submarines in trouble spots around the world, such as South-East Asia in 2040, the Iceland dispute in 2042 and the Panama Isthmus rebellion of 2043. When the British Civil War broke out in 2047, Gray was the captain of a destroyer in the Atlantic, siding with the rebels and helping them to overthrow the military dictatorship which had ruled the island since the 2028–9 Atomic War. When the fighting finally ended, the revolutionary government recommended his promotion to Admiral of the Fleet.

The announcement of Gray's retirement from active service at only thirty years of age came as a surprise to the public at large, but this was a carefully planned cover story to camouflage his appointment to the Universal Secret Service. After two years of active field duty, he became Chief of the British section of the USS, in command of the London headquarters, where he transformed a disorganized and inefficient collection of agents into a compact fighting machine. His record of superb leadership ability and dedication to a cause spoke for itself when he was selected by the World Government to become the first commander-in-chief of the newly formed Spectrum organization, with the codename Colonel White.

Dedicated and sincere, Gray finds little time to relax completely as he feels unable to set aside his responsibilities to Cloudbase, even temporarily. However, in his off-duty moments, he enjoys playing war games and chess, as well as both reading and writing crime fiction.

LIEUTENANT GREEN

Born on 18 January 2041 at Port of Spain, Trinidad, Seymour Griffiths was the oldest of nine siblings who, at the age of twelve, suddenly found himself in sole charge of bringing up his five brothers and three sisters when their parents were killed in an air disaster. Organizing the family to work together, Griffiths had to deal with the welfare authorities, who were determined to disperse the children among different foster homes. First educated at the local high school and then at Kingston University, Jamaica, he gained degrees in music, telecommunications and technology. While studying for his postgraduate diploma, he constructed the world's first pocket radio-telescope.

After university, Griffiths enrolled in the newly formed World Aquanaut Security Patrol as a junior hydrophones operator in the Submarine Corps, but he later took an advanced course in communications and was then promoted to commander of communications installations at the Marineville Control Tower. His efficiency in this role impressed the WASP officials, who created a new communications section manned by twenty skilled operators directly under his command. The Spectrum selection board recognized Griffiths's expert knowledge and experience in communications and invited him to join the organization as chief controller, with the codename Lieutenant Green.

On duty, Griffiths is alert and calm, taking great care not to allow himself to appear flustered, worried or annoyed. Off duty, however, he is boisterous and full of fun, with a particular fondness for West Indian calypso music. He often delights his Spectrum colleagues by playing his guitar and singing traditional songs.

CAPTAIN OCHRE

Born in Detroit, USA, on 23 February 2035, Richard Fraser was not a man destined for academic achievement. Hating high school work, he preferred to spend his valuable study time designing

and building model aircraft, and by the time he was sixteen he had learned to fly and qualified for his pilot's licence. Unfortunately, his general education suffered badly. On leaving school at eighteen, he failed to acquire the grades necessary for university entry and, without a degree, could not pursue his dream of enrolling in the World Army Air Force.

Bitterly disappointed, he joined the World Government Police Corps, where his real character and ability emerged. After three years' hard training, initially as a cadet and then as an officer, Fraser became fascinated by detective work. He was transferred to the Chicago area, where his amazing ingenuity, vivid imagination and natural flair for detection led him to become instrumental in breaking one of the toughest crime syndicates in the USA. Promotion rapidly followed promotion and ultimately he was seen as the natural choice to replace the retiring Supreme Commander of the Police Corps, so it was much to everyone's surprise that he turned down the position, preferring to command his own small division rather than be tied to a desk by tedious paperwork. This loyalty to his convictions, inspired detecting ability and common sense encouraged Spectrum to seek him out for a position with the organization, one which he readily accepted under the codename Captain Ochre.

Off duty, Fraser is quick-witted and a brilliant conversationalist, and he is very fond of practical jokes. Popular with the Angels, he still manages to find time for making model planes and maintaining his

CAPTAIN BLACK

Born in Manchester, England, on 17 March 2029, Conrad Turner became an orphan at the age of only seven months when both his parents were killed in a devastating atomic war. He was left in the care of a distant relative who, while unable to offer the affection and comfort of normal family life, ensured that he received a good education. At fifteen, Turner entered the Manchester Technical Academy, where he gained diplomas in physics, space navigation and international law, but he also became something of a recluse, cutting himself off from his fellow students and developing the single-minded drive and ambition that were to take him to the top in his chosen career.

At the age of eighteen, after graduating from Northern University with degrees in science and technology, Turner joined the British Air Force. When Britain was plunged into civil war in the winter of 2047, his flair for independent action soon enabled him to make a name for himself as a fearless and deadly combatant. He later joined the World Space Patrol as Commander of Fireball XL3, one of the principal craft in the WSP fleet, and he soon became one of the WSP's most famous officers.

Turner's achievements were noted in high places and he was seconded from the WSP after several years' service to become one of Spectrum's first agents, with the codename Captain Black. Here he once again distinguished himself, to the point that he was an automatic choice to lead a Zero X mission to Mars to investigate the source of strange alien signals which had been monitored by Spectrum. Discovering the Mysteron complex, he made a fatal error when he mistook the Mysterons' scanning device for a weapon and opened fire, completely destroying the complex.

Captain Black prior to his reconstruction as a Mysteron agent.

The Mysterons swore vengeance for this unprovoked attack and killed Turner, reconstructing him using their powers of retro-metabolism to act as their primary agent in a war of nerves against the people of Earth. Receiving his orders directly from Mars, Turner executes them with the precision, skill and swiftness that he had developed in Earth's service.

Far left: Captain Black engineers the death of Major Gravener (Treble Cross).

Left: Captain Black coordinates the plan to destroy Nuclear City (Special Assignment).

DESTINY ANGEL

Juliette Pontoin was born in Paris on 23 August 2040, the daughter of a wealthy textile manufacturer. She was educated in a convent there and then at Rome University, but was all too keen to allow her social life to take precedence over her studies. Her work suffered as a consequence, but she still managed to graduate with degrees in weather control and telecommunications.

With these unusual qualifications, Juliette joined the World Army Air Force, but she found that her true calling was in the Intelligence Corps. Training as a pilot was an important part of her job, and she soon became known to the WAAF officials for her flying skills and her brilliant handling of intelligence work. She was promoted to commanding officer of the newly formed Women's Fighter Squadron, where she excelled in fighter tactics and exhibited superb leadership qualities.

After three years in the force, however, Juliette grew tired of the lack of personal freedom afforded to her and left the WAAF to set up her own firm of flying contractors. It was not long before her tremendous prowess in the field of intelligence and her faultless flying record drew her to the attention of Spectrum and she was invited to join the organization as Destiny Angel, one of the five members of Spectrum's élite air-combat fighting force.

Utterly ruthless and totally efficient at work, Juliette is charming and sophisticated as soon as she goes off duty. Extremely fashion-conscious, she has a flair for designing and making her own clothes.

SYMPHONY ANGEL

Karen Wainwright was born in Cedar Rapids, Iowa, USA, on 6 January 2042. Always top of her class at school in Boston, Karen entered Yale University at only sixteen years of age. There she attained no fewer than seven degrees in the study and employment of mathematics and technology, and was voted 'Student of the Year' by the Combined University Committee.

After graduation, she was contacted by the Universal Secret Service and successfully completed their comprehensive five-year training course in just two years. Sent on active duty as an agent dealing solely with industrial espionage, Karen became a true credit to the USS and her brilliant handling of tricky assignments made her their number-one secret agent.

While training as a pilot for a special USS mission, Karen fell in love with flying and realized that this was her one ambition in life. Leaving the service, she joined a charter airline that existed purely to ferry customers around the world. So superlative were her flying skills that she gained world recognition and her exploits were frequently reported as headline news. Spectrum saw Karen's potential and invited her to become an Angel pilot with the codename Symphony. She passed the gruelling entrance exam with ease and was immediately enrolled in the organization.

On duty, Karen is dedicated and thoroughly proficient. Off duty, she is sympathetic and quick-witted, with a keen interest in hairdressing, often designing fabulous new hairstyles for the other Angels.

RHAPSODY ANGEL

Dianne Simms was born in Chelsea, London, on 27 April 2043, the daughter of World Government official Lord Robert Simms. Educated at a girls' public school, she graduated from London University with degrees in law and sociology, but initially made no attempt to exploit her achievements, choosing instead to be drawn into the swinging party life of a débutante. However, she soon became bored and longed for adventure and excitement. She found them when she met Lady Penelope Creighton-Ward, then head of the Federal Agents Bureau and one of Britain's top secret agents, who invited Dianne to join the FAB.

After her initial training course, Dianne was sent on many dangerous assignments, both alongside Lady Penelope and on her own, and succeeded in bringing several notorious espionage agents to justice. Delighted with her protégée's development into one of the FAB's most trusted agents, Lady Penelope handed over supreme command of the organization to Dianne when she left to join International Rescue. Under Dianne's command, the FAB became a highly distinguished and respected secret organization and Dianne herself became the most sought-after agent in Europe. When the FAB was forced to close, she joined the European Charter airline company as chief security officer, but Spectrum had followed Dianne's career with interest and, realizing her tremendous potential, selected her to become one of the Angel pilots, with the codename Rhapsody.

Dianne is full of charm, sophistication and responsibility, both on and off duty. Flying has become a way of life for her and even off duty she likes nothing better than to relax by soaring through the clouds in a glider. She also enjoys playing chess and has found a worthy opponent in Colonel White.

MELODY ANGEL

Born on a cotton farm in Atlanta, Georgia, USA, on 10 January 2043, Magnolia Jones grew up as the only girl in a family of four elder brothers. She became something of a tomboy and often played truant with her brothers, eventually leaving school at fifteen to take up professional motor-racing. Her parents had other ideas and packed her off to a Swiss finishing school to learn how to become a lady. There she discovered flying and, after she was expelled from the school for unruly behaviour, she joined the World Army Air Force and trained as a test pilot.

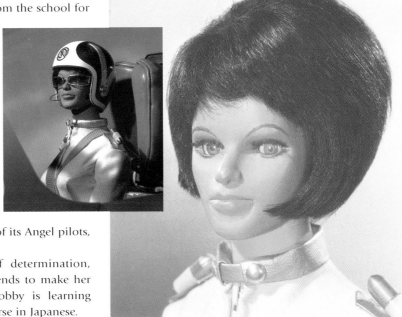

Her courage and nerves were tested to the limit when an XKF 115 that she was piloting ditched over the South Sea Islands. Magnolia was stranded for more than a year, but she managed to build her own plane from the remains of the wrecked test aircraft and flew back to civilization. She left the WAAF shortly after and, backed by her father, set up a freelance flying-taxi service aimed at luxury inter-city flights for business executives. Approached by Spectrum, she readily agreed to join the organization as one of its Angel pilots, with the codename Melody.

A tower of strength, tough and full of determination, Magnolia has a powerful personality which tends to make her dominate her social circle. Her favourite hobby is learning languages and she recently embarked on a course in Japanese.

HARMONY ANGEL

Born in Tokyo on 19 June 2042, Chan Kwan is the only daughter of a wealthy flying-taxi owner, so she grew up in a world of high-speed jets. Educated at Tokyo High School and then at a finishing school in London, she soon realized that flying was the only career she was interested in. However, at her father's wishes, she attended Tokyo University and graduated with a degree in physics and aerodynamics.

Chan spent the next two years perfecting her flying skills and modifying a second-hand single-seater plane in preparation for a solo round-the-world flight. She set off on 2 March 2064, but after thirty-six hours she abandoned her attempt when she received an SOS call from three men stranded on a blazing tanker. She landed on the tanker deck, rescued the men and flew back to land, where she received a hero's welcome. She finally realized her ambition to fly around the world six months later, breaking all previous records for a solo flight.

Later that year her father retired, leaving her to manage his business, Peking Taxi Corps, and within a year she had expanded the company into the largest and fastest flying-taxi service in the world. Her amazing skill, dedication to a cause and fantastic flying ability soon prompted an invitation from Spectrum's selection board to join the organization as an Angel pilot, with the codename Harmony.

Right: The Angels relax in the Amber Room.

Off duty, Chan is full of Eastern charm and femininity. She loves sport and spends hours in the gym practising and teaching karate and judo, at which she has achieved the level of black belt fourth dan.

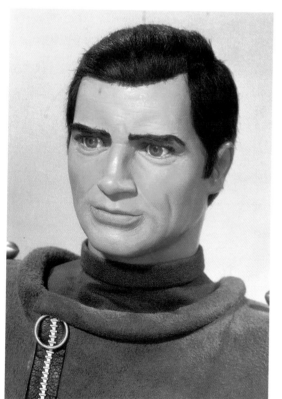

CAPTAIN GREY

Bradley Holden was born in Chicago, USA, on 4 March 2033. Educated at the World Naval Academy in San Diego, he graduated with degrees in navigation, aqua-technology and computer control, and immediately enrolled in the submarine service attached to the World Navy. Stationed in Sydney, Australia, Holden trained as an officer and was given command of a World Navy submarine. Tackling a number of dangerous assignments, he and his crew were often in danger, but his level-headedness, valour and quick thinking saved their lives on more than one occasion and prevented the submarine from falling into enemy hands.

When the World Aquanaut Security Patrol was established in 2061, Holden was transferred and promoted to security commander of the new organization. Put in charge of the prototype submarine which was later to become Stingray, Holden was a true credit to the service, fighting in many daring campaigns against numerous threats from under-sea enemies. His brilliant reputation in active service and superb handling of security drew the attention of the Spectrum selection committee and he was accepted into the organization as a field agent, with the codename Captain Grey.

Off duty, Holden's only hobby is swimming and he spends many hours in the Cloudbase pool, developing new styles and strokes. He has also embarked on a programme of research into the miniaturization of aqualung diving gear.

CAPTAIN MAGENTA

Patrick Donaghue was born in Dublin on 17 May 2034. When he was three, his parents emigrated to America and settled in a poor New York suburb. Donaghue grew up in an atmosphere of poverty and crime, but he was encouraged by his mother to work hard at the local high school and won a scholarship to Yale University. There he fell in with a dare-devil group of extremists known as Group 22 and served a short prison term for his part in the Anti-Bereznik riots of 2053. However, his academic work was of a consistently high standard and he graduated with degrees in physics, electrical engineering and technology.

Donaghue joined a large Brooklyn firm as a computer programmer, but he found the work boring and routine. Turning to crime for excitement and big money, he organized a small but efficient crime syndicate operating in New York and became highly respected in the New York underworld, eventually controlling two-thirds of the city's crime organizations. The Spectrum selection committee realized that he was the perfect candidate for the new security organization because of his intimate knowledge of criminal activity. Interested and excited by their offer, Donaghue was granted a free pardon by the World Government and assumed his new responsibilities with the codename Captain Magenta.

Dedicated, meticulous and utterly ruthless, Donaghue makes each assignment a personal challenge. Off duty, however, he is charming and witty and in his spare time, he designs ways of making World Government security buildings even more impregnable.

Left: Captain Magenta and Dr Fawn in the Officers' Lounge with Captains Scarlet, Blue and Ochre.

DR FAWN

Edward Wilkie was born in Yalumba, Australia, on 10 July 2031, the son of a prominent Australian medical specialist. It was only natural that he should follow in his father's footsteps and, after acquiring honours degrees in biology and medicine from Brisbane University, he joined the World Medical Organization as Medical Assistant Controller in the Australian sector. During his short tenure in this sector, he recognized a growing need to modernize the service, and after a promotion to Health Controller of the Scandinavian sector he devoted all his spare time to planning the reorganization of the WMO.

Within two years, he had outlined a revolutionary system that would introduce robot doctors capable of diagnosing patients' ailments in seconds. The WMO made Wilkie Administrator for the Advancement of Medicine, with all the resources and manpower he required to put his plans into practice. His totally unselfish attitude to medicine and his outstanding ability to develop and discover new ways of healing drew the attention of the Spectrum selection committee, who offered him the post of the organization's chief medical officer, codenamed Dr Fawn.

Completely dedicated to work that frequently occupies him twenty-four hours a day, Wilkie never tires and refuses to stop working until every problem has been solved. Even in his rare off-duty moments he can be found buried in research, looking for ways to perfect and improve his robot doctors.

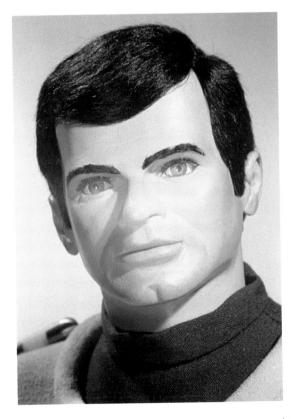

THE VEHICLES

SPECTRUM CLOUDBASE

Cloudbase is the aerial headquarters of the Spectrum organization, hovering at a height of 40,000 feet above sea level. Some 630 feet long and 330 feet wide, it is a unique, completely self-contained engineering marvel, an aircraft carrier in the sky where members of Spectrum live and work. Formerly designed as a submarine, a floating island and then a space station, Cloudbase was ultimately developed as a floating headquarters on the edge of the Earth's atmosphere. Constructed at the World Government research depot in Stockholm, it was prefabricated and assembled in outer space.

Thanks to solar energy, a vast complex of enormous engines in the Engine Room at Cloudbase is able each day to produce enough energy to supply Unity City's needs for a fortnight. Propelled by atomic jets powered by air-intake nacelle jet cloud-conversion engines, Cloudbase's location is variable, but the base is normally kept moored in a geostationary position by vast hover combines.

Cloudbase is home to 593 Spectrum personnel whose every need is catered for by a variety of facilities. The base is fully equipped with a range of computers, radar and radio communications systems, and information-monitoring and filing equipment, enabling the personnel to deal swiftly and effectively with data gathered from around the globe.

The nerve centre of Cloudbase is the Control Room, which is fitted with a computer of the most advanced design that acts as a complete information and communications centre. Over 20 feet long, the Cloudbase computer features components and circuitry which are encapsulated in a specialized transparent plastic for easy visual and physical access. It is directly linked to memory banks on Earth and has a storage access time of 10 nano-seconds.

Cloudbase also houses an aircraft hangar for the maintenance and repair of Spectrum's Angel Interceptor strike aircraft. This hangar is situated directly beneath the flight deck, enabling the vehicles to be raised quickly into position for launch. Other facilities include a Conference Room, Monitor Room, Lounge, Sick Bay, Room of Sleep, Agents' Training Bay, Arms Store, Design and Testing Laboratory, Analysis and Research Centre and the Amber Room, a ready room for the Angel pilots. Cloudbase also includes the Relaxabay, a vast centrally located area which incorporates a heated swimming pool, tennis courts, squash courts, miniature ski slopes, table-tennis tables and billiard tables.

Colonel White briefs his officers in the Cloudbase Conference Room.

SPECTRUM SALOON CAR (SSC)

The Spectrum Saloon Car is a five-seater patrol vehicle available for use by all Spectrum personnel. An 18-foot-long independent four-wheel-drive vehicle capable of speeds of up to 200 m.p.h., the SSC is powered by a gas turbine situated under the rear floor. Hot gas from the combustion chamber drives compressor and power turbines before being ejected through the rear grille.

The car's bodywork is made from lightweight, resilient fleetonium alloy fitted to a specially strengthened chassis, with the main rib following the contour of the vehicle as a safety measure in case of overturning. The nose is strengthened for use as a ram and the tyres and windscreen are all bullet-proof.

The car is equipped with powerful quartz headlights, a long-distance viewing laser projector with optical telescope coupled to a TV screen in the cabin, and an infra-red beam with centrally mounted detector eye, sidelights and trafficators. The vehicle also boasts transverse gearing, independent suspension and magnetic brake drums which provide powerful controlled braking by means of electromagnetically generated opposing magnetic fields.

Road/tyre friction heat at high speeds is countered by wing intakes, while a central housing and a rear-mounted fin maintain the vehicle's stability at speed. Safety airbags are fitted as standard.

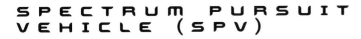

SPECTRUM PURSUIT VEHICLE (SPV)

Fast, armed, armoured and amphibious, the Spectrum Pursuit Vehicle is Spectrum's major Earth-bound combat force. A ten-wheeled two-seater bullet-proof vehicle capable of speeds of over 200 m.p.h., the 25-foot-long SPV has no windscreen and is driven from an aircraft-type bucket seat with the driver sitting facing the rear, steering the lightweight multi-purpose motors by television monitor. Entry to the vehicle is via a sliding side panel which incorporates the driver's seat.

Powered by hydrogenic electrical fuel cells, the SPV features a detachable power unit, held in position by twin clamps and coupled independently to all road wheels. This arrangement enables the unit to be used to power small personal vehicles, such as jet-packs, carried aboard all Pursuit Vehicles. Stand-by batteries provide motive force for the vehicle when the power unit is being used for other purposes.

When used amphibiously, the SPV's wheels retract upwards and propulsion is provided by twin water turbo jets, positioned at the rear. The vehicle is fitted with a magnetic disc reverse-thrust braking system and twin tank tracks which enable it to climb all but vertical obstacles.

Each SPV is equipped with revolutionary radar installations, super-sensitive two-way radios, an air-conditioning plant and a proteinized food supply, enabling the crew to remain entirely self-sufficient for long periods. The SPV's armaments consist of laser cannons, ground-to-air missiles and electrode ray cannons – the only truly effective anti-Mysteron weapons.

Spectrum maintains a vast fleet of SPVs hidden at secret strategic locations around the globe, including all major airports and Delta filling stations. Maintained and guarded by undercover Spectrum agents, the vehicles can be requisitioned by any member of the organization.

ANGEL INTERCEPTOR

The Angel Interceptor aircraft is a single-seater strike aircraft developed by International Engineering from the World Army Air Force Viper Jet, but the final blueprint of the Angel is vastly different from the original Viper, having been specially adapted for Cloudbase requirements. The plane is 60 feet long, precision-engineered and incredibly compact, carrying extra electronic instruments and mammoth fuel tanks which enable it to fly at a top speed of 3,000 m.p.h. and complete any mission without refuelling.

With a wingspan of 35 feet and weighing in at 40,100 lb, each aircraft costs £1,250,000 and takes nine months to build. The tail assembly houses twin turbo-jet compressors (one on each side of the fuselage) which serve the rear-mounted ram jet. Bled air serves the pitch jets, which give control at supersonic speeds in rarefied air and are also used for Cloudbase landing manoeuvres. For normal landing or reducing air speed quickly, bled air is used for braking jets, while a small but powerful retro rocket can be brought into play in case of an emergency.

Three Angel aircraft are always positioned on the aerial launch platform on Cloudbase ready for immediate take-off. Entry to the cockpit is by hydraulic lift from the Cloudbase Amber Room up through the hull of the craft, so that the pilot is injected into the cockpit complete with her seat. Instruments and gunsights are arranged within easy view of the pilot, who has all-round visibility. The craft is equipped with a flight computer auto-pilot fitted behind the pilot's seat.

The aircraft's nose probe houses hyper-sensitive instruments such as air and skin temperature monitors, wind speed and gust detectors, and radar and radio aerials. A main cannon is mounted on the nose just in front of the cockpit. This fires a variety of computer pre-selected ammunition, such as tracer, armour-piercing or rocket shells. The craft is also equipped with a battery of air-to-air/air-to-ground missiles.

SPECTRUM PASSENGER JET (SPJ)

The Spectrum Passenger Jet is a high-speed, non-combatant personnel transport aircraft, used for rapid transit of Spectrum agents to the scene of enemy action, and for special personnel and equipment manoeuvres. It can seat seven passengers, with a two-seater pilot cabin, and flies at a speed of 1,125 m.p.h.

At 78 feet long, with a wing-span of 37 feet and weighing 630,427 lb, the Passenger Jet is a refinement of Universal Aero's revolutionary TVR 24 civil aircraft, but is now patented and manufactured solely for Spectrum. Vast fuel tanks hold enough high-octane petrolene to give the craft a range of 12,000 miles, powering a main induction plant fitted with twin reheat turbo jets, either one of which will keep the plane airborne. The craft incorporates an unusual rear-wing assembly in which the entire outer wing turns through 90 degrees to act as an airbrake, rotated on a high-tensile actuating rod.

The cockpit is fitted with a computer which takes the place of the navigator, co-pilot and radio operator, enabling the craft to be flown by a single pilot if necessary. The nose cone houses an instrument compartment containing radar antennae and flight computer links which serve gust detectors and air-speed indicators in the nose probe.

SPECTRUM HELICOPTER

The Spectrum Helicopter is a general-purpose vehicle that is used primarily for high-speed transportation of Spectrum personnel over short distances. Its rugged construction makes it especially suitable for landing on rough terrain, shifting sand and heavy seas. At 45 feet in length, with rotor blades 39 feet in diameter that rotate at 2,000 r.p.m., the helicopter can carry up to five people flying at a maximum speed of 302 m.p.h.

The rotor blades are driven by twin air-induction turbo jets housed behind and above the cabin. An unusual ring-shaped wing tail gives the helicopter great stability and, in conjunction with the other airflow surfaces of the craft, enables the plane to glide for a considerable distance in the event of power failure. Bled air from the gearbox cooling intake feeds a compressor which inflates airbags inside a pair of floats fitted to either side of the craft so as to correct pressure for landing on water and on smooth or rough ground.

The cabin houses the pilot's seat, with seating for passengers behind. The main feature of the pilot's control panel is an omni-scanner navigation screen which displays the terrain below the craft and pinpoints the position of all Spectrum agents outside Cloudbase. Although principally a non-combatant vehicle, Spectrum Helicopters none the less pack a veritable artillery. The vehicle's main armament is a gun situated immediately in front of the cockpit which fires high-explosive rocket projectiles.

MAXIMUM SECURITY VEHICLE (MSV)

The Spectrum Maximum Security Vehicle is a four-seater, bullet-proof, high-speed vehicle used specifically for the transportation of Mysteron-threatened VIPs in the utmost safety to their destinations. Although it is 24 feet long and weighs 8 tons, the MSV is nevertheless capable of speeds of up to 200 m.p.h.

Hand-built by expert coach-builders, the vehicle was declared indestructible after exhaustive tests by the World Army Air Force under the severest battle conditions. Very much a combat vehicle, carrying a lethal armament of laser cannons and anti-Mysteron electrode-ray cannons, the MSV is fitted with radar and two-way radio, and is complete with survival food kit. Powered by a main transverse diesel engine, the vehicle is also equipped with a stand-by motor driven by the batteries, which can be recharged by solar collector strips.

The shell of the vehicle is constructed in layers of armour plating, refrigeration honeycomb, radiation-damping sandwich and an internal steel wall. Windows are constructed of a special heat-resistant anti-radiation lead quartz. The vehicle is mounted on twin bullet-proof tyres which are tubeless and filled with self-sealing compound, and the whole wheel assembly incorporates hydraulic brakes, power-assisted steering and hydraulic clamped link independent suspension.

Fitted with its own pressurized air-filtration plant, the MSV can be hermetically sealed from all outside contact in the event of threat by gas or radiation. The passenger compartment is entirely self-contained, with heavily padded seats, safety straps and an intercom/external TV. This is separated from the driver's compartment by a thick bulkhead.

*The Magnacopter en route
to Glen Garry Castle
in Scotland (The Trap).*

*Right: Spectrum Detector
Truck 6 is instrumental in
the manhunt for Captain
Black (Manhunt).*

*A Spectrum Hovercraft
on manoeuvres in the
Australian Outback
(Traitor).*

OTHER VEHICLES

In addition to these primary service vehicles, Spectrum is equipped with a range of specialized support vehicles.

The **Yellow Fox Security Tanker** offers an alternative method of ultra-secure transportation for VIPs in circumstances when the use of a Maximum Security Vehicle would be too conspicuous. Ingeniously disguised as a tanker carrying high-octane fuel, Yellow Fox conceals a cahelium-strengthened double-walled passenger lounge within the 'container tank'. Furnished with a conference table and seating for six in comfort and secrecy, the lounge is accessed from the rear of the vehicle through a hermetically sealed entry hatch. Powered by a transverse diesel engine, Yellow Fox travels at speeds of up to 120 m.p.h.

The **Spectrum Detector Truck** (also known as a Radar Van) is a squat four-wheeled vehicle packed with sophisticated scanning and communications equipment for tracking a signal source and directing Spectrum ground forces to the target. The vehicle is 24 feet long and mounted with a multi-wavelength antenna with 360-degree rotation which feeds a constant stream of signal data to a compact radar room in the rear. A unit of eight Detector Trucks can be mobilized at any one time, enabling a signal source to be targeted with pinpoint accuracy by cross-referencing directional co-ordinates from each vehicle.

The **Magnacopter** is a large-scale airborne maximum security vehicle which affords comfortable air transport for VIPs. At 200 feet in length and with rotor blades 150 feet in diameter, the Magnacopter can seat up to twenty delegates in the passenger lounge and is fully equipped with a galley area, toilet facilities and a control room fitted with computers and communications consoles. A vehicle-storage bay beneath the Magnacopter carries a Maximum Security Vehicle as standard equipment. Powered by twin turbo jets and a rocket motor, the Magnacopter is capable of air speeds of up to 200 m.p.h.

The **Spectrum Hovercraft** is the optimum mode of high-speed transport in desert regions, such as North Africa and the Australian Outback, and for short-range travel over water. Some 62 feet long, the Hovercraft uses a neutron generator powering a compressor turbine to propel the vehicle to speeds in excess of 100 m.p.h. on a cushion of air. The control cabin seats a pilot and co-pilot, with two passengers at the rear. A fleet of Spectrum Hovercraft is permanently maintained at the organization's Koala Training Base in Australia.

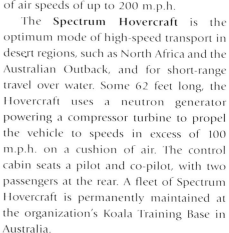

SCREEN ADVENTURES 3

REGULAR VOICE CAST

Captain Scarlet	**Francis Matthews**
Captain Blue	**Ed Bishop**
Colonel White	**Donald Gray**
Destiny Angel	**Liz Morgan**
Symphony Angel	**Janna Hill**
Lieutenant Green	**Cy Grant**
Captain Black	**Donald Gray**
Captain Ochre	**Jeremy Wilkin**
Rhapsody Angel	**Liz Morgan**
Melody Angel	**Sylvia Anderson**
Harmony Angel	**Liz Morgan and Lian Shin**
Captain Grey	**Paul Maxwell**
Captain Magenta	**Gary Files**
Dr Fawn	**Charles Tingwell**
The Voice of the Mysterons	**Donald Gray**

CREDITS

Executive Producer	**Gerry Anderson**
Produced by	**Reg Hill**
Format	**Gerry and Sylvia Anderson**
Director Supervising Series	**Des Saunders**
Supervising Visual Effects Director	**Derek Meddings**
Associate Producer	**John Read**
Characters Created by	**Sylvia Anderson**
Lighting Cameraman	**Julien Lugrin**
	Paddy Seale
	Ted Catford
Visual Effects Lighting Cameraman	
Harry Oakes	**Derek Black**
Bert Mason	**Les Paul**
Camera Operators	
Tom Fletcher	**Ron Gallifant**
Les Paul	**Alan McDonald**
Nick Procopides	**Derek Black**
	Ted Cutlack
Supervising Art Director	**Bob Bell**
Script Editor	**Tony Barwick**
Music Composed and Directed by	**Barry Gray**
Puppetry Coordination	**Mary Turner**
Production Manager	**Frank Hollands**
Assistant Director	
Leo Eaton	**Peter Anderson**
Keith Lund	**Ian Griffiths**
Ray Atcheler	**Ian Spurrier**
Puppetry Supervision	**Christine Glanville**
	Wanda Webb

Puppet Operators	
Peter Johns	**Mel Cross**
Judith Morgan	**John Lane**
Wanda Webb	**Jan King**
Visual Effects Director	**Shaun Whittaker-Cooke**
	Jimmy Elliott
Art Director	**Grenville Nott**
Designer	**Keith Wilson**
	John Lageu
Sculpting Supervision	**John Brown**
Sculptors	**Tim Cooksey**
	Terry Curtis
	Plugg Shutt
Visual Effects Production Manager	**Harry Ledger**
	Brian Burgess
Wardrobe	**Iris Richens**
Dialogue Synchronization	**Ian Spurrier**
	James Cowan
	Antony Bell
Editor	
Len Walter	**Harry McDonald**
John Beaton	**Bob Dearberg**
Supervising Editor	**Len Walter**
Supervising Sound Editor	**Peter Pennell**
Music Editor	**George Randall**
Dialogue Editor	**Don Brill**
Property Master	**Arthur Cripps**
Sound	**Anvil Films Ltd**
Visual Effects 2nd Unit Director	**Peter Wragg**
Visual Effects 2nd Unit Lighting Cameraman	**Les Paul**
	Ted Wooldridge
Visual Effects 2nd Unit Camera Operator	**Ted Cutlack**
John Shann	**Noel Rowlands**
Electronic Development	**Jack Kensley**
Electronic Collaboration	
Standard Telecommunication Laboratories, Harlow	
Captain Scarlet Sung by	**The Spectrum**

The episodes that follow are listed in the official ITC recommended broadcast order.

1. THE MYSTERONS

Written by **Gerry and Sylvia Anderson**
Directed by **Desmond Saunders**

'We can only hear them over our radios, but I've got a feeling they're with us all the time.'

Mars – AD 2068. Aboard the Zero X Martian Exploration Vehicle, Spectrum agent Captain Black leads a mission to investigate the source of extraterrestrial signals which have been monitored by Spectrum. Black's team discovers a strange alien complex controlled by advanced computers that prepare to welcome the visitors, focusing on a sensor device on the MEV, but Black

mistakes the device for a weapon and opens fire on the city. The complex is completely destroyed, but a projection device casts a beam over the ruins and restores the complex to its original form. The voice of the Mysterons promises that the people of Earth will pay for this act of aggression with the destruction of all life on Earth. Captain Black falls under the Mysterons' control to become their Earth agent and instrumental in their vengeance. Transmitting a message on all radio and television frequencies, the Mysterons announce that their first act of retaliation will be the assassination of the World President.

Captain Brown and Captain Scarlet are assigned to escort the World President to the Spectrum Maximum Security Building, but their Spectrum Saloon Car is sabotaged by the Mysterons and crashes. Both men are killed instantly and reconstructed as Mysteron *doppelgängers*, indistinguishable from the original Spectrum officers. While the Mysteron Scarlet reports to Colonel White, the Mysteron Brown accompanies the World President in a Maximum Security Vehicle to the heavily guarded Maximum Security Building in New York. After passing through an electronic checkpoint which ensures that Brown is not carrying any weapons, the President is escorted to a luxury suite deep underground. Suddenly,

The clock at the London Car-Vu indicates that the time is 9.30 a.m. when Captain Scarlet arrives there with the World President. A few minutes later, Scarlet falls from the sky park and the Mysterons' hold over him is broken. But as we learn in the next episode, Winged Assassin, Scarlet was under the control of the Mysterons for six hours, so the crash in which the original Scarlet was killed must have taken place at about 3.30 a.m. GMT which would be 10.30 p.m. New York time. Yet is it daylight when Scarlet is killed and continues to be daylight throughout the attempt on the World President's life at the Maximum Security Building.

A mid-1960s stock photograph of New York is used as an establishing shot of the city, apparently unchanged in 100 years. The Empire State Building is clearly visible, but if this is the same fictional world as that seen in THUNDERBIRDS, the Empire State would have been demolished three years beforehand (in the THUNDERBIRDS episode Terror in New York City).

The film is flopped when Destiny announces that Scarlet has turned off the M21: the Spectrum badge on her helmet is reversed. In the closing scene, all five Angels are present in the Cloudbase Conference Room, but one of them should always be on stand-by in Angel One.

smoke begins to pour from Captain Brown and he spontaneously explodes, totally destroying the building.

Safe on Spectrum's Cloudbase headquarters, the World President is shown a video recording of the attempt on his life which illustrates how his chair quickly moved him behind a protective steel wall just as Brown exploded. Captain Scarlet is entrusted with the President's safety and accompanies him to London in a Spectrum Passenger Jet, escorted by the Angel flight. After the SPJ has left Cloudbase, Spectrum's New York office reports that the body of Captain Brown has been found near the scene of the SSC crash, and Colonel White realizes that whatever happened to Captain Brown could also have happened to Captain Scarlet. He immediately instructs Destiny Angel to escort the SPJ back to Cloudbase, but Scarlet refuses to cooperate. As the SPJ crosses the English coast, Colonel White orders Destiny to make a dummy attack on the jet, but Scarlet responds by knocking the President unconscious before ejecting them both from the plane. Once on the ground, Scarlet forces the President at gunpoint into a nearby car and heads for London on the M21.

Captain Blue requisitions Spectrum Pursuit Vehicle A69 and sets off in pursuit. As there are only two roads that Scarlet can take from the M21, Rhapsody Angel destroys a viaduct on the London road, forcing Scarlet to turn on to a road which leads only to the London Car-Vu, a huge sky park overlooking the city. With Scarlet now trapped, Colonel White diverts Spectrum Helicopter A42 to the Car-Vu, unaware that the Helicopter has been taken over by the Mysterons.

Arriving at the top of the Car-Vu, Scarlet forces the President out on to a girder structure at the edge of the platform. Blue straps on a jet-pack in an attempt to rescue the World President, but the Mysteronized Helicopter opens fire on him. Destiny shoots down the Helicopter and it crashes into the Car-Vu with a massive explosion which damages the support structure. A gun battle ensues between Scarlet and Blue, but Scarlet is shot in the chest and slips off the girder, falling 800 feet to the ground. Blue dives in and rescues the President from the girder just as the structure collapses.

Despite his fatal injuries, Captain Scarlet makes a complete recovery and Dr Fawn reports that he is no longer under the control of the Mysterons. This new Captain Scarlet is now indestructible and will become Spectrum's greatest asset in the fight against the Mysterons.

Notes

The main title sequence of this episode includes a voice-over by Ed Bishop which does not appear on the opening titles of any other episode: 'The finger is on the trigger, about to unleash a force with terrible powers beyond the comprehension of man. This force we shall know as the Mysterons. This man will be our hero, for fate will make him indestructible. His name: Captain

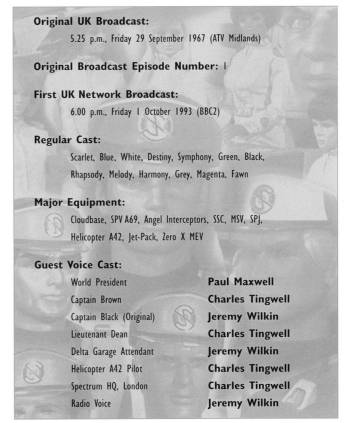

Original UK Broadcast:
    5.25 p.m., Friday 29 September 1967 (ATV Midlands)

Original Broadcast Episode Number: 1

First UK Network Broadcast:
    6.00 p.m., Friday 1 October 1993 (BBC2)

Regular Cast:
    Scarlet, Blue, White, Destiny, Symphony, Green, Black, Rhapsody, Melody, Harmony, Grey, Magenta, Fawn

Major Equipment:
    Cloudbase, SPV A69, Angel Interceptors, SSC, MSV, SPJ, Helicopter A42, Jet-Pack, Zero X MEV

Guest Voice Cast:

World President	**Paul Maxwell**
Captain Brown	**Charles Tingwell**
Captain Black (Original)	**Jeremy Wilkin**
Lieutenant Dean	**Charles Tingwell**
Delta Garage Attendant	**Jeremy Wilkin**
Helicopter A42 Pilot	**Charles Tingwell**
Spectrum HQ, London	**Charles Tingwell**
Radio Voice	**Jeremy Wilkin**

Scarlet.' The episode has no on-screen title caption but is referred to in all production documentation as *The Mysterons*.

The Zero X MEV previously appeared in the feature film *Thunderbirds Are Go* (1966). A foreword to the shooting script for *The Mysterons* indicates that the producers intended this to be seen as the same vehicle and that CAPTAIN SCARLET AND THE MYSTERONS therefore exists in the same fictional universe as the THUNDERBIRDS television series and films.

For the opening scenes in the MEV, the original Captain Black is voiced by Jeremy Wilkin. Although the puppet's head is a duplicate cast of the regular Mysteronized Captain Black puppet, it has modified finishing in the skin tone, eyes and eyebrows which emphasizes the difference in the character once he has become a Mysteron agent. The revamp puppet seen here as the blond Spectrum security guard at the Maximum Security Building later became WIN commander-in-chief Shane Weston in JOE 90.

Just before the SSC crash which kills Scarlet and Brown, the picture slowly changes from full colour to a blue monotone so as to indicate the presence of the Mysterons, and then suddenly reverts to full colour again as the SSC's tyre bursts. This effect was lost on the series' original television audience in 1967 as the episode was transmitted in black and white in the UK.

2. WINGED ASSASSIN

Written by **Tony Barwick**
Directed by **David Lane**

'There's some sort of trouble with Delta Tango One Niner. They won't open the doors.'

At London's Nelson Hotel, an attempt on the life of the Director General of the United Asian Republic is foiled by Captain Grey. Shortly after, the Mysterons announce that they intend to assassinate the Director General and Spectrum is assigned to protect him as he leaves the hotel for London Airport. Captain Blue is placed in charge of the operation.

Meanwhile, Dr Fawn completes his tests on Captain Scarlet. Scarlet is able to recall the crash in which he died but everything after that is a blank. Fawn explains to him that his mind and body were controlled by the Mysterons for six hours and that in human terms he was killed several times over. However, his injuries have healed without a trace and he is now exactly as he was before the crash, with one exception: he has retained the ability of retro-metabolism and even a fatal wound will heal completely within only a few hours. Colonel White decides to take a calculated risk and places Scarlet back on duty, assigning him to join Blue in London. The pair requisition SPV 105 and head for London Airport.

Intercontinental Airlines Stratojet DT19 is en route from New York to London when it suddenly loses all power and crashes into the sea. The passenger jet is reconstructed by the Mysterons and the duplicate DT19 continues the journey to London under Mysteron control. In London, a lookalike of the Director General sets off in a decoy motorcade while Captain Grey escorts the real Director General to London International Airport in Spectrum's Yellow Fox Tanker. As the Mysteronized DT19 lands on the runway and makes its way to the terminal building, the Director General arrives at the airport and boards his personal jet. The Airport Controller discovers that the DT19 is completely empty – the crew and passengers have vanished – and as the aircraft begins to move away from the terminal building, Blue realizes that the plane is a Mysteron booby trap and orders the Director General's plane to take off immediately.

In the SPV, Scarlet and Blue race to stop the DT19 as it sets off down the runway on a collision course with the Director General's plane. The Angels open fire on the Stratojet, but to no effect, so Blue aims the SPV cannon at the plane's tyres. Unfortunately, the cannon mechanism is jammed, so Scarlet ejects Blue and rams the DT19's wheels with the SPV's nose, wrecking the landing gear. The SPV careers out of control and

crashes into a radar building, but the Stratojet's landing gear collapses. The DT19 slides to a halt on the runway right in the path of the Director General's plane, which clips the tail fin of the Stratojet as it takes off, crashing and killing the Director General. Scarlet sustains fatal injuries in the SPV crash, but Blue is confident that he will make a complete recovery.

Notes

The flashback footage from *The Mysterons*, seen here as Scarlet recalls his death in the SSC crash, is subtly different in its presentation: in *The Mysterons*, the footage slowly changes to a blue monotone leading up to the explosion of the SSC's tyre, but in *Winged Assassin* this footage remains in full colour throughout.

The Airport Controller was previously seen as Lieutenant Dean in *The Mysterons*, while the DT19 co-pilot appeared in that episode as Dean's MEV colleague Space Navigator Conway. The puppet that became Shane Weston in JOE 90 appears here as a Spectrum guard at London Airport.

Original UK Broadcast:
5.25 p.m., Friday 6 October 1967 (ATV Midlands)

Original Broadcast Episode Number: 2

First UK Network Broadcast:
6.00 p.m., Friday 8 October 1993 (BBC2)

Regular Cast:
Scarlet, Blue, White, Destiny, Green, Black, Ochre, Rhapsody, Melody, Harmony, Grey, Magenta, Fawn

Major Equipment:
Cloudbase, SPV 105, Angel Interceptors, SSC, MSV, SPJ, DT19, Yellow Fox Tanker

Guest Voice Cast:

Director General	**Jeremy Wilkin**
Captain Brown	**Charles Tingwell**
DT19 Pilot	**Paul Maxwell**
DT19 Co-pilot	**Martin King**
Airport Controller	**Martin King**
Airport Operator	**Charles Tingwell**
Agent 042	**Charles Tingwell**
Intercontinental Airlines Tannoy	**Janna Hill**

3. BIG BEN STRIKES AGAIN

Written by **Tony Barwick**
Directed by **Brian Burgess**

'Now let's assume Macey counted correctly and heard Big Ben strike thirteen. What's the only explanation?'

Under police escort, transporter driver Macey is ferrying a nuclear device through the streets of London when his transporter suddenly goes out of control. In the hands of the Mysterons, the transporter evades the police escort and Macey is powerless to stop it as it twists and turns through the narrow streets, finally coming to rest in an underground car park. Macey is thrown forward on to the windscreen as the transporter brakes violently and he is knocked unconscious.

Spectrum receives notification of the Mysterons' next act of retaliation: the destruction of the city of London. A full-scale search begins for the missing transporter but it has still not been found two and a half hours later. Macey recovers consciousness and switches on the radio to check the time. He counts the chimes as Big Ben strikes midnight and is astonished to hear a thirteenth chime! The rear door of the transporter opens by itself and Macey watches horrified as the five-key electrical trigger mechanism on the atomic device slots into place, activating it to detonate in twelve hours. Macey tries to stop the spinning dials but is struck down from behind. Searching London in an SSC, Captain Scarlet comes across Macey lying in the gutter. The driver is taken to Cloudbase, where he relates his story, but he is unable to say where the car park is situated. There are about 2,000 car parks in London that fit his description and time is running out.

Captain Blue considers Macey's remarks about hearing Big

Ben strike thirteen and suddenly hits upon the solution, calculating that the car park must be within a 1,500-yard radius of Big Ben. There are only two car parks in the area that fit the description, so Colonel White dispatches Captain Ochre to Jupiter Way while Scarlet and Blue take an SPV to check out Park View. There they find the transporter, but with only nineteen minutes to go before the device detonates, the lengthy defusing procedure is no longer an option. Colonel White instructs Scarlet to drive the transporter to its original destination, a construction site 10 miles outside London with a prepared excavation 2 miles underground. Escorted by Blue in the SPV, Scarlet arrives at the construction site and takes the transporter down in a lift to the underground silo. With seconds to spare, he races to the surface, but is only three-quarters of the way up in the lift when the device explodes.

Scarlet is fatally injured in the blast, but later joins Blue, Melody and Destiny at a restaurant just a few yards from the car park in Park View. There, Blue demonstrates how he was able to pinpoint the car park: the park is about a mile away from Big Ben, so the clock chimes take approximately four and a half seconds to reach it, but Macey also heard the chimes instantaneously over the radio, so after the last chime sounded on the radio, he heard it again live four and a half seconds later.

Notes

Several minor scenes from Tony Barwick's original script for *Big Ben Strikes Again* were omitted from the finished episode. As Cloudbase is placed on red alert, viewers would have seen that Spectrum has agents codenamed Yellow and Purple, and would have also seen the Room of Sleep, a section of Cloudbase that is referred to in other episodes but never appears on screen.

Lieutenant Dean and Space Navigator Conway, Black's MEV colleagues from *The Mysterons*, both appear in *Big Ben Strikes Again* as police officers. The Director General of the United Asian Republic from *Winged Assassin* is seen alive and well dining in the restaurant at the end of the episode.

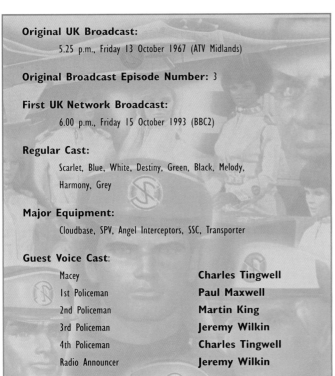

Original UK Broadcast:
5.25 p.m., Friday 13 October 1967 (ATV Midlands)

Original Broadcast Episode Number: 3

First UK Network Broadcast:
6.00 p.m., Friday 15 October 1993 (BBC2)

Regular Cast:
Scarlet, Blue, White, Destiny, Green, Black, Melody, Harmony, Grey

Major Equipment:
Cloudbase, SPV, Angel Interceptors, SSC, Transporter

Guest Voice Cast:

Macey	Charles Tingwell
1st Policeman	Paul Maxwell
2nd Policeman	Martin King
3rd Policeman	Jeremy Wilkin
4th Policeman	Charles Tingwell
Radio Announcer	Jeremy Wilkin

As the episode opens, a shot of Big Ben shows that the time is 11.45 p.m. and within a few minutes Macey's transporter has been taken over by the Mysterons. Colonel White then states that the search for the missing transporter has been going on for two and half hours, and after this we see Macey recover consciousness in the transporter cabin. It must be at least 2.15 a.m., but Macey's watch reads 11.58 p.m. and he hears Big Ben strike midnight.

4. MANHUNT

Written by **Tony Barwick**
Directed by **Alan Perry**

'The tables are turned. The manhunt for Captain Black is on!'

Captain Black breaks into the Culver Atomic Centre, but is discovered by a security guard who sounds the alarm. With all the exits sealed and guards closing in on his position, Black is forced to take refuge in a radioactive area and is exposed to a short-life atomic isotope. A concealed security camera takes a picture of the intruder and this is sent to Spectrum, who can finally confirm that Black has been working for the Mysterons from the moment of his return to Earth. Colonel White explains to Captain Scarlet, Captain Blue and Symphony Angel that, although he has escaped from the Atomic Centre, Black's exposure to the radioactivity means that he can be detected for the next forty-eight hours. Colonel White dispatches detector trucks to the area equipped with directional long-range Geiger counters as the manhunt for Captain Black is launched.

Scarlet and Blue head for Stone Point Village to requisition

an SPV, but Black arrives ahead of them, killing a garage mechanic at the local filling station. When Scarlet and Blue arrive at the garage to collect an SPV, they are greeted by a Mysteron reconstruction of the mechanic, but Scarlet suspects a trap when the man fails to ask them for identification. Scarlet shoots the mechanic down when he pulls a gun on them. Black has taken SPV 0782, but the Detector Trucks are able to get a fix on his position. Symphony makes visual contact with the SPV as it heads directly towards Captain Ochre's checkpoint, but the Mysterons warn Black of the roadblock ahead, instructing him to turn off the road and return to the Atomic Centre. Scarlet and Blue trail Black to a forest clearing, where they find SPV tracks and a medallion given to Symphony by Blue on her birthday. The pair realize that Symphony must have spotted the SPV and landed her Angel Interceptor, only to be captured by Black.

Captain Grey reports from Detector Truck 3 that Black has returned to the Atomic Centre. Colonel White realizes that Black must know that he is radioactive – at the Atomic Centre he is effectively hidden by all the free radiation. Black forces Symphony into a radiation chamber and exposes her to radiation which will kill her in minutes. However, he switches off the radiation emitter after only a few seconds, telling her that he is going to give her a chance to escape. Shortly after, the stolen SPV crashes the gates of the Atomic Centre and heads straight towards a roadblock half a mile from the plant, where it crashes off the highway into a tree. The SPV is surrounded, but when the door is opened, Scarlet and Blue are surprised to discover the irradiated Symphony inside – she has been used as a decoy to draw the Spectrum officers away from the gate, leaving it unguarded while Black makes his escape.

Notes

The music heard on the radio in the Delta garage when Black murders the mechanic was composed as the main titles music for Gerry Anderson's live-action film *Crossroads to Crime* (1960). Lieutenant Dean and Space Navigator Conway from *The Mysterons* make their fourth consecutive appearance in the series, here as a Spectrum Geiger operator and a guard at the Culver Atomic Centre respectively.

Original UK Broadcast:
5.25 p.m., Friday 20 October 1967 (ATV Midlands)

Original Broadcast Episode Number: 4

First UK Network Broadcast:
6.00 p.m., Friday 22 October 1993 (BBC2)

Regular Cast:
Scarlet, Blue, White, Symphony, Green, Black, Ochre, Grey

Major Equipment:
Cloudbase, SPV 0782, Angel Interceptors, SSC, MSV, Detector Truck 3, Detector Truck 5, Detector Truck 6

Guest Voice Cast:

Harris	**Charles Tingwell**
Richards	**Gary Files**
Geiger Operator	**David Healy**
Garage Mechanic	**Gary Files**
Security Chief	**Martin King**
Guard	**Paul Maxwell**
Guard Voice 1	**Jeremy Wilkin**
Guard Voice 2	**David Healy**

After Colonel White thanks Scarlet and Blue for their courage and devotion, the two Captains can be heard speaking with each other's voices.

Oddly, Scarlet shows no sign of nausea in the presence of the Mysteron agent at the Delta garage. The agent is also apparently killed by Scarlet's standard-issue Spectrum gun, which doesn't fit with what we later learn about high-voltage electricity being the only thing that can kill Mysteron agents.

5. POINT 783

Written by **Peter Curran and David Williams**
Directed by **Robert Lynn**

'Do you mean to tell me that it was Major Brooks himself who exploded?'

The Mysterons threaten to destroy the Supreme Commander of Earth Forces within twenty-four hours. Spectrum assumes responsibility for his safety and he is escorted by Captain Scarlet and Captain Blue to Supreme Headquarters Earth Forces in New York to chair a briefing on the new Unitron tank, a computer-controlled vehicle designed for use against other mechanized forces. Meanwhile, the Supreme Commander's personal aide, Major Brooks, is travelling to New York by car with Colonel Storm. As the two SHEF officers approach the single-lane Grand Catskill Tunnel, the Mysterons take control of the driver of a methane tanker who runs a red light at the opposite end of the tunnel. The two vehicles collide head-on in the tunnel and the SHEF officers are killed instantly, but they are reconstructed by the Mysterons.

Major Brooks meets the Supreme Commander, Scarlet and Blue as they arrive at SHEF HQ and the four men make their way to the conference room, where the Supreme Commander begins his briefing. Brooks suddenly reveals himself to be a Mysteron agent and smoke begins to pour from his neck, but Scarlet quickly activates security shields which fall into place just as Brooks explodes.

Blue escorts the Supreme Commander to Point 783, a command post in the Sahara Desert which is being used as a base for the Unitron test programme. There, Blue is introduced to General Cope and Colonel Storm, unaware the Storm is a Mysteron agent. The test exercise begins and Cope explains that the Unitron can be controlled by a trained operator or programmed to seek and destroy a predetermined target automatically. The group assembles on the observation deck, but it soon becomes apparent that the Unitron has been pre-programmed to target the command post. Blue ushers the Supreme Commander back inside as shells begin to rain down on Point 783. Colonel White sends in the Angels to engage the

hostile Unitron, but their missiles prove ineffective.

Scarlet requisitions SPV 428 and soon arrives at Point 783 to escort the Supreme Commander to safety. Storm joins Scarlet and the Supreme Commander in the SPV, but as they leave the command post, the Unitron sets off in pursuit and Storm reveals that he has programmed the Unitron to target on himself. He pulls a gun and shoots Scarlet in the chest when he tries to reach for his own gun, but Scarlet ejects himself and the Supreme Commander from the SPV. The Unitron pursues the SPV and both vehicles hurtle over the edge of a cliff. Scarlet is fatally wounded but Blue assures the Supreme Commander that he will soon recover and return to active duty.

Notes

This episode marks the first appearance of a revamp puppet who later became WIN agent Sam Loover in JOE 90, seen here as the Supreme Commander of Earth Forces. Lieutenant Dean from *The Mysterons* appears again, this time as a guard in the conference room at SHEF Headquarters, while the Director General of the United Asian Republic from *Winged Assassin* appears as the Arab Spectrum agent guarding SPV 428. Major Brooks was previously seen as the Delta garage mechanic murdered by Captain Black in *Manhunt*.

When the Mysteron Major Brooks spontaneously explodes in the conference room, safety shields activated by Scarlet drop into place over Captain Blue before the Supreme Commander. As the security of the Supreme Commander is paramount, he should have received priority protection.

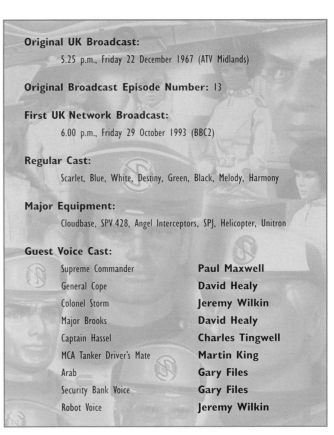

Original UK Broadcast:
5.25 p.m., Friday 22 December 1967 (ATV Midlands)

Original Broadcast Episode Number: 13

First UK Network Broadcast:
6.00 p.m., Friday 29 October 1993 (BBC2)

Regular Cast:
Scarlet, Blue, White, Destiny, Green, Black, Melody, Harmony

Major Equipment:
Cloudbase, SPV 428, Angel Interceptors, SPJ, Helicopter, Unitron

Guest Voice Cast:

Supreme Commander	**Paul Maxwell**
General Cope	**David Healy**
Colonel Storm	**Jeremy Wilkin**
Major Brooks	**David Healy**
Captain Hassel	**Charles Tingwell**
MCA Tanker Driver's Mate	**Martin King**
Arab	**Gary Files**
Security Bank Voice	**Gary Files**
Robot Voice	**Jeremy Wilkin**

6. OPERATION TIME

Written by **Richard Conway and Stephen J. Mattick**
Directed by **Ken Turner**

'That Magnus should keep his hands out of the way.'

At London Hospital, top surgeon Dr Theodore Magnus conducts a brain operation using a cerebral pulsator, a device that eliminates most of the risk in this type of surgery: the patient is given only a local anaesthetic and is conscious throughout the operation. The operation is a success and the patient is expected to make a complete recovery.

Spectrum receives the latest Mysteron threat, a cryptic warning that they intend to 'kill time' which has the Spectrum officers baffled. While the computer compiles a list of possible targets, Colonel White dispatches his top officers to set up field headquarters in key cities. Meanwhile, Dr Magnus prepares for an operation on General Tiempo, the Commander of Western Region World Defence. Tailed by Captain Black, Magnus visits Tiempo at the Westbourne Clinic to confirm that the operation is scheduled for the next day. Leaving the clinic, Magnus becomes involved in a car chase with Black, who shoots out a tyre on Magnus's car. Out of control, the car skids over the edge of a cliff and Magnus is killed when the car explodes on impact. He is re-created by the Mysterons and receives orders from Black to kill time...

Captain Magenta reads about General Tiempo's operation in a newspaper and realizes that the General is the Mysterons' target: *tiempo* is the Spanish word for time. Colonel White decides to relocate the operation to Cloudbase and Captain Scarlet escorts Tiempo and Magnus to the Spectrum base. Dr Fawn suggests that the operation should be postponed for a week or so, but Magnus insists that it must take place immediately. The Sick Bay is prepared and the cerebral pulsator is installed while Magnus takes a series of X-rays of Tiempo's head. The operation then begins, with Magnus connecting an exposed area of his patient's forehead to his cerebral pulsator while the rest of the patient is covered with a sheet.

Meanwhile, in the X-ray room, the radiographer discovers that one of the X-rays of Tiempo's head also features a normal view of Magnus's hand. Realizing that the only explanation is that Magnus is a Mysteron agent, the radiographer rushes to tell Colonel White. In the Sick Bay, the voltage on the pulsator is set too high and the condition of the patient deteriorates. Despite Dr Fawn's protests, Magnus insists on continuing until the order comes through from Colonel White that the surgeon is to be arrested. It is too late for the patient, however, as he is already dead, but to Magnus's dismay the dead man is revealed to be Scarlet, who has been substituted in the General's place.

Magnus escapes from the Sick Bay, knocking down Fawn and Magenta. Pursued by Grey, he locks himself in the generator room but Blue gains access to the room via the maintenance door. Blue tries to persuade Magnus to give himself up, but when Magnus opens fire the Captain knocks a ladder down on to him and Magnus falls back into the generator. He is killed by the high-voltage electricity.

Notes

The London Hospital building seen at the start of the episode previously appeared as the SHEF Headquarters building in *Point 783*. Magnus's colleague Dr Turner is named after episode director Ken Turner. The puppet portraying him was previously seen as General Cope in *Point 783*. Magnus's other colleague, Dr Harrison, is the puppet that later became Sam Loover in JOE 90, first seen as the Supreme Commander in *Point 783*.

The original shooting script suggested that footage of Tiempo's X-rays being developed might be shot on location at Wexham Park Hospital, Stoke Green, only a few miles from the Century 21 Studios, but this did not prove to be necessary.

When Dr Fawn reveals that Magnus has killed Scarlet instead of General Tiempo, he is heard speaking with Magnus's voice.

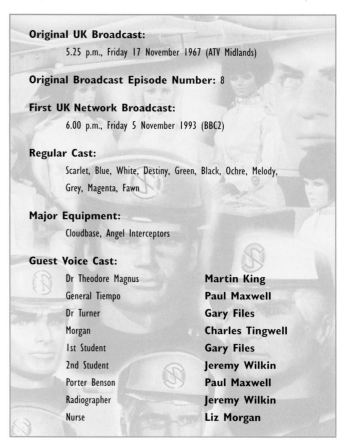

Original UK Broadcast:
5.25 p.m., Friday 17 November 1967 (ATV Midlands)

Original Broadcast Episode Number: 8

First UK Network Broadcast:
6.00 p.m., Friday 5 November 1993 (BBC2)

Regular Cast:
Scarlet, Blue, White, Destiny, Green, Black, Ochre, Melody, Grey, Magenta, Fawn

Major Equipment:
Cloudbase, Angel Interceptors

Guest Voice Cast:

Dr Theodore Magnus	**Martin King**
General Tiempo	**Paul Maxwell**
Dr Turner	**Gary Files**
Morgan	**Charles Tingwell**
1st Student	**Gary Files**
2nd Student	**Jeremy Wilkin**
Porter Benson	**Paul Maxwell**
Radiographer	**Jeremy Wilkin**
Nurse	**Liz Morgan**

7. RENEGADE ROCKET

Written by **Ralph Hart**
Directed by **Brian Burgess**

'Remember, time is against us. Every second takes that rocket nearer its target.'

Space Major Reeves is travelling by power launch to Base Concord when he suddenly feels unwell. He steps out on to the deck for some air, but a safety barrier slips loose and he falls into the sea. Caught in the wake of the launch, Reeves drowns and is reconstructed by the Mysterons. Arriving at Base Concord, a rocket base sited on a remote island, Reeves seals the doors of the rocket control room and reprogrammes the telemetry of an experimental Variable Geometry Rocket. Setting the four-letter destruct code as 'ZERO', he launches the VGR before escaping in an interceptor jet with the flight programme unit.

The Mysterons warn of their intention to launch one of Earth's incendiary rockets in such a way that Spectrum will be unable to determine its target. Cloudbase tracks a rocket which appears to have been launched from Base Concord, and Colonel White is subsequently contacted by the Base Commander, who explains what has happened. The Angels are dispatched to track down Major Reeves and, before long, Melody makes visual contact with Reeves's jet. Captain Scarlet and Captain Blue arrive at Base Concord, where they learn that no tracking station has been able to locate the VGR. The Base Commander tells the Spectrum officers that this doesn't make sense: the VGR should be invisible to radar only on its final approach to its target when it flies under the radar screen. Then

the Base Sergeant realizes that the VGR must be flying on an absolutely vertical flight path, which would render it invisible to radar. This being so, the VGR must be programmed to come straight down and the only target within 300 miles of the area is Base Concord itself!

As evacuation procedures are put into practice, the Angels continue to track Reeves's jet, but Reeves takes evasive action and shoots down Melody's Angel Interceptor. Melody ejects safely and her Angel crashes into the sea. At Base Concord, a new flight programme unit is fitted to the control board, but without the destruct code the rocket cannot be prematurely detonated. The destruct code is based on four-letter words, but there are 10,000 possible combinations of letters in the codebook. The Sergeant starts at 'ABLE' and plans to work systematically through the book, even though the chances of finding the correct codeword before the rocket hits are slim.

The Angels close in on Reeves and Rhapsody urges him to surrender, but he refuses and deliberately crashes his jet into the sea. There is now no chance of recovering the flight programme unit, which sinks to the sea bed. With only three minutes to go before the rocket strikes, Scarlet and Blue disobey Colonel White's orders and remain behind after the rest of the personnel have been evacuated to continue working through the destruct codes. The VGR makes its final approach to the base, but just seconds before impact the programme unit shifts position on the sea bed and the jolt switches the unit to 'ZERO', transmitting the correct destruct code. Scarlet and Blue have just punched 'AMEN' into the flight programme unit at the base when the rocket explodes.

Notes

Major Reeves previously appeared as Captain Brown in *The Mysterons*. The captain of the launch that ferries Reeves to Base Concord previously appeared as General Tiempo in *Operation Time*, while the Base Controller shot by Reeves was seen as transporter driver Macey in *Big Ben Strikes Again*. The Base Captain appeared as Richards, the security chief in *Manhunt*, and the sergeant who starts to type in the destruct codes is the puppet that later became Shane Weston in JOE 90.

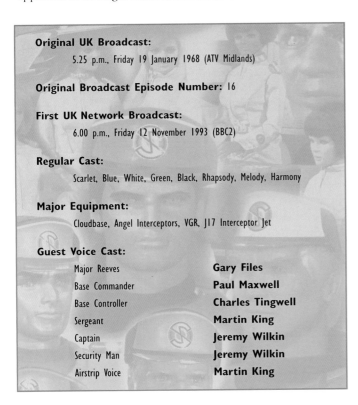

Original UK Broadcast:

    5.25 p.m., Friday 19 January 1968 (ATV Midlands)

Original Broadcast Episode Number: 16

First UK Network Broadcast:

    6.00 p.m., Friday 12 November 1993 (BBC2)

Regular Cast:

    Scarlet, Blue, White, Green, Black, Rhapsody, Melody, Harmony

Major Equipment:

    Cloudbase, Angel Interceptors, VGR, J17 Interceptor Jet

Guest Voice Cast:

Major Reeves	**Gary Files**
Base Commander	**Paul Maxwell**
Base Controller	**Charles Tingwell**
Sergeant	**Martin King**
Captain	**Jeremy Wilkin**
Security Man	**Jeremy Wilkin**
Airstrip Voice	**Martin King**

Major Reeves normally has two gold stars on his uniform, but when his Mysteron reconstruction appears in the wheelhouse of the launch ferrying him to Base Concord, he has only one star on his chest. When he arrives at Base Concord, the missing star is back again.

8. WHITE AS SNOW

Written by **Peter Curran and David Williams**
Directed by **Robert Lynn**

'Sir, I don't think you appreciate that the man is dead.'
'That's no excuse!'

Communications satellite TVR-17 is destroyed when Captain Black takes over the Control Centre and brings the satellite into a premature re-entry. TVR-17 is reconstructed by the Mysterons as the first stage of their latest act of retaliation. Colonel White arrives in the Cloudbase Control Room to find Captain Scarlet and Lieutenant Green listening to the TVR-17 radio broadcast. He asks Green to turn the music down but the signal keeps getting louder. Radar picks up the satellite on a collision course with Cloudbase and, realizing that it could be a Mysteron booby trap, Colonel White orders it to be shot down. Scarlet refuses to act on the Colonel's order, arguing that it could mean the deaths of the twelve crewmen on board, but White insists, dispatching Symphony Angel to shoot it down.

With Colonel White himself the target of the Mysteron threat, the Spectrum commander elects to leave Cloudbase for a secret destination. He offers Scarlet temporary command of Cloudbase but Scarlet refuses, angry that the Colonel apparently disregarded the lives of the men on the TVR-17. The Colonel places Captain Blue in charge before leaving the base. Green then reveals that a report on the wreckage of the TVR-17 has concluded that the satellite was destroyed three hours before the attack on Cloudbase. Realizing that he was wrong to criticize Colonel White, Scarlet asks Green where the Colonel has gone, but Green has orders to keep the destination secret.

Colonel White charters a helijet to fly him to a rendezvous with atomic submarine USS Panther II. Winched aboard the vessel, he introduces himself to the crew as Robert Snow, for only the captain is aware of his true identity. The submarine prepares to dive, but Ensign Soames traps his foot in a chain on the deck and drowns when the vessel submerges. He is reconstructed by the Mysterons and assigned by the submarine captain to act as Colonel White's personal steward.

Soames seals the bulkhead door that is the only access to the submarine's 'E' Section and makes his way to the Colonel's quarters. There, he attempts to carry out the Mysterons' threat, but the man in the cabin returns his gunfire and a gun battle ensues between the two men. As the submarine officers cut through the bulkhead door with a blowtorch, Soames's target is hit, but the dying man manages one last shot which brings down the Mysteron agent. The submarine officers discover that the man Soames had assumed to be the Colonel is actually Scarlet in disguise. The real Colonel White is found bound and gagged in a wardrobe.

Back on Cloudbase, Scarlet admits that he pulled rank on Lieutenant Green to learn the Colonel's destination, then used his Spectrum pass to get through naval security and finally stowed away on board the submarine before it left the World Navy base. Colonel White finds Scarlet guilty of gross insubordination and sentences him to death, but since Scarlet is indestructible an execution would be a waste of time, so he is returned to active duty instead.

Notes

The shooting script for this episode originally began with the Mysterons simply using their influence to take control of the TVR communications satellite. All of the scenes with the DJ and TVR Control, Black engineering the satellite's destruction and its subsequent reconstruction were late additions that did not appear in the script.

TVR-17 DJ Bob Lynn is named after episode director Robert Lynn. Lieutenant Dean and his MEV Space Navigator Conway from *The Mysterons* appear together again here, as Panther II seamen Clark and Davidson. Colonel White's 'smiler' head is seen for the first time here but appears only rarely in subsequent episodes.

Original UK Broadcast:

5.25 p.m., Friday 3 November 1967 (ATV Midlands)

Original Broadcast Episode Number: 6

First UK Network Broadcast:

6.00 p.m., Friday 19 November 1993 (BBC2)

Regular Cast:

Scarlet, Blue, White, Destiny, Symphony, Green, Black, Ochre, Rhapsody, Melody, Harmony, Grey, Magenta

Major Equipment:

Cloudbase, Angel Interceptors, Helijet, USS Panther II, TVR-17

Guest Voice Cast:

Captain, USS Panther II	**Paul Maxwell**
Lieutenant Belmont	**Charles Tingwell**
Ensign Soames	**Gary Files**
DJ Bob Lynn	**Gary Files**
TVR-17 Control	**Martin King**
Pilot	**Jeremy Wilkin**

9. SEEK AND DESTROY

Written by **Peter Curran and David Williams**
Directed by **Alan Perry**

'Look – Angels! The girls have come to escort us!'

A transporter from the Fairfield Engine Company ferries a large crate to a warehouse in a deserted part of the countryside. Two other crates have already been left there and, curious about their contents, the driver, Jackson, is on the point of looking inside when he is shot down by Captain Black. Black sets fire to the warehouse and, shortly after, the Mysterons issue their latest threat, to kill one of the Spectrum Angels. Captain Blue suspects that Destiny, on vacation in Paris, is the most likely target. Colonel White agrees and dispatches Scarlet and Blue to Paris to escort Destiny back to Cloudbase. The two Captains make their way to Destiny's Paris hotel, but she is not in her room. Blue suggests that she is probably out shopping and Scarlet spots a book of matches which directs them to the Café de la Paix. There, they find Destiny, and once Scarlet has explained the situation the three Spectrum agents are soon en route for the airport in a Spectrum Saloon Car.

At the scene of the warehouse fire, the local fire chief reports to managing director Fairfield that the entire warehouse and its contents are a complete write-off. Fairfield reveals that the crates contained top-secret Spectrum aircraft constructed by a number of different factories, none of which holds a complete set of drawings. Fairfield's factory is responsible for the manufacture of the engines and once they have been fitted to the aircraft, they are crated up and left for collection by the last company in line, which will make final flight tests and spray them before delivery to Cloudbase. Three jets overfly the warehouse and Fairfield recognizes them as the three Angel Interceptors destroyed in the fire. The aircraft have been reconstructed by the Mysterons...

Fifteen minutes away from the airport, Scarlet suddenly senses danger nearby and tells Blue to stop the car. The trio dive for cover in a ditch at the side of the road just as the SSC comes under fire from the three Mysteron Interceptors and is destroyed. Scarlet reports the situation to Cloudbase and

Colonel White immediately dispatches Harmony, Rhapsody and Melody to seek and destroy the Mysteron jets. Scarlet, Blue and Destiny are buzzed by the Mysteron aircraft as they make a targeting run before coming around for a final attack. Fortunately, the Angels arrive just in time and an aerial dogfight ensues. Harmony shoots down the first Mysteron jet, but is then shot down herself – she ejects safely and her Interceptor crashes. Rhapsody manages a direct hit on the second Mysteron jet, leaving only one Mysteron Interceptor in the air. This last enemy aircraft draws Melody into a kamikaze nose dive, but while the Mysteron plummets headlong into the ground and explodes, Melody is able to pull out of the dive safely.

Notes

In the shooting script by Peter Curran and David Williams, the operation of the transporter picking up the crate containing an Angel Interceptor is described as 'like Thunderbird 2 picking up a pod'. Destiny's Paris hotel is the SHEF Headquarters building from *Point 783*, now adorned with four gold stars. Transporter driver Jackson was first seen in the series as the pilot of the DT19 in *Winged Assassin*, although prior to his appearance here he also portrayed Benson, the porter at London Hospital in *Operation Time*. The fire chief was previously seen as the TVR-17 Controller in *White as Snow*, and the waiter at the Café de la Paix first appeared as the Director General of the United Asian Republic in *Winged Assassin*.

When Rhapsody shoots down the second Mysteronized Angel Interceptor, it crashes and the explosion very visibly shakes the foreground of the model countryside set. Although Melody is as dark-skinned as Lieutenant Green, her hands are white in the close-up shots of real hands operating the Angel Interceptor controls.

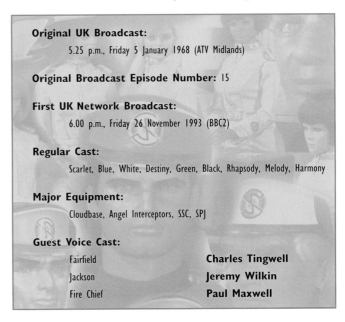

Original UK Broadcast:
    5.25 p.m., Friday 5 January 1968 (ATV Midlands)

Original Broadcast Episode Number: 15

First UK Network Broadcast:
    6.00 p.m., Friday 26 November 1993 (BBC2)

Regular Cast:
    Scarlet, Blue, White, Destiny, Green, Black, Rhapsody, Melody, Harmony

Major Equipment:
    Cloudbase, Angel Interceptors, SSC, SPJ

Guest Voice Cast:

Fairfield	Charles Tingwell
Jackson	Jeremy Wilkin
Fire Chief	Paul Maxwell

  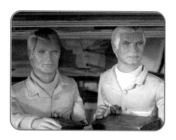 

10. SPECTRUM STRIKES BACK

Written by **Tony Barwick**
Directed by **Ken Turner**

'This is a priority message, codeword Ark – Captain Indigo is in the hands of the Mysterons.'

On a special assignment in a private game reserve in Africa, Captain Scarlet and Captain Blue are directed to a hunting lodge, where they are joined by Colonel White, the World President, Space General Peterson, Dr Giadello and Captain Indigo. On the President's instructions, Indigo operates a control console on the bar and the entire building sinks below ground. The floor of the lounge separates from the bar area and deposits the group in the conference room of the Spectrum Intelligence Agency. Then Indigo raises the lodge building back to its normal position above ground and a false floor slides into place where the floor of the lounge had previously been.

The World President announces that this conference has been called to assess Spectrum's knowledge of the Mysterons and to demonstrate two new devices for use against them, a Mysteron Gun and a Mysteron Detector. Giadello explains the principle of the Mysteron Gun, developed from the discovery that Mysteron agents can be killed by high-voltage electricity. He then calls Indigo on the intercom and asks him to bring the C38 Detector down in the elevator, but the Captain is surprised by the arrival of Captain Black, who shoots him in cold blood. Indigo is reconstructed by the Mysterons and his *doppelgänger* arrives in the conference room to deliver the detector. Colonel White explains that Mysteron agents are impervious to X-rays and, using this information, Giadello has developed a camera that takes an instant X-ray picture of a suspect. Demonstrating the detector on Scarlet, Giadello shows how it takes a normal picture of a Mysteron reconstruction instead of an X-ray photo. Peterson tries out the detector using Indigo as his subject, but Indigo makes his escape before the picture develops and he is revealed to be a Mysteron agent.

Scarlet sets off in pursuit with the Mysteron Gun, but he discovers that Indigo has locked the lift mechanism in the down position and taken the master key. Scarlet races after the Mysteron agent while the lodge descends on to the conference room with the false floor locked in place, threatening to crush the men trapped below. Scarlet is joined by a game warden and the pair give chase. The warden manages to shoot out a rear tyre on Indigo's car, which skids to a halt near a rock formation. Indigo takes cover in the rocks, but Scarlet draws his fire while the warden creeps round behind him and guns him down. The warden is convinced that Indigo is dead, but when the Mysteron agent suddenly revives and reaches for his gun, Scarlet shoots him with the Mysteron Gun. Scarlet returns to the lodge with the lift master key, climbs through a hatch in the roof and stops the lift just in time.

Notes
Captain Indigo is portrayed by the puppet that previously appeared as Macey, the transporter driver in *Big Ben Strikes Again*. The World President makes his second and final appearance here – the next time that the puppet appears it is as Dr Sommers in *Expo 2068*. There is something slightly bizarre about the scene where Colonel White talks about the Mysteron agent Dr Magnus in front of Space General Peterson, as the puppet that appears here as Peterson also portrayed Magnus in *Operation Time*.

Original UK Broadcast:
  5.25 p.m., Friday 24 November 1967 (ATV Midlands)

Original Broadcast Episode Number: 9

First UK Network Broadcast:
  6.00 p.m., Friday 3 December 1993 (BBC2)

Regular Cast:
  Scarlet, Blue, White, Destiny, Symphony, Green, Black, Rhapsody

Major Equipment:
  Cloudbase, Angel Interceptors, Mysteron Detector, Mysteron Gun

Guest Voice Cast:

World President	**Paul Maxwell**
General Peterson	**Charles Tingwell**
Captain Indigo	**Gary Files**
Dr Giadello	**Jeremy Wilkin**
1st Warden (Post 14)	**Gary Files**
2nd Warden (Post 28)	**Martin King**
3rd Warden (Post 40)	**Gary Files**

Captain Blue fires fourteen shells into the ceiling in an attempt to destroy the lift mechanism control console, but when we see the ceiling descending on the occupants of the conference room, it has only eight bullet holes in it.

11. AVALANCHE

Written by **Shane Rimmer**
Directed by **Brian Burgess**

'Believe me, before this day is out you'll need all the help you can get.'

In Northern Canada, Eddie, a maintenance engineer, is making his regular tour of the Frost Line Outer Space Defence System bases when he suddenly finds a fallen tree in the path of his maintenance truck. Slamming on the brakes, he loses control on the icy mountain road and is killed when his truck crashes down the mountainside. Eddie and his truck are both reconstructed by the Mysterons and are soon en route to Red Deer Base. Spectrum receives notification of the Mysterons' next act of retaliation: the destruction of key links in the Frost Line network. Colonel White advises the Frost Line commander-in-chief, General Ward, to put every base on red alert, but Ward is overly confident of the army's ability to deal with the threat from outer space.

Despite the alert, a sentry at Red Deer allows Eddie access to the base. By the time he realizes his mistake, it is too late and Eddie guns him down as he leaves the base. At the Command Base, Lieutenant Burroughs receives an emergency code from Red Deer but is unable to make contact with the base. Colonel White dispatches Captain Scarlet and Lieutenant Green to investigate. Using an airlock, they enter the base's hermetically sealed dome wearing respirators, and make their way to the control room. They find the personnel dead and the corridors filled with a strange mist, but Green's instruments read radiation and toxicity negative and the mist is just water vapour. Meanwhile, Eddie gains access to Cariboo Base, where he inserts a small canister into an air-conditioning inspection hatch. Shortly after, Cariboo transmits an emergency message and then contact is lost. General Ward tells Colonel White that if Big Bear, the next base on the Frost Line, is similarly targeted, he will order a retaliatory missile strike on Mars.

Scarlet and Green are baffled by the deaths of the Red Deer personnel until Green removes his respirator and finds that he cannot breathe. Scarlet realizes that the Mysterons have removed all of the oxygen from Red Deer's self-contained atmosphere! Destiny locates the wreckage of Eddie's truck and, recognizing that this is the same vehicle that called at Red Deer and Cariboo, Colonel White deduces that it is now in the hands of the Mysterons and must be stopped before it gets to Big Bear. Requisitioning SPV 503, Scarlet and Green race to Big Bear, but when they get there they discover that Eddie has left only a few minutes beforehand, heading for the Command Base. While Scarlet sets off in pursuit, Green recovers the strange canister from the air-conditioning duct.

With Scarlet's SPV close behind him, Eddie releases liquid oxygen on to the mountain road. Skidding on the icy road, Scarlet loses control of the SPV and crashes into a snow bank. Colonel White realizes that if Eddie rams the Command Base with a truck full of liquid oxygen, he will blow it sky high, but with his SPV out of action Scarlet has just one last chance to stop Eddie. He fires his pistol into an overhang of snow above the mountain road in front of the maintenance truck, starting an avalanche. A wall of snow and ice sweeps down the mountain, taking Eddie's truck with it.

Notes

Maintenance man Eddie made his first appearance in CAPTAIN SCARLET as the Delta petrol attendant in *The Mysterons*, but prior to his appearance here, he was also seen as the tanker driver's mate in *Point 783* and a guard at the Culver Atomic Centre in *Manhunt*. The sentry at Red Deer Base was initially seen as Harris, another of the guards at the Atomic Centre in *Manhunt*, while the sentry at Cariboo Base is the puppet that later became Shane Weston in JOE 90. Frost Line commander General Ward previously appeared as General Tiempo in *Operation Time*.

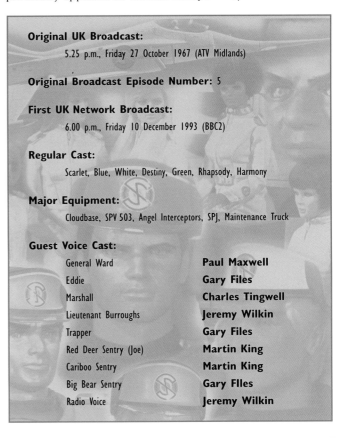

Original UK Broadcast:
5.25 p.m., Friday 27 October 1967 (ATV Midlands)

Original Broadcast Episode Number: 5

First UK Network Broadcast:
6.00 p.m., Friday 10 December 1993 (BBC2)

Regular Cast:
Scarlet, Blue, White, Destiny, Green, Rhapsody, Harmony

Major Equipment:
Cloudbase, SPV 503, Angel Interceptors, SPJ, Maintenance Truck

Guest Voice Cast:

General Ward	**Paul Maxwell**
Eddie	**Gary Files**
Marshall	**Charles Tingwell**
Lieutenant Burroughs	**Jeremy Wilkin**
Trapper	**Gary Files**
Red Deer Sentry (Joe)	**Martin King**
Cariboo Sentry	**Martin King**
Big Bear Sentry	**Gary Flles**
Radio Voice	**Jeremy Wilkin**

12. SHADOW OF FEAR

Written by **Tony Barwick**
Directed by **Robert Lynn**

'Gentlemen, we're about to obtain the best close-up shots of Mars ever taken by man.'

Captain Scarlet and Captain Blue observe the activities at the K14 Observatory in the Himalayas, where astronomers Breck, Carter and Angelini are monitoring signals from a satellite that has been sent to orbit Mars and relay pictures to Earth. The Mysterons destroy the satellite and the signals never reach K14, but Scarlet and Blue are unconcerned as phase one of Spectrum's plan is complete.

Cloudbase moves to a position 50 miles west of the Himalayas so as to be within Angel Interceptor range of K14 and Colonel White launches the Angels to patrol the airspace above the observatory. The first satellite is revealed to have been a decoy for Mini-Sat 5, a second, smaller satellite that makes a successful soft-landing on the Martian moon Phobos. This hidden satellite will transmit close-up pictures of Mars back to Earth as the prologue to a larger Spectrum project, Operation Sword.

Shortly after midnight, Dr Breck is observing Mars through the observatory telescope when the planet appears to give off a bright pulsing light. Breck falls dead and is reconstructed as a Mysteron agent. With only forty minutes until the first pictures of Mars are to be received at the observatory, Breck is discovered to be missing. Realizing that Breck is almost certainly in the hands of the Mysterons, Colonel White dispatches Captain Grey and Melody Angel in a Spectrum Helicopter to search the surrounding area for Breck, while Scarlet and Blue set out on foot.

Grey locates Breck in the rocks above the observatory and Scarlet and Blue intercept him. As the transmission countdown begins, Breck tells Scarlet that he has attached a bomb to the radio telescope's rotation gear – when the dish is moved into position to receive the signals from Phobos, the observatory will be blown to pieces. Breck exchanges gunfire with the Spectrum officers but is shot down by Scarlet. Scarlet and Blue race to warn the astronomers at K14, but it is too late and the observatory is totally destroyed. Despite this setback, Colonel White announces that Operation Sword will proceed as scheduled.

Notes

Colonel White states that the mission to land Mini-Sat 5 on Phobos is part of a larger plan, Operation Sword. However, we never learn what Operation Sword is all about and it is never mentioned again in the series.

A merchandising concept entitled *Project SWORD* was developed and marketed by Century 21 Merchandising in 1967 for a range of space vehicle toys which spawned a comic strip in *Solo* comic and a *Project SWORD* annual. Set in the year 3031, *Project SWORD* told of the adventures of the operatives of the Space World Organization for Research and Development, searching deep space for new sources of power, food and minerals to replenish Earth's drained natural resources. As such, *Project SWORD* had no conceptual connection to CAPTAIN SCARLET AND THE MYSTERONS, so the mention of Operation Sword in *Shadow of Fear* is entirely unrelated.

This is the only episode in which we see Cloudbase mobile in horizontal flight as the Spectrum base moves to a new position over the Himalayas. Captains Blue and Grey are seen using Mysteron Detectors, so this episode must be set after the events of *Spectrum Strikes Back*.

Two of the K14 astronomers have been seen before in the series. Carter first appeared as Space Navigator Conway in *The Mysterons*, while Angelini was previously Fairfield, the managing director of the Fairfield Engine Company in *Seek and Destroy*, but Breck appears for the first time here.

Original UK Broadcast:
5.25 p.m., Friday 2 February 1968 (ATV Midlands)

Original Broadcast Episode Number: 18

First UK Network Broadcast:
6.00 p.m., Friday 17 December 1993 (BBC2)

Regular Cast:
Scarlet, Blue, White, Destiny, Symphony, Green, Ochre, Melody, Harmony, Grey, Magenta

Major Equipment:
Cloudbase, SPV, Angel Interceptors, Helicopter, Mysteron Detector, Mini-Sat 5

Guest Voice Cast:

Dr Breck	**Paul Maxwell**
Dr Carter	**Charles Tingwell**
Dr Angelini	**Jeremy Wilkin**

13. THE TRAP

Written by **Alan Pattillo**
Directed by **Alan Perry**

'Tomorrow morning, on the stroke of ten, the entire supreme command of the World Air Force will be wiped out – here in this room!'

As Melody Angel escorts World Air Force staff plane XQR to Cloudbase, she loses visual contact with the jet in a freak storm. The XQR is struck by lightning and crashes, but within minutes the plane and its passengers, Commodore Goddard and his aide Holt, are reconstructed by the Mysterons. Shortly after, the Mysterons issue a cryptic challenge in their war of nerves, threatening to 'clip the wings of the world'.

Goddard arrives on Cloudbase in order to discuss security arrangements with Colonel White for the International Air Conference, where all the high-ranking officers of the World Air Force will meet to consider methods of dealing with the Mysteron menace. Goddard announces that he has changed the location of the conference to the loneliest spot in Europe, Glen Garry Castle in Scotland. There, Captain Scarlet and Goddard meet Morton, the caretaker, who will be the only other person in the castle apart from the delegates. In the conference room, Scarlet admires a large portrait which dominates the room and Morton reveals that it covers an access stairway to the castle battlements which was filled in by the previous owners.

The delegates arrive on Cloudbase and are checked through security before continuing on to Glen Garry in a Magnacopter piloted by Symphony. Melody is convinced that she saw Goddard's jet struck by lightning en route to Cloudbase, so Colonel White sends her to search the area. He then informs Scarlet that he will wait for the Captain's final clearance before allowing the Magnacopter to land at the castle. From his bedroom, Scarlet spots someone walking along the battlements and realizes that the access stairway from the conference room must have been opened up. In an alcove concealed behind the painting, Scarlet discovers Holt with a machine gun trained on the conference table, but he is captured by Goddard, who impersonates his voice to give the all-clear for the Magnacopter. As the delegates assemble in the conference room, Symphony is puzzled by Scarlet's disappearance and decides to check his bedroom, but she too is captured and is thrown in the castle dungeons with Scarlet.

Meanwhile, Melody has discovered the wreckage of Goddard's XQR plane and Colonel White deduces that Goddard and Holt are Mysteron agents. Captain Blue is dispatched to Glen Garry, where he requisitions an SPV before making his way to the castle. Chained to the dungeon wall, Scarlet and Symphony work together to alert Morton by tapping on a grille in the ceiling with an antique pike. Morton frees the Spectrum agents and Scarlet bursts into the conference room just as Holt is about to gun down the delegates. In an exchange of gunfire, Holt is killed but Goddard escapes on to the battlements, where he trains a machine gun on the Magnacopter. Using the SPV jet-pack, Scarlet flies up to the battlements and draws Goddard's fire away from the Magnacopter for long enough to let Symphony get clear with the delegates. Then Scarlet orders Blue to fire the SPV rockets at the battlements and Goddard is killed as the castle explodes.

Notes

Glen Garry Castle is partially constructed from a model of McGregor Castle built for the STINGRAY episode *Loch Ness Monster*, which also appeared as Glen Carrick Castle in the THUNDERBIRDS episode *30 Minutes After Noon*.

Commodore Goddard was initially seen in the series as Major Brooks in *Point 783*, while his colleague Holt originally appeared as Fairfield in *Seek and Destroy*. Morton, the castle retainer, was previously seen as Colonel Storm in *Point 783*.

This is the first episode in the ITC recommended broadcast order to feature the revised end title sequence with 'Captain Scarlet' sung by The Spectrum. However, it was not the first episode to be completed with this alternative end title sequence – that honour fell to *Lunarville 7*.

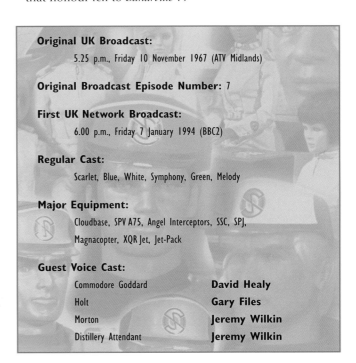

Original UK Broadcast:
  5.25 p.m., Friday 10 November 1967 (ATV Midlands)

Original Broadcast Episode Number: 7

First UK Network Broadcast:
  6.00 p.m., Friday 7 January 1994 (BBC2)

Regular Cast:
  Scarlet, Blue, White, Symphony, Green, Melody

Major Equipment:
  Cloudbase, SPV A75, Angel Interceptors, SSC, SPJ, Magnacopter, XQR Jet, Jet-Pack

Guest Voice Cast:

Commodore Goddard	**David Healy**
Holt	**Gary Files**
Morton	**Jeremy Wilkin**
Distillery Attendant	**Jeremy Wilkin**

14. SPECIAL ASSIGNMENT

Written by **Tony Barwick**
Directed by **Robert Lynn**

'A Spectrum officer is outside the ranch. If you are with us... kill him!'

In Arizona, Captain Black murders a garage attendant who then becomes a Mysteron agent and sabotages the brakes on a car driven by opportunists Steele and Kramer. The car crashes and both men are killed instantly, only to be reconstructed as Mysteron agents. Shortly after, the Mysterons announce their intention to obliterate the subcontinent of North America. After briefing the Spectrum officers on this latest Mysteron threat, Colonel White takes Captain Scarlet to one side and tells him that he has a special assignment for him based on a report from Spectrum Intelligence...

With Captain Blue, Scarlet visits the Dice Club casino, where he loses badly at roulette. He owes the casino 5,000 credits and when this is reported to Spectrum, Colonel White asks for Scarlet's resignation as gambling is a serious breach of the Spectrum code of conduct. Taking up residence at the Gregory Hotel, Scarlet is contacted by Kramer and Steele

posing as gangsters planning a major operation. They offer to pay off his debt and throw in an extra 5,000 if he will requisition an SPV for them. Suspecting that Scarlet may be in some kind of trouble, Blue learns of his whereabouts from a barman who overheard his conversations with Steele and Kramer. The three men have departed for an old ranch house 10 miles north of the city, where Scarlet learns that Kramer and Steele are Mysteron agents whose plans are being coordinated by Captain Black. They intend to use the SPV to carry an atomic device into Nuclear City, Nevada, where it will be detonated and start a chain reaction which will destroy North America. Apparently reluctant at first, Scarlet agrees to ally himself with the Mysteron agents and, to prove his loyalty, he shoots down Blue when he arrives at the ranch house.

Blue recovers consciousness to discover that Scarlet has shot him with an anaesthetic dart, and Colonel White reveals that Scarlet has been working undercover. Searching for some kind of clue left by Scarlet, Blue finds a relief map and a pointer indicating Nuclear City. Colonel White deduces that this is the Mysterons' target and dispatches the Angels to overfly the area. In SPV 104, Scarlet sets off for Nuclear City with Steele and Kramer, who carries a compact atomic device in a case. Some 5 miles south of Nuclear City, Scarlet releases smoke from the rear of the SPV, a signal to the Angels to target and destroy the vehicle. As the Angels open fire on the SPV, Scarlet is shot by Steele, but he pulls the ejector-seat control and is launched to safety as the Angels score a direct hit on the vehicle.

Notes

The original draft script for this episode began with Scarlet losing all his money at the casino. The final shooting script added the scenes with Kramer and Steele's car accident, their reconstruction and Colonel White's brief to the Spectrum officers after receiving the Mysterons' threat. The scenes with Captain Black murdering the garage attendant and the attendant then sabotaging Steele's car were later additions.

Following the continuity established in *The Mysterons*, Mason's Autos is a Delta petrol station and SPV 104 is hidden beneath the forecourt of another Delta garage. The ranch house where Scarlet shoots Blue is adapted from the model of the hunting lodge seen in *Spectrum Strikes Back*.

Original UK Broadcast:

5.25 p.m., Friday 1 December 1967 (ATV Midlands)

Original Broadcast Episode Number: 10

First UK Network Broadcast:

6.00 p.m., Friday 14 January 1994 (BBC2)

Regular Cast:

Scarlet, Blue, White, Symphony, Green, Black, Ochre, Melody, Harmony, Grey, Magenta

Major Equipment:

Cloudbase, SPV 104, Angel Interceptors

Guest Voice Cast:

Steele	**Martin King**
Kramer	**Gary Files**
Croupier	**Gary Files**
Barman	**Jeremy Wilkin**
Mason	**Shane Rimmer**
Security Chief	**Gary Files**
Attendant	**Martin King**

When Blue arrives at the ranch house, in the establishing model shot he is driving a black and grey car, but the close-up puppet shot clearly shows Blue driving a Spectrum Saloon Car.

15. LUNARVILLE 7

Written by **Tony Barwick**
Directed by **Robert Lynn**

'They are trapped in Lunarville 7. We will deal with them at our leisure.'

The Lunar Controller announces that he has been able to contact the Mysterons and come to a peaceful settlement with them: the Moon will now be independent of Earth and will take no part in the war of nerves. Interested to learn exactly how the Controller has managed to negotiate with the Mysterons, Colonel White sends Captain Scarlet, Captain Blue and Lieutenant Green to Lunarville 7 in an XK3 rocket with instructions to also investigate reports of an unauthorized complex being constructed in the Humboldt Sea.

Arriving at Lunarville 7, the Spectrum officers meet the Lunar Controller and his aide, Orson, who equips them with recognition discs. These discs enable them to be identified by the control computer SID, which is programmed to obey verbal instructions. SID controls everything in Lunarville 7, from the air-conditioning to the power supplies. Scarlet requests a trip on the lunar surface and with Orson the three agents travel by Moonmobile to view Lunarville 4. Scarlet is keen to go on to the Humboldt Sea, but Orson refuses as it is getting late. They return to Lunarville 7, where Orson shows them to their quarters, but Scarlet finds the room bugged and rips out the microphone. When Orson reports this to the Controller, the Controller announces that he has programmed SID to accept only his authorization and keep all exits sealed.

That night, Scarlet tries to requisition a Moonmobile from SID but is told that the Controller has declared a state of emergency. Lunarville 7 has been evacuated and all except

Class-C instructions require the Controller's authorization. Scarlet makes his way to the Controller's room and switches their recognition discs, enabling him to authorize SID to open an airlock and allow access to a Moonmobile. The Spectrum officers travel to the Humboldt Sea, where Green spots a strange light coming from Crater 101. Investigating, they find alien machines building a Mysteron complex.

Back at Lunarville 7, Scarlet places the Controller under arrest on the authority of the World President. The Controller responds by revealing that he and Orson are Mysteron agents, telling the Spectrum officers that they will never leave the Moon alive. He orders SID to seal all the exits but the computer is unable to recognize the Controller's authority as he is still wearing Scarlet's recognition disc. Just as the Spectrum agents escape from Lunarville 7 in the XK3, the Lunar Controller shoots SID in frustration. The computer explodes, setting off a chain reaction which totally destroys the base.

Notes
Part of the Lunar Controller's speech was omitted from the final cut of *Lunarville 7*. After he describes how there are '...some 4,000 people living and working on the lunar surface,' he originally continued, 'Many of us have been here for several years. I myself have lived in Lunarville 7 for the past eight years and have come to regard the Moon as my home. We were all born on Earth, but I see a future where men will be born, spend all their lives and die on the Moon. We have now developed our centres to the extent of being self-sufficient, able to support all their inhabitants.'

The rocket that ferries Scarlet, Blue and Green to the Moon is clearly labelled XK3 and referred to by Magenta as an XK3, but the pilot oddly describes it as an XK5.

It is a handy design feature of the Moonmobiles that the seat belts match the colours of the Spectrum agents' uniforms – apart from when Scarlet's and Green's belts inexplicably change colour between shots during their journey to the Humboldt Sea.

When the Spectrum agents arrive back at Lunarville 7 after visiting Crater 101, SID reports that Captain Scarlet has re-entered the complex with Blue and Green. But Scarlet is not wearing his own recognition disc – SID should be able to identify him only as the Lunar Controller.

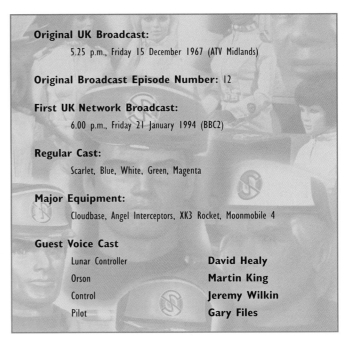

Original UK Broadcast:
5.25 p.m., Friday 15 December 1967 (ATV Midlands)

Original Broadcast Episode Number: 12

First UK Network Broadcast:
6.00 p.m., Friday 21 January 1994 (BBC2)

Regular Cast:
Scarlet, Blue, White, Green, Magenta

Major Equipment:
Cloudbase, Angel Interceptors, XK3 Rocket, Moonmobile 4

Guest Voice Cast

Lunar Controller	**David Healy**
Orson	**Martin King**
Control	**Jeremy Wilkin**
Pilot	**Gary Files**

16. THE HEART OF NEW YORK

Written by **Tony Barwick**
Directed by **Alan Perry**

'I think I know how to make the Mysterons work for us.'

A pair of crooks, Kruger and Doig, stage a raid on the Spectrum Security Vaults, gassing the guard and breaking into the strongroom with explosives. Captain Scarlet and Captain Blue are sent to the vaults to find out if the theft of Grade-A Security documents has any connection to the latest Mysteron threat to destroy 'the heart of New York'. Blue suspects an inside job, but evidence suggests that the thieves did not know what they were looking for. Colonel White is satisfied that this is not the work of the Mysterons and dispatches Scarlet and Blue to New York.

Kruger and Doig are joined by Carl, a worker at the plant where the vault was made, who had believed that they might find something more valuable in the vault. However, Kruger has been reading the documents which detail the Mysterons' war of nerves and their power of retro-metabolism. He devises a plan to get the Mysterons to work for them. First, the trio fake their own deaths, staging a car crash for the benefit of a fire warden at a lookout tower in the hills. Then they pretend to have been Mysteronized and announce that they will rob the head office of the Second National Bank in New York, which

holds the gold reserve for the whole eastern seaboard. The warden reports the incident to Spectrum.

New York has been evacuated and Scarlet and Blue are searching the city for booby traps when they receive notification that the Mysterons have narrowed their attack to the Second National Bank. Colonel White refuses to risk Spectrum lives to save a bank and orders all personnel to pull back to roadblocks at the city limits. Kruger, Doig and Carl arrive at a checkpoint and Captain Ochre photographs them with a Mysteron Detector while Kruger flashes fake FBI identification, telling Captain Magenta that they know that the Mysterons have limited their target to one area downtown. Ochre confirms that the three men are not Mysteron agents, so Magenta allows them to enter the city.

When Scarlet and Blue arrive at the checkpoint, Scarlet queries how these 'Government agents' knew of the Mysterons' plans, since that information was only circulated to Spectrum personnel. As he and Blue race into the city to stop the crooks, Kruger, Doig and Carl arrive at the bank and set about breaking into the vault, unaware that they are being observed by Captain Black. He locks the three men inside the vault and then sets explosives to blow up the bank. Scarlet and Blue spot Black as he makes his escape and give chase through the city streets. As Black heads straight for a roadblock with Scarlet and Blue close behind, the Mysterons instruct him to pull into a blind alley. When Scarlet and Blue turn the corner into the alley, Black and his car have vanished into thin air! Back at the bank, the explosives detonate, killing the three men inside the vault.

Notes

The puppet that portrays Kruger appeared in minor roles in six earlier episodes: *Winged Assassin, Big Ben Strikes Again, Point 783, Avalanche, The Trap* and *Special Assignment*. Carl originally appeared as Lieutenant Belmont in *White as Snow*, but the puppet that takes the role of the third member of their team, Doig, is seen only in this episode. The Spectrum guard at the security vaults is the puppet that later became Shane Weston in JOE 90. The lookout warden was previously Major Brooks in *Point 783* and Commodore Goddard in *The Trap*.

Original UK Broadcast:
   5.25 p.m., Friday 8 December 1967 (ATV Midlands)

Original Broadcast Episode Number: 11

First UK Network Broadcast:
   6.00 p.m., Friday 28 January 1994 (BBC2)

Regular Cast:
   Scarlet, Blue, White, Green, Black, Ochre, Magenta

Major Equipment:
   Cloudbase, Angel Interceptors, SSC, SPJ, Mysteron Detector

Guest Voice Cast:

Kruger	**David Healy**
Doig	**Gary Files**
Carl	**Martin King**
Lookout Warden	**Jeremy Wilkin**
Guard	**Martin King**

In the puppet shots of Scarlet, Blue and Black driving through New York, the background (a rolling painted backdrop) shows trees and bushes in front of the city buildings, but in the model shots there is no vegetation whatsoever lining the city streets.

17. TRAITOR

Written by **Tony Barwick**
Directed by **Alan Perry**

'We've heard you've had a little trouble at the base recently.'

During an exercise, a Hovercraft from the Spectrum cadet school at Koala Base in Australia malfunctions inexplicably, overheating and going out of control. The cadets, Joe Johnson and Phil Machin, jump clear just as the vehicle explodes. This is the third such incident in six days and sabotage is suspected, possibly from inside the Spectrum organization itself in the light of the most recent Mysteron threat, a cryptic warning that a traitor within Spectrum will create havoc and destroy morale.

Captain Scarlet and Captain Blue are sent to Koala Base, ostensibly to give a series of lectures to the new recruits, but really to establish whether sabotage has occurred without alerting Major Stone, the base commander, to their investigations. During their first lecture, Blue relates the sequence of events that led to Scarlet becoming indestructible and Machin begins to suspect that Scarlet might still be working for the Mysterons. He suggests to Johnson that, as one of the organization's top officers, Scarlet would have access to all sections of Spectrum, including the plant where the Hovercraft are made. During the night, Scarlet and Blue awake to find their bedroom on fire, but they escape unharmed.

The next day, Stone announces that Hovercraft exercises will resume as part of a plan to bring the traitor out into the open, so Scarlet and Blue decide to accompany Johnson and Machin in Hovercraft 4. Before they leave, Blue confides in Scarlet that he has his suspicions about Major Stone, as he is in the best position to sabotage the base. Johnson tells Major Stone that he believes that Machin could have started the fire in Scarlet's room, and that Machin's suspicions about Scarlet could be a deliberate attempt to distract attention from himself.

During the exercise, Scarlet, Blue and the two cadets pass the crash site of Hovercraft 2 in which both crewmen were killed. Suddenly, Hovercraft 4 starts to lose control and overheat, just like the previous three vehicles, and Machin pulls a gun on Scarlet, threatening to shoot him if he refuses to reveal how the Hovercraft has been sabotaged. Machin loses his gun when the Hovercraft lurches violently and it is recovered by Blue. Scarlet orders Blue, Machin and Johnson to jump clear of the vehicle while he stays on board to retrieve the instrument recorder. The Hovercraft crashes and explodes but Scarlet manages to get clear just in time.

From the instrument recorder, Spectrum scientists are able to discover that the 'traitor' is just a tiny valve in the hydraulic system of the Hovercraft. Its molecular structure has been altered in a way that can be attributed only to the Mysterons, who have otherwise relied on man's inherently suspicious nature to do their work for them.

Notes

The original script for this episode closes with a clear indication that the Mysterons' only influence on events has been to make the Spectrum officers and cadets suspicious of each other by suggesting the presence of a traitor. The valves in the hydraulic systems of the Hovercraft are discovered to have broken down due to the extreme heat of the Australian Outback, and the fire in Scarlet's bedroom is revealed to have been an accident.

As Blue relates how Scarlet became indestructible, we are treated to flashback footage from *The Mysterons*. Although it establishes a reason for Machin to suspect Scarlet, the function of this footage was really just to provide five minutes of filler material in an episode that ran under time.

Major Stone previously appeared as Jason Smith in *Fire at Rig 15*, Cadet Johnson was seen as Mason, the garage attendant in *Special Assignment*, and Cadet Machin previously appeared with red hair as the radiographer who discovered that Dr Magnus was a Mysteron agent in *Operation Time*.

This episode was originally scheduled for broadcast as episode 16 on 12 January 1968 during the series' original UK broadcast run, but was postponed and finally broadcast three months later as episode 29 on 23 April 1968.

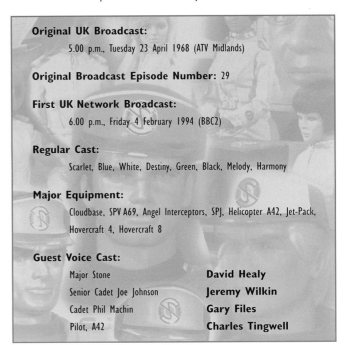

Original UK Broadcast:
5.00 p.m., Tuesday 23 April 1968 (ATV Midlands)

Original Broadcast Episode Number: 29

First UK Network Broadcast:
6.00 p.m., Friday 4 February 1994 (BBC2)

Regular Cast:
Scarlet, Blue, White, Destiny, Green, Black, Melody, Harmony

Major Equipment:
Cloudbase, SPV A69, Angel Interceptors, SPJ, Helicopter A42, Jet-Pack, Hovercraft 4, Hovercraft 8

Guest Voice Cast:

Major Stone	**David Healy**
Senior Cadet Joe Johnson	**Jeremy Wilkin**
Cadet Phil Machin	**Gary Files**
Pilot, A42	**Charles Tingwell**

18. MODEL SPY

Written by **Bill Hedley**
Directed by **Ken Turner**

'This is an official meeting, not the Folies-Bergères!'

Top fashion models Gabrielle and Helga are killed when the monotrain on which they are travelling inexplicably crashes. Both girls are reconstructed as Mysteron agents. Shortly after, Cloudbase receives the latest Mysteron threat, which warns that they are about to attack the House of Verdain and kill André Verdain. Colonel White reveals that the House of Verdain is the cover for the European Area Intelligence Service, and that fashion designer André Verdain is the controller of the whole operation. The Colonel suspects that the attempt on Verdain will be made at a fashion show in Monte Carlo, so he assigns Destiny and Symphony to go undercover as models attached to the House of Verdain, with Scarlet and Blue as press officer and photographer respectively.

The four Spectrum agents are scheduled to land in Paris, but the capital is fog-bound so they fly direct to Monte Carlo. There they meet Verdain, who invites them to join him and his models, Gabrielle and Helga, on his cabin cruiser. As Verdain takes the cruiser for a trip around the bay, Gabrielle starts a fire in the engine room, but Scarlet spots the smoke and orders Verdain to get everyone overboard. Once they have jumped clear, Scarlet takes the cruiser out to sea and leaps from the deck just seconds before the boat explodes.

Scarlet suspects that Gabrielle is a Mysteron agent as Symphony saw her near the engine room just before the fire started, but Verdain insists upon attending a press reception at the Hotel Imperial. At the cocktail party before the reception, Scarlet slips a bug into Verdain's drink which will enable them to track his movements. Gabrielle engages Scarlet in conversation, mentioning that she flew down from Paris the previous day. This is all Scarlet needs to convince him that she is a Mysteron agent: he knows that Paris was fog-bound all day

so Gabrielle is obviously lying.

From a maintenance cradle outside the window, Black targets Verdain with a rifle, but Scarlet spots him and shouts a warning to Verdain, who ducks out of the line of fire as Gabrielle turns out the lights. In the darkness, Black and Helga force Verdain through the window into the cradle and make their escape in Black's saloon car. Scarlet gives chase in a convertible while Blue requisitions an SPV. Symphony and Destiny track Verdain from a helicopter and relay his position to Scarlet. Black soon realizes that Verdain must have a homing device on him, but Helga is unable to find it. Black drops a grenade in Scarlet's path and the Spectrum officer loses control of his car as he swerves to avoid the explosion. He crashes off the road and the convertible is wrecked, but Blue arrives in the SPV and the pair continue the pursuit. Entering a tunnel with the SPV close behind them, Black realizes that the homing device is inside Verdain and orders Helga to throw him out of the car. The tunnel exit is blocked and the two Mysteron agents are trapped, but Verdain regains consciousness just in time to see Black's car vanish into thin air.

Notes

The Monte Carlo backdrop seen in the establishing model shots and scenes of Verdain's cruiser was created for the THUNDERBIRDS episode *The Man from MI.5*. The jet that overflies Verdain's cruiser previously appeared as Commodore Goddard's XQR plane in *The Trap*.

When the Spectrum agents meet Verdain, Scarlet decides to drop their Spectrum codenames so as to maintain their cover, but everyone still continues to call the two Angels Destiny and Symphony.

When the lights go out at the reception, Colonel White is briefly visible being waggled about on the right of the picture – he wasn't at the reception before the lights went out, and he isn't there when they come back on.

Original UK Broadcast:
5.25 p.m., Friday 29 December 1967 (ATV Midlands)

Original Broadcast Episode Number: 14

First UK Network Broadcast:
6.00 p.m., Friday 11 February 1994 (BBC2)

Regular Cast:
Scarlet, Blue, White, Destiny, Symphony, Green, Black

Major Equipment:
Cloudbase, SPV, Angel Interceptors, Search Helicopter, Monotrain

Guest Voice Cast:

André Verdain	Jeremy Wilkin
Helga	Liz Morgan
Gabrielle	Sylvia Anderson
Commissionaire	Jeremy Wilkin
Confused Partygoer	Shane Rimmer

19. FIRE AT RIG 15

Written by **Bryan Cooper**
Directed by **Ken Turner**

'Don't worry. He's too old a hand to get near an explosion. He'll be all right.'

Ultra-sonic drilling Rig 15 in the Middle East has finally struck oil, a very particular kind of oil needed by Spectrum at their Bensheba refinery to produce the specialized fuel used by all Spectrum vehicles. But the Mysterons use their powers to open the master valve and the rig is almost shaken to pieces by the sudden increase in pressure. The rig workers manage to get clear just as oil gushes out and explodes, turning Rig 15 into a column of fire 1,000 feet high.

The latest Mysteron threat declares their intention to immobilize Spectrum and Colonel White realizes that they may intend to target the ultra-sonic oil wells or the Bensheba refinery, for if either was destroyed it would be disastrous for Spectrum. Captain Scarlet and Captain Blue fly out to Bensheba, where they meet Rig Controller Kinley. He introduces them to fire-control expert Jason Smith, who has been hired to put out the Rig 15 blaze. Smith enters the raging inferno in a specially equipped tractor to place explosives which will blow out the flames like a candle. With the tractor in position, Smith leaves his vehicle, but Captain Black is watching from a vantage point nearby and uses his powers to mesmerize the man. Smith collapses near the tractor and is killed when the explosives detonate. The fire is successfully extinguished, but Smith is reconstructed as an agent of the Mysterons. Later, in his explosives truck, Smith receives his instructions from the Mysterons, relayed by Captain Black: he is to drive his truck to the refinery and blow it to pieces.

Smith leaves Rig 15 at dawn and the Spectrum officers prepare to return to Cloudbase, but then Kinley discovers Smith's body in the debris and Scarlet realizes that there is only one explanation: Jason Smith is in the hands of the Mysterons – and with the amount of explosive that he has on board, his truck is like a four-wheeled time bomb! Scarlet requisitions SPV 1034 and sets off in pursuit. Melody Angel reports sighting Smith on the Bensheba road, about 15 miles from the refinery, but she cannot launch an attack for fear of rupturing the oil pipeline which runs parallel to the road. Scarlet cuts across the desert and heads off Smith near some oil storage tanks on the perimeter of the refinery. Smith throws explosives into the path of the SPV but Scarlet manages to force the truck off the road and away from the pipeline. The truck hits a sand dune and explodes, but Scarlet loses control of the SPV and crashes into one of the oil storage tanks. Scarlet suffers fatal injuries but Spectrum's fuel supply is secure.

Notes

The location of the Spectrum refinery is given in Bryan Cooper's original script as Bethsheba rather than Bensheba.

Jason Smith made his first appearance in the series as the TVR-17 Controller in *White as Snow*, but prior to the puppet's appearance here he has also been seen as the fire chief in *Seek and Destroy* and Major Stone in *Traitor*. Charlie Hansen was previously seen as Captain Brown in *The Mysterons*, while Kinley took the role of Colonel Storm in *Point 783*.

This was the last episode to be completed with the original arrangement of the end titles music.

Original UK Broadcast:
5.25 p.m., Friday 16 February 1968 (ATV Midlands)

Original Broadcast Episode Number: 20

First UK Network Broadcast:
6.00 p.m., Friday 25 February 1994 (BBC2)

Regular Cast:
Scarlet, Blue, White, Green, Black, Melody, Grey, Fawn

Major Equipment:
Cloudbase, SPV 1034, Angel Interceptors, SPJ, Fire Tractor, Explosives Truck

Guest Voice Cast:

Jason Smith	**David Healy**
Kinley	**Jeremy Wilkin**
Charlie Hansen	**Gary Files**
Oil Worker	**Martin King**

20. FLIGHT TO ATLANTICA

Written by **Tony Barwick**
Directed by **Leo Eaton**

'What a bang! Can we do that again?'

To celebrate the first anniversary of the formation of Spectrum, the officers host a party with the help of some anonymously donated non-alcoholic champagne. As they toast the organization, Captain Scarlet drops his glass by accident and, before he can get a replacement, the party ends abruptly when Colonel White discovers what is going on.

The latest Mysteron threat targets the World Navy Complex at Atlantica, an impregnable base defended by a ring of sea-to-air missiles and killer submarines. Colonel White orders Symphony Angel to patrol the area, but Lieutenant Green loses contact with her shortly after she leaves Cloudbase. Captain Blue and Captain Ochre are assigned to disperse a wreck being carried by heavy currents towards Atlantica, flying a V17 Air Force bomber out of Maxwell Field. However, both men are uncharacteristically rude during the Air Force briefing and as they leave the briefing room Ochre drops the bombing orders when he bumps into Captain Black. Ochre fails to recognize the Mysteron agent, who switches the top page before handing the papers back.

Concerned for Symphony, Colonel White sends Destiny and Harmony to investigate, but Green loses contact with them too and, one by one, the remaining Spectrum officers all become erratic and irresponsible. Only Colonel White and Scarlet are unaffected and they soon realize that they were also the only ones who didn't drink the champagne at the celebration earlier. They use the Sick Bay auto-analyser to discover that the champagne was spiked with an organic compound which causes sporadic amnesia and general irresponsibility. Aboard the V17, Ochre reads the bombing orders, which direct them to bomb the defence system control tower and then Atlantica Base itself. Colonel White receives a report that the Angels have landed safely, but the V17 has altered course and is heading for Atlantica. Scarlet and the Colonel set off in pursuit in an SPJ.

Using the V17's computer-controlled bombing system, Blue and Ochre destroy the Atlantica defence system tower, causing the ring of tracker missiles to go haywire. Ochre passes out, but Blue flies on towards Atlantica Base. Colonel White orders Scarlet to shoot the V17 down, but he refuses and tries to raise Blue on the radio. Blue sets the bomb release for ninety seconds and Scarlet is eventually left with no alternative but to fire a missile at the bomber. Fortunately, Blue ejects himself and Ochre just before the V17 crashes into the sea.

Three days later, Colonel White holds a second celebration, this time according to regulations, and the Spectrum personnel toast the organization's proper first anniversary with bottles of Captain Scarlet champagne.

Notes

This is the first of only two episodes in which all fourteen of the regular cast appear. The other is *Attack on Cloudbase*.

Colonel White reveals here that Spectrum was formed in July 2067 – the inaugural charter was drawn up on 7 July and the World President signed it on 10 July. Writer Tony Barwick was particularly fond of using the date 10 July in his scripts as it was his birthday.

The music heard in the conference room at the start of the episode is a jazz piece composed for the STINGRAY episode *Tune of Danger*. The radio in the cockpit of the V17 plays 'Dangerous Game', a tune composed for the THUNDERBIRDS episode *The Cham-Cham*.

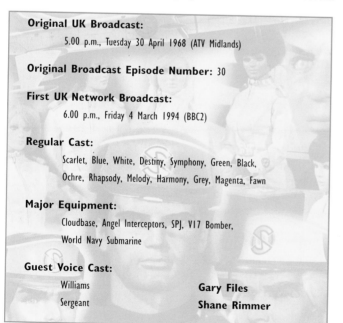

Original UK Broadcast:
5.00 p.m., Tuesday 30 April 1968 (ATV Midlands)

Original Broadcast Episode Number: 30

First UK Network Broadcast:
6.00 p.m., Friday 4 March 1994 (BBC2)

Regular Cast:
Scarlet, Blue, White, Destiny, Symphony, Green, Black, Ochre, Rhapsody, Melody, Harmony, Grey, Magenta, Fawn

Major Equipment:
Cloudbase, Angel Interceptors, SPJ, V17 Bomber, World Navy Submarine

Guest Voice Cast:
Williams
Sergeant

Gary Files
Shane Rimmer

The date of the formation of Spectrum given in this episode conflicts with other background information published by the Century 21 Organization (primarily in TV Century 21 magazine and the CAPTAIN SCARLET annuals) which details that Spectrum was launched on 28 September 2065, after nine months of planning and preparation.

21. CRATER 101

Written by **Tony Barwick**
Directed by **Ken Turner**

'If we ever get out of this, Lieutenant, I'll buy you all the coconuts you can eat.'

Colonel White organizes an operation to destroy the Mysteron complex discovered by Captain Scarlet, Captain Blue and Lieutenant Green in Crater 101 on the Moon during their visit to Lunarville 7, but a volunteer party must first be sent into the complex to remove its power source, otherwise the complex will simply reconstruct itself after destruction. The Mysterons threaten to destroy anyone who dares to enter, but Scarlet, Blue and Green volunteer for the mission none the less.

The trio journey to Lunarville 6, where they meet Linda Nolan, a veteran of the CB29 Neptune Probe mission of 2058. Extensive aerial reconnaissance of Crater 101 has tracked the movements of unmanned lunar vehicles programmed to carry out the construction of the complex, all controlled by one larger vehicle. On arrival at the crater, the Spectrum agents will have just four hours to penetrate the complex, remove the power source and get clear before a low-yield atomic device, ferried by Nolan's colleague Frazer in a Lunar Tank, is detonated at midnight Standard Earth Time. Nolan asks Scarlet to take her lucky charm with him, a memento of the Neptune mission inscribed, 'We made it – ahead of schedule.' The Spectrum officers set off in a Moonmobile, followed an hour later by Frazer in the Lunar Tank, but, unknown to everyone, the real Frazer has been killed and replaced with a Mysteron agent...

Scarlet, Blue and Green arrive at Crater 101 and transfer to a Lunar Tractor for the final assault on the complex. Fighting their way past the robot construction vehicles, Green uses the Tractor's missile gun to knock out the Mysteron control vehicle, clearing the way into the complex. Meanwhile, Frazer contacts Nolan to inform her that the detonator on the atomic device has been set to explode two hours earlier than planned. Nolan realizes that Frazer is a Mysteron agent, but cannot warn the Spectrum officers as Crater 101 is below the lunar horizon and beyond radio contact.

Scarlet, Blue and Green enter the Mysteron complex and find themselves in a strange, alien environment filled with light, colour and sound. A screen showing a hypnotic pattern transfixes the three men, but Scarlet fights its influence and manages to destroy it. They finally locate the power source, a diamond pulsator attached to a control console, and Scarlet

attempts to disconnect it. Back at Lunarville 6, Nolan launches an unmanned CB29 rocket in an attempt to warn Scarlet of the danger. The rocket comes to rest near the complex and Blue investigates. When Scarlet learns of Blue's discovery, he realizes that this is a coded message from Nolan relating to the inscription on the lucky charm, meaning that the bomb will explode ahead of schedule. Blue checks the detonation time on the atomic device and finds it set to go off at 10.00 p.m. With just five minutes before the whole crater goes up, Scarlet orders Blue and Green to return to the Moonmobile and get clear while he disconnects the pulsator. As time runs out, Scarlet finally succeeds in prising the crystal loose and escapes in the Lunar Tractor just before the bomb explodes, completely destroying the Mysteron complex.

Notes
Crater 101 continues the story which began in *Lunarville 7* and concludes in *Dangerous Rendezvous*. There is yet another mention of 10 July, this time as the date in 2058 when the first Neptune Probe was launched from the Moon.

When Frazer leaves Lunarville 6 in the Lunar Tank, we can see that part of the base is made from Mini-Sat 5 (*Shadow of Fear*) and the Frost Line Command Base domes (*Avalanche*).

Linda Nolan was briefly seen attending André Verdain's reception in *Model Spy*. Her German colleague, Shroeder, previously appeared as General Tiempo in *Operation Time*, while Mysteron agent Frazer was formerly Captain Hassel in *Point 783*, although he has also been seen as a guard at Base Concord in *Renegade Rocket*.

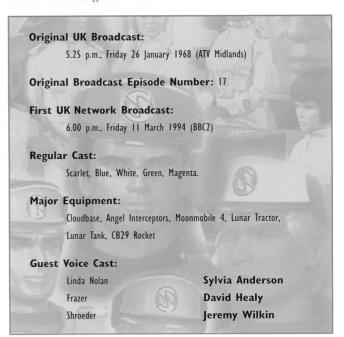

Original UK Broadcast:
5.25 p.m., Friday 26 January 1968 (ATV Midlands)

Original Broadcast Episode Number: 17

First UK Network Broadcast:
6.00 p.m., Friday 11 March 1994 (BBC2)

Regular Cast:
Scarlet, Blue, White, Green, Magenta.

Major Equipment:
Cloudbase, Angel Interceptors, Moonmobile 4, Lunar Tractor, Lunar Tank, CB29 Rocket

Guest Voice Cast:
Linda Nolan — **Sylvia Anderson**
Frazer — **David Healy**
Shroeder — **Jeremy Wilkin**

22. DANGEROUS RENDEZVOUS

Written by **Tony Barwick**
Directed by **Brian Burgess**

'Let's hope the Mysterons listen to reason when you talk to them.'

In a maximum security operation, Captain Scarlet is asked to escort Dr Kurnitz of the Nash Institute of Technology's Radio Communications Division to the airport in the Yellow Fox Tanker as the first stage in their journey to Cloudbase. While they are still en route, Spectrum receives a message from the Mysterons threatening to destroy Cloudbase itself at midnight. The Spectrum headquarters is placed on a maximum security alert and the only aircraft allowed to land is the one carrying Scarlet and Kurnitz.

Kurnitz has been studying the Mysteron pulsator recovered by Scarlet from the complex in Crater 101 on the Moon and, following the doctor's instructions, Spectrum has constructed a transmission device that simulates the exact conditions inside the Mysteron complex. With the diamond pulsator in place, Colonel White will be able to speak directly to the Mysterons for the first time.

Speaking on behalf of the World Government and the peoples of Earth, Colonel White transmits a message to the Mysterons in an attempt to explain the misunderstanding that led to the destruction of the Mysteron complex on Mars. He admits and says he deeply regrets the error made by the Zero X team, and offers the hand of friendship in the hope that there may be a way of finally ending the war of nerves. While they wait for the Mysterons' reply, Colonel White demonstrates the Spectrum communications system to Kurnitz and shows him an Angel launch from the flight deck.

Some two hours later, the Mysteron response comes through. They have decided to allow one member of Spectrum to meet with their representative, on condition that he carries no weapons or communication equipment. The rendezvous is set for a desolate volcanic area in Greenland and Scarlet takes up the challenge, even though he knows he may be walking into a trap.

Scarlet flies to Greenland, where the Mysterons instruct him to eject from his SPJ. On landing, he is met by an unmanned black saloon car which drives him to a deserted shack. Inside, Scarlet is invited to sit in front of a screen which conceals Captain Black on the other side. Black tells him to relay a message to the world, but the message is merely a recording which reiterates the Mysterons' intention to take their revenge against the Earth. Black leaves the shack with the recording still

running, but Scarlet recognizes the deception and breaks through the screen to the room behind. There, he finds a glowing diamond pulsator identical to the one on Cloudbase and, sensing that it is about to explode, he races from the shack just seconds before it is completely demolished by the blast.

Scarlet suddenly realizes that the pulsator is the key to the Mysterons' threat to destroy Cloudbase: a release of energy of the kind that he has just seen will obliterate the base! Frantically, he drives the saloon car to the nearby Renvick Radar Station, where he rigs up a Morse code signalling device to alert Cloudbase to the danger. With only seconds to spare, Captain Ochre hurls the pulsator through the nearest porthole and it explodes as it falls to the ground below.

Notes

Dangerous Rendezvous concludes the story that began with *Lunarville 7* and continued in *Crater 101*. During Colonel White's message to the Mysterons, flashback footage from the opening sequence of *The Mysterons* illustrates how the war of nerves began.

Apart from the characters seen in the flashback footage from *The Mysterons*, this episode features only two revamp puppets: Dr Kurnitz, the puppet that later became Shane Weston in JOE 90, and his receptionist, who had previously appeared as the Mysteron agent Helga in *Model Spy*.

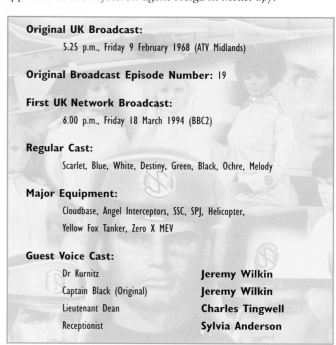

Original UK Broadcast:
    5.25 p.m., Friday 9 February 1968 (ATV Midlands)

Original Broadcast Episode Number: 19

First UK Network Broadcast:
    6.00 p.m., Friday 18 March 1994 (BBC2)

Regular Cast:
    Scarlet, Blue, White, Destiny, Green, Black, Ochre, Melody

Major Equipment:
    Cloudbase, Angel Interceptors, SSC, SPJ, Helicopter,
    Yellow Fox Tanker, Zero X MEV

Guest Voice Cast:

Dr Kurnitz	**Jeremy Wilkin**
Captain Black (Original)	**Jeremy Wilkin**
Lieutenant Dean	**Charles Tingwell**
Receptionist	**Sylvia Anderson**

23. NOOSE OF ICE

Written by **Tony Barwick**
Directed by **Ken Turner**

'We're pretty isolated, but we don't leave anything to chance. The Mysterons won't succeed here.'

At the Hotspot mining base at the North Pole, Neilson, the maintenance man, is caught in a raging blizzard during an inspection of the base's Eskimo booster station. Buried by the snow, his body is reconstructed by the Mysterons and his replacement leaves the booster station to return to Hotspot Control in a Snow Cougar vehicle. Shortly after, Spectrum receives the latest threat from the Mysterons that dooms a much-vaunted new Space Fleet to failure.

At Space Administration Headquarters, the commander-in-chief, General Rebus, explains to Captain Scarlet and Captain Blue that in order to cut down the transit time to Mars by a third, the fleet's rocket nose casings must be constructed from tritonium so as to withstand the higher stresses involved. The only natural source of tritonium in commercial quantities lies at the bottom of the sea under the North Pole, so the Hotspot mining base would seem to be the most likely target for the Mysteron threat. Scarlet and Blue travel in an SPV to Hotspot Tower, crossing the long bridge that spans the ring of water around the tower. As they enter a lift that will take them 1,000 feet below the ice to the base control centre, they pass Neilson, on his way to make another inspection of the Eskimo booster station. Rhodes, the station commander, welcomes Scarlet and Blue to the mining complex and explains that the tritonium mining is made possible only by the use of huge heating elements, fed by 100,000 volts from the booster station, which keep the temperature of the water around the tower above freezing point. If the current failed, the sea would freeze within half an hour and the expanding ice would crush the tower.

Captain Black relays instructions from the Mysterons to Neilson in the booster station. The maintenance man turns off the main heating elements and unplugs the power cables from the main circuits, cutting off all power to the mining complex. At Hotspot Tower, Rhodes and the Spectrum officers soon realize that this is no ordinary power failure as the sea begins to freeze, like a frozen noose tightening around the neck of the tower. With the elevators out of action, Scarlet dons a heated suit and ventures through a waterlock into the freezing Arctic water, braving the enormous pressure variation to make his way to the surface. In the SPV, Scarlet races across the bridge as it collapses around him and drives at breakneck speed to the booster station. There, Scarlet confronts Neilson, who shoots him in the chest as he throws one of the live power cables at the Mysteron agent, but Neilson is electrocuted when the cable makes contact with the metal stairway that he is standing on. Scarlet is fatally wounded but manages to reconnect the cables and restore power to the main heating elements. The ice melts, leaving Hotspot Tower intact but badly damaged and out of operation for at least six months.

Notes

The incidental music that accompanies Neilson's death in the snow storm was originally composed for STINGRAY. More incidental music from STINGRAY can be heard as the temperature drops around Hotspot Tower.

Maintenance man Neilson originally appeared as Captain Brown in *The Mysterons*. This is the puppet's third role as a character who is reconstructed as a Mysteron agent: he also appeared as Major Reeves in *Renegade Rocket*. Hotspot Controller Rhodes is portrayed by the puppet that later became Sam Loover in JOE 90. General Rebus was first seen as the Commander of Base Concord in *Renegade Rocket*, although he has also been seen patronizing both the Café de la Paix in *Seek and Destroy* and the Dice Club in *Special Assignment*. The guard at Hotspot Tower was formerly Jason Smith in *Fire at Rig 15*.

Original UK Broadcast:
5.00 p.m., Tuesday 12 March 1968 (ATV Midlands)

Original Broadcast Episode Number: 24

First UK Network Broadcast:
6.00 p.m., Friday 25 March 1994 (BBC2)

Regular Cast:
Scarlet, Blue, White, Green, Black (voice only)

Major Equipment:
Cloudbase, SPV, Angel Interceptors, Snow Cougar 21

Guest Voice Cast:

General Rebus	David Healy
Neilson	Gary Files
Rhodes	Jeremy Wilkin
Hotspot Control	Martin King
Guard	Martin King

   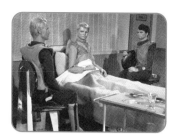

24. TREBLE CROSS

Written by **Tony Barwick**
Directed by **Alan Perry**

'I'd say Major Gravener was a lucky man – a very lucky man.'

Chief test pilot Major Gravener is en route to Slaton Air Base with his driver, Harris, when their car is approached at high speed by Captain Black at the wheel of a truck fitted with false headlights on an extended arm. Believing that they are about to collide head-on with another vehicle, Harris swerves off the road and the car crashes into a lake. Gravener drowns but is reconstructed as a Mysteron agent and the Mysterons issue Spectrum with their latest threat, to destroy the World Capital, Futura City. However, shortly after the Mysteron Gravener and Captain Black have left the scene, a pair of doctors, Mitchell and Baxter, are driving home from a lecture when they come upon the crash site. They recover Major Gravener's body from the water, connect him to a resuscitator and take him to Slaton Hospital in an ambulance. There he is placed in a recovery unit and is miraculously revived two hours later.

The next morning at Slaton Air Base, Gravener's Mysteron *doppelgänger* commandeers an XK107 fighter with a live nuclear warhead. Fortunately, the hospital contacts the air base to tell them that they have the real Gravener there and, realizing that the pilot of the XK107 is an impostor, the base authorities block the runway and the XK107 crashes on take-off. Spectrum receives a report on the incident from Slaton Air Base and Captain Scarlet and Captain Blue leave for Slaton Hospital immediately. Explaining to Gravener what has happened to him, the two officers persuade him to help them find out how the Mysterons intend to attack Futura City, by replacing his Mysteron double. It is just possible that the Mysterons may not realize that Gravener is still alive or that their agent has already failed in his attempt to steal the XK107.

Gravener takes off from the air base in a second XK107 fighter and the plan to deceive the Mysterons appears to have worked when he is contacted by Captain Black, who instructs him to land at Weston Airstrip, a disused airfield some 30 miles outside Futura City. As he and Blue race to the airfield in an SSC, Scarlet deduces that the Mysterons plan to transfer the warhead from the XK107 to another vehicle and then use the XK107 as a decoy. The airstrip is completely surrounded by Spectrum ground vehicles and the Angels patrol overhead, targeting Captain Black's truck as it attempts to leave the area. Scarlet and Blue cut off the truck's only exit from the airfield and give chase as it heads for the east road. Destiny opens fire on the truck, diverting it on to the runway just as Gravener is bringing the XK107 in to land. Swerving to avoid colliding with the aircraft, the truck crashes into an airfield building, but the driver of the vehicle is discovered to be a Mysteron reconstruction of Gravener's driver Harris, not Captain Black. Black has escaped again, but Futura City is safe.

Notes
You have to admire writer Tony Barwick's attention to detail: when Dr Mitchell announces that the date is Tuesday 10 July, that date in 2068 will indeed be a Tuesday. Although this episode is mainly set on 10 July, it is not beyond the bounds of credibility that the closing scene of *Flight to Atlantica* (also set on 10 July) takes place on the same day.

The revamp puppet that is seen for the first time here as Dr Mitchell later appeared as BISHOP agent Matthew Harding in the 1969 Supermarionation series THE SECRET SERVICE. Major Gravener originally appeared as Major Brooks in *Point 783* and also as Commodore Goddard in *The Trap*. Dr Mitchell's nurse was formerly Mysteron agent Helga in *Model Spy*, while his colleague Dr Baxter was previously General Tiempo in *Operation Time*.

A montage of footage from *Manhunt* is used to illustrate the Spectrum ground forces closing in on Weston Airstrip.

Original UK Broadcast:
5.25 p.m., Friday 23 February 1968 (ATV Midlands)

Original Broadcast Episode Number: 21

First UK Network Broadcast:
6.00 p.m., Friday 8 April 1994 (BBC2)

Regular Cast:
Scarlet, Blue, White, Destiny, Green, Black, Rhapsody, Harmony

Major Equipment:
Cloudbase, SPV, Angel Interceptors, SSC, Detector Truck 3, Detector Truck 6, XK107

Guest Voice Cast:

Major Gravener	**Jeremy Wilkin**
Dr Mitchell	**David Healy**
Dr Baxter	**Martin King**
Nurse	**Liz Morgan**
Sergeant	**Gary Files**

25. INFERNO

Written by **Tony Barwick and Shane Rimmer**
Directed by **Alan Perry**

'There's something strange going on, sir. He just seemed to cut off.'

An SKR4 recovery craft, on a mission to destroy a live rocket with a faulty destruct system, is involved in a collision with a meteorite. Packed with explosives, the SKR4 blows up and is totally obliterated, but the craft is reconstructed by the Mysterons, who then issue Spectrum with a warning of their next act of retaliation: the destruction of the Najama complex.

Colonel White briefs his officers on the target of this latest Mysteron threat, a giant desalination plant in the foothills of the Andes mountains. This plant processes sea water from the Pacific to irrigate the interior and without it hundreds of square miles would revert to wasteland. Captain Ochre and Captain Magenta are assigned to cover the north and south entries to the Najama valley, while Captain Scarlet and Captain Blue mount their surveillance from an ancient temple on the rim of the valley overlooking the complex. The crumbling temple is filled with ancient artefacts, stone carvings and statues, one of which topples from the wall, narrowly missing Scarlet and Blue as they search for the best vantage point. Finding a balcony which looks out over the plant, they note that the complex contains a number of large liquid-oxygen tanks – one explosion could start a chain reaction that would turn the whole valley into a blazing inferno.

The SKR4 continues on its return flight path but the sergeant monitoring the craft's descent at the Euro-Space Tracker Station expresses his belief to Major Moran that something is wrong with the two men piloting the vehicle. Night falls, and at the temple Scarlet takes the first watch while Blue gets some sleep. Captain Black arrives at the temple and climbs a huge sun-god statue which dominates the main chamber to plant a homing device in the mouth of the idol. Blue is woken by rocks falling from above, but Black vanishes into thin air before he can be discovered.

The next morning, the SKR4 is on its final orbital approach but refuses to answer calls from the Euro-Space Tracker Station.

> When Lieutenant Green launches the Angels, we see Destiny set off in Angel One and then Harmony and Melody boarding Angels Two and Three. But when the Angels arrive at Najama, Angels Two and Three are piloted by Rhapsody and Symphony!

Major Moran alerts Colonel White and reports that the SKR4 re-entry signal is being jammed in some way. Lieutenant Green confirms that the craft is homing in on a transmission from the Najama area, so the Colonel immediately dispatches the Angels to Najama and contacts Scarlet to explain the situation. As the SKR4 re-enters Earth's atmosphere, Ochre and Magenta monitor the homing signal and relay the bearings on the source to Blue so that he can pinpoint the position of the homing device. He soon realizes that the transmitter is somewhere in the temple, but with impact due in just five minutes, there is not enough time to find it so Scarlet orders the Angels to destroy the temple.

Destiny, Symphony and Rhapsody begin their bombing run, quickly destroying the temple and leaving only the sun-god statue still standing. A final strike topples the statue, but it is too late to alter the trajectory of the SKR4, which crashes into the temple ruins. The resulting explosion starts a landslide which wipes out the Najama complex.

Notes

Inferno opens with a piece of incidental music that was originally composed for the THUNDERBIRDS episode *Pit of Peril*. Other incidental tracks from THUNDERBIRDS can be heard during the episode as well as music originally composed for SUPERCAR.

General Tiempo from *Operation Time* makes another appearance here as the pilot of the SKR4 recovery vehicle. Major Moran of the Euro-Space Tracker Station is portrayed by Dr Angelini from *Shadow of Fear*.

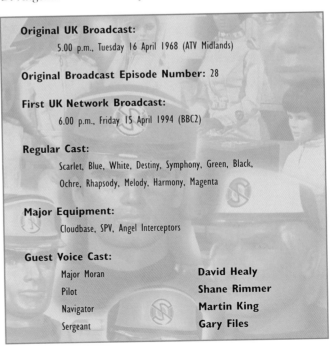

Original UK Broadcast:
5.00 p.m., Tuesday 16 April 1968 (ATV Midlands)

Original Broadcast Episode Number: 28

First UK Network Broadcast:
6.00 p.m., Friday 15 April 1994 (BBC2)

Regular Cast:
Scarlet, Blue, White, Destiny, Symphony, Green, Black, Ochre, Rhapsody, Melody, Harmony, Magenta

Major Equipment:
Cloudbase, SPV, Angel Interceptors

Guest Voice Cast:

Major Moran	David Healy
Pilot	Shane Rimmer
Navigator	Martin King
Sergeant	Gary Files

26. Flight 104

Written by **Tony Barwick**
Directed by **Robert Lynn**

'This whole thing gets stranger every minute. We might be on to something big.'

Captain Scarlet and Captain Blue escort the world's leading astrophysicist, Dr Conrad, to a conference with the World President at Lake Toma in Switzerland. This conference, which will determine the method of Earth's return to Mars, has been targeted by the Mysterons for their next act of retaliation. So as not to attract attention, Scarlet and Blue travel incognito without using Spectrum transport, but during a stopover at the Adelphi Hotel, they arouse the curiosity of a reporter, Harry, and his photographer, Joe, who tail them to Novena Airport. Scarlet and Blue are aware that the pressmen are following them but allow the pair to string along to keep tabs on them.

At Novena Airport, Scarlet, Blue and Conrad prepare to board Flight 104, on which all of the seats have been booked by Spectrum under different names. When Harry and Joe attempt to reserve seats on the flight, they are initially told that the plane is fully booked, but Scarlet allows the men to board the plane so as not to make them suspicious. Meanwhile, Captain Black accesses the quarters of the flight crew, drugs them and locks them in a storage room. When Flight 104 leaves Novena, it is under Mysteron control...

Airport security discovers the flight crew and Williams alerts Colonel White, but with Scarlet and Blue in mufti, the Colonel cannot contact them on Spectrum wavebands to warn them. He dispatches the Angels to intercept the plane. Scarlet and Joe discover that there is no stewardess aboard and when Scarlet tries to access the cockpit, he finds the cabin door locked. Making visual contact with the jet, Destiny releases a trail of red smoke which alerts Scarlet and Blue to the danger. Blue shoots out the lock on the cockpit door and he and Scarlet take the controls, but the airliner fails to respond and rapidly descends towards a crash-landing in the Alps. The officers fight with the locked controls, but as the plane passes over a power station the controls suddenly come free and Scarlet realizes that the Mysterons' influence has been cancelled out by the high voltage. However, a stray bullet from Blue's gun has broken the electrical circuit on the landing gear and they are unable to release the undercarriage. Scarlet orders Blue, Conrad and the two newsmen to the rear of the plane as he brings Flight 104 in for an emergency landing at Geneva Airport. The plane touches down, skids out of control along the runway and crashes nose-first into an outbuilding. Scarlet is fatally injured but Blue and the other passengers are safe.

Notes

Incidental music composed for Stingray can be heard as Flight 104 passes over the power station, and when the plane comes in for its crash-landing at Geneva Airport, footage from the Thunderbirds episode *Trapped in the Sky* shows the crash tenders moving into position.

Captain Brown from *The Mysterons* is cast here as Dr Conrad. Lieutenant Dean from *The Mysterons* reappears as Bill Williams, security chief at Novena Airport. Reporter Harry was previously seen as Eddie, the maintenance man in *Avalanche*. His colleague photographer, Joe, initially appeared as the DT19 pilot in *Winged Assassin*.

When Angel One is launched, we hear the normal launch sound but the craft stays exactly where it is. The Angel Interceptor has only just started to move when the scene cuts to a different shot and suddenly we see the aircraft flying off the end of the flight deck.

After Scarlet and Blue break into the cockpit of the passenger jet, Destiny reports the situation to Cloudbase speaking with Rhapsody's voice.

Original UK Broadcast:
  5.25 p.m., Friday 1 March 1968 (ATV Midlands)

Original Broadcast Episode Number: 22

First UK Network Broadcast:
  6.00 p.m., Friday 22 April 1994 (BBC2)

Regular Cast:
  Scarlet, Blue, White, Destiny, Green, Black, Ochre, Harmony, Grey, Magenta

Major Equipment:
  Cloudbase, Angel Interceptors, Passenger Jet Flight 104

Guest Voice Cast:

Dr Conrad	David Healy
Reporter Harry	Jeremy Wilkin
Photographer Joe	Gary Files
Bill Williams	Martin King
Flight Desk	Gary Files
Airport Tannoy	Liz Morgan

27. PLACE OF ANGELS

Written by **Leo Eaton**
Directed by **Leo Eaton**

'This bacillus is a totally new strain. The human body has no defence against it.'

A phial of deadly K14 virus is being stored at Biological Research Station 'D' near Manchester, England. Captain Black sets a booby trap for the station's research assistant, Judy Chapman, parking a petrol tanker across the road on a blind bend. Chapman crashes into it and the tanker explodes, killing her instantly. She is reconstructed by the Mysterons and returns to the Research Station to steal the virus, using mechanical grabs to strangle the guard on duty in the isolation room.

When the Mysterons threaten to destroy 'the Place of the Angels', the Spectrum officers are baffled by the cryptic reference. Lieutenant Green receives a call for assistance from the Research Station, so Captain Scarlet and Captain Blue are sent to Manchester, where they meet project coordinator Dr Denton. He tells them that the phial of K14, for which there is no known antidote, has been taken by Judy Chapman, and if

she breaks the test tube, the virus could wipe out a city of 10 million people. Chapman is sighted at New York International Airport, so Scarlet and Blue fly to New York and requisition SPV 021. Colonel White dispatches the Angels to locate Chapman's car and maintain aerial contact, and soon Scarlet and Blue are on her trail. As she makes her way along Interstate Highway 180, Chapman is warned by Captain Black that the SPV is close behind her, so she abandons her car and pushes it down an embankment. When Scarlet and Blue arrive a few minutes later, Chapman has vanished, but they find broken glass in the car that could be the remains of the test tube.

The area is closed off amid fears that the K14 has been released into the surrounding countryside. Scarlet and Blue are flown back to Cloudbase and placed in isolation in the Sick Bay until tests are completed. The crash area is sprayed with an anti-viral foam in an attempt to prevent the virus from spreading but Dr Denton's tests prove negative – the Mysterons have deliberately engineered a false alarm to decoy Spectrum.

The search for Chapman continues, but three hours later there is still no clue to her actual whereabouts, as she has apparently been sighted in Miami, Los Angeles and Moose Bay, Canada. Suddenly, Scarlet solves the riddle of the Mysterons' cryptic threat: Los Angeles translates as 'The Angels', so this must be the Mysterons' target. Scarlet and Blue fly there in an SPJ and pick up Chapman's trail as she heads for the Boulder Dam, the city's main reservoir. Once there, Chapman intends to contaminate the water with the K14 as the most effective method of spreading the virus. Scarlet parachutes on to the dam, only to be shot by Chapman just before he lands. The Mysteron agent holds a gun on the injured Scarlet as she prepares to pour the culture into the reservoir, but she misses her footing on a grille and falls over the edge of the dam. The phial of K14 comes to rest on a ledge and Scarlet manages to recover it before it topples into the water.

Original UK Broadcast:
5.25 p.m., Friday 8 March 1968 (ATV Midlands)

Original Broadcast Episode Number: 23

First UK Network Broadcast:
6.10 p.m., Friday 29 April 1994 (BBC2)

Regular Cast:
Scarlet, Blue, White, Destiny, Symphony, Green, Black, Rhapsody, Harmony

Major Equipment:
Cloudbase, SPV 021, Angel Interceptors, SSC, SPJ, Bio-Hazard Containment Helicopters, Air Ambulance

Guest Voice Cast:

Judy Chapman	Sylvia Anderson
Dr Denton	Jeremy Wilkin
Captain	Martin King
Engineer	Gary Files
Security Guard	Gary Files
Spectrum, New York	Jeremy Wilkin

Notes

The original title of this episode was 'The City of Angels' and in Leo Eaton's script the Mysterons' threat was to 'destroy the population of the City of Angels'.

Mysteron agent Gabrielle from *Model Spy* takes the role of Judy Chapman here, while Dr Denton is portrayed by the puppet that later became Sam Loover in JOE 90.

The UK television network premiere of this episode on BBC2 was delayed for ten minutes by live coverage of the 1994 World Snooker Championship semifinal between Stephen Hendry and Steve Davis.

28. EXPO 2068

Written by **Shane Rimmer**
Directed by **Leo Eaton**

'Sorry to break my appointment, Doctor, but there's been a little change in plan...'

Transporter 43 is ferrying a new core reactor to the Manicougan Power Complex when it is diverted by Captain Black on to a route that takes it over the edge of a demolished bridge into a gorge. Driver, transporter and core reactor are all reconstructed by the Mysterons as the prelude to their next act of retaliation, which threatens to deal a heavy blow to the prestige of the world with a strike on the Atlantic seaboard of North America.

As the core reactor transit appears to be the only security risk in the threatened area, Captain Scarlet and Captain Blue are dispatched in SPV 442 to Highway 83, the route being taken by Transporter 43, to escort it to the Manicougan Dam site. But before Scarlet and Blue can rendezvous with the transporter, the driver leaves the highway and cuts along a dirt track that leads to a clearing in the adjacent forest. At the nearby construction site of the forthcoming Expo 2068 exhibition, Black holds the controller of a fleet of supply

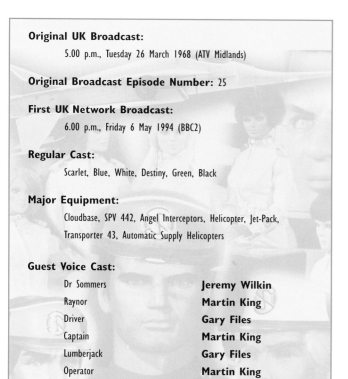

Original UK Broadcast:
    5.00 p.m., Tuesday 26 March 1968 (ATV Midlands)

Original Broadcast Episode Number: 25

First UK Network Broadcast:
    6.00 p.m., Friday 6 May 1994 (BBC2)

Regular Cast:
    Scarlet, Blue, White, Destiny, Green, Black

Major Equipment:
    Cloudbase, SPV 442, Angel Interceptors, Helicopter, Jet-Pack,
    Transporter 43, Automatic Supply Helicopters

Guest Voice Cast:

Dr Sommers	**Jeremy Wilkin**
Raynor	**Martin King**
Driver	**Gary Files**
Captain	**Martin King**
Lumberjack	**Gary Files**
Operator	**Martin King**

helicopters at gunpoint, ordering him to programme one of the vehicles to fly as he instructs. Black then relays instructions to the transporter driver for removing the reactor's thermic safety valve before transferring the reactor to a crate carried by the supply helicopter. A passing lumberjack witnesses the transfer but is shot down by the driver.

Security reports that the transporter has missed the final checkpoint, so Scarlet and Blue backtrack to find where it turned off the highway and soon come upon the clearing. Here they come across the injured lumberjack, who keeps repeating the word 'Seneca' before he passes out. Blue also finds the thermic safety valve and project controller, Dr Sommers, confirms that without it the temperature of the reactor may rise to over 200 degrees, causing a nuclear explosion. Destiny Angel locates the transporter heading away from the Manicougan site and Scarlet and Blue set off in pursuit, but when the transporter crashes off the road on a bend, they find it empty.

Colonel White informs Scarlet and Blue that the whole area has been cordoned off and the only activity is the movement of the Seneca Construction Company supply helicopters at the Expo 2068 site. Hearing this, Scarlet makes the connection with what the lumberjack was trying to tell them and realizes that the reactor has been transferred to one of the helicopters. Racing to the Expo site, Scarlet finds the helicopter containing the reactor hovering directly above the Expo Tower and uses a jet-pack to reach it, but Black shoots the helicopter operator and, with no one to programme its movements, the vehicle begins to veer randomly about the construction site. Scarlet cuts his way into the supply crate held beneath the helicopter and gains access to the reactor. Using instructions relayed by Dr Sommers, he attempts to shut down the reactor, but this proves to be a difficult operation with the helicopter swinging violently out of control. He finally disconnects the last wire from the primary circuits just seconds before the reactor goes critical, but the helicopter collides with the Expo Tower and explodes. Although he has saved the Atlantic seaboard, Scarlet is fatally injured, but his body is ferried back to Cloudbase, where he is expected to make a full recovery.

Notes

Shane Rimmer's script for *Expo 2068* included additional scenes to show Scarlet and Blue collecting SPV 442 from a village store managed by a Spectrum agent wearing an old-fashioned nightgown and a baseball cap. This script also makes it clear that the Mysterons' intention is to deal a heavy blow to the prestige of the world by crashing the core reactor into the Expo 2068 site - their target is *not* the Manicougan Power Complex – but the dialogue that imparts this information was deleted from the finished episode.

29. THE LAUNCHING

Written by **Peter Curran and David Williams**
Directed by **Brian Burgess**

'I get threatened every day of the week – phone calls, letters...If I took any of them seriously, I'd never get any work done!'

Tribune reporter Mervin Brand is travelling to a press conference with President Roberts when his jet is struck by lightning and crashes. Brand is killed but reconstructed as a Mysteron agent and resumes his journey. Shortly after, Spectrum receives word of the latest Mysteron threat: to destroy President Roberts within the next twelve hours. Captain Scarlet is assigned to explain the danger of this threat to a sceptical President Roberts, while Captain Blue and Captain Ochre impose a maximum security cordon around the Presidential Residence and the Angels patrol overhead. Scarlet requests the President not to leave the residence for the next twelve hours, but Roberts insists on holding his weekly press conference. Scarlet agrees to this, but all attendees will be screened with a Mysteron Detector on entering the building.

Brand's plane is intercepted by the Angels and he is escorted to an airstrip outside the restricted area. After proving his identity to Harmony, he is cleared to continue on to the conference by road. Driving a black saloon car, Brand pulls up near the Presidential Residence but makes no attempt to approach the building. Blue becomes suspicious of Brand's parked car, but when Ochre points the Mysteron Detector at him Brand drives off, almost running Blue down. The President expresses his dismay that he cannot attend the launching of a new atomic liner, confiding to Scarlet that the ship is to be named after him. Scarlet suddenly realizes that the Mysterons' threat could be directed at the ship rather than the President himself! As Scarlet races to the shipyard, Brand makes his way to the launch platform, from which the wife of the Vice-President of Trans-Pacific Shipping will release the traditional champagne bottle during the launch ceremony. When Brand gets close enough to the champagne bottle, he uses his Mysteron powers to alter the molecular structure of its contents, turning it into a powerful explosive. Scarlet arrives at the launch platform as the Vice-President's wife is about to press the launch release. Brand pulls a gun but is shot down in an exchange of fire with Scarlet. Scarlet orders the shipyard to be evacuated and, just as the last civilian leaves the area, Brand revives and lunges for the launch release button. The bottle swings towards the ship but the liner has already been released from its moorings, and the deadly bottle swings back into the launch platform and explodes. Scarlet is fatally injured but makes a complete recovery, much to the President's surprise.

Notes

The jazz instrumental that opens this episode was originally composed for STINGRAY. Incidental tracks composed for THUNDERBIRDS can be heard throughout, but the music that plays during the launching of the President Roberts was originally composed for the FIREBALL XL5 episode *Flying Zodiac*.

President Roberts is played by the puppet that later appeared as Sam Loover in JOE 90. Mervin Brand was previously seen as Macey in *Big Ben Strikes Again* and Captain Indigo in *Spectrum Strikes Back*. The Trans-Pacific Vice-President formerly portrayed Steele in *Special Assignment*, while his wife was Judy Chapman in *Place of Angels*.

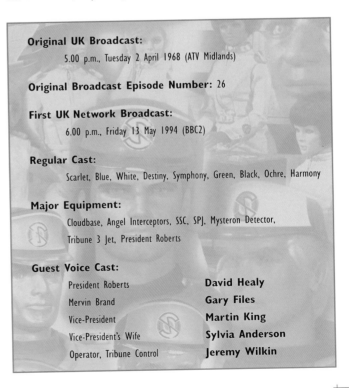

Original UK Broadcast:
  5.00 p.m., Tuesday 2 April 1968 (ATV Midlands)

Original Broadcast Episode Number: 26

First UK Network Broadcast:
  6.00 p.m., Friday 13 May 1994 (BBC2)

Regular Cast:
  Scarlet, Blue, White, Destiny, Symphony, Green, Black, Ochre, Harmony

Major Equipment:
  Cloudbase, Angel Interceptors, SSC, SPJ, Mysteron Detector, Tribune 3 Jet, President Roberts

Guest Voice Cast:

President Roberts	**David Healy**
Mervin Brand	**Gary Files**
Vice-President	**Martin King**
Vice-President's Wife	**Sylvia Anderson**
Operator, Tribune Control	**Jeremy Wilkin**

When Captain Scarlet leaves the Presidential Residence, the shot of Captain Blue turning to look at the approaching SSC is flopped. As the camera slowly pulls back from Scarlet sitting in the SSC, we can see that the section of the puppet-sized SSC doesn't properly match the design of the same section on the model vehicle.

30. CODENAME EUROPA

Written by **David Lee**
Directed by **Alan Perry**

'This Mysteron agent is one of the most dangerous we have ever faced.'

Professor Gabriel Carney, an electronics genius, is assassinated by Captain Black at his gadget-filled home. He is reconstructed as a Mysteron agent with instructions to kill John L. Henderson, Conrad Olafson and Joseph Meccini, the three joint presidents of the Congress of Europe. Known as the Triumvirate of Europe, these men are the target of the latest Mysteron threat. Colonel White activates plan XB, codenamed Europa, an operation to protect the three presidents by sending them each to different places of maximum security.

Captain Ochre is assigned to protect President Olafson, who is sequestered in an underground suite at Vandon Maximum Security Base. Carney sets up speakers in the woods beyond the west fence and broadcasts taped sound effects of a military assault. Believing the base to be under attack, Ochre transfers the guards from the east perimeter to the west fence, enabling Carney to cut a hole in the electrified fence in the east sector. When the guards report hearing a tank formation closing in, the Angels are launched with orders to attack and destroy, and while all attention is focused at the opposite side of the base, Carney drops a bomb in an air vent which appears to lead to Olafson's underground room. The bomb explodes, demolishing the building, but the air vent was a dummy inlet which went no deeper than ground level and Olafson is safe.

Colonel White receives a report that Professor Carney's body has been discovered and, although he has clearly been dead for some time, a second Carney was seen elsewhere less than an hour earlier. Captain Scarlet and Captain Blue search Carney's bungalow and find a set of file cards and video footage of the Triumvirate. They also discover a pad with a handwritten note that reads '123 OHM' and Scarlet deduces that if the letters are the initials of the presidents' surnames, then President Henderson is Carney's second target. They leave immediately for the Maximum Security Centre, where Henderson is located. Driving a grey saloon car, Carney crashes Captain Magenta's roadblock 20 miles east of the Security Centre. Scarlet and Blue are diverted to intercept Carney, but the Mysteron agent uses an electronic jamming device on their SPV, blacking out the driving monitor. Unable to see where they are going, Blue crashes the SPV off the road.

That night, Carney flies a model plane trailing strips of foil over the Security Centre, jamming the radio communication network. A well-placed incendiary device cuts off the electricity supply and the centre's lights go out, but Carney wears infra-red goggles which enable him to see in the dark and bypass the guard. He makes his way to the Security Suite, where Scarlet and Blue are guarding Henderson, but trips over a length of wire that the Spectrum agents have taped across the doorway. Caught off balance, Carney is shot and killed by Scarlet.

Notes

The original script for this episode featured additional scenes in which the Mysteron Carney disposes of the body of the original Carney with a remote-controlled lawn mower. The script also makes it clear that Carney was the chief designer of the electronic security systems at Spectrum's maximum security bases, a point that was lost in transition to the screen.

For the fourth time, Captain Brown from *The Mysterons* appears as a Mysteron agent, here playing Professor Carney. For this appearance, a new 'agony' head was sculpted for the scene in which he is shot by Captain Black. President Henderson was initially seen in the series as General Cope in *Point 783*, President Meccini was previously the Captain of the USS Panther II in *White as Snow*, and President Olafson was formerly Major Gravener's driver, Harris, in *Treble Cross*.

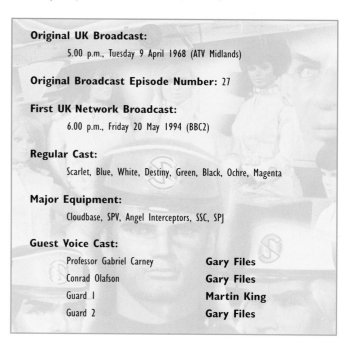

Original UK Broadcast:
5.00 p.m., Tuesday 9 April 1968 (ATV Midlands)

Original Broadcast Episode Number: 27

First UK Network Broadcast:
6.00 p.m., Friday 20 May 1994 (BBC2)

Regular Cast:
Scarlet, Blue, White, Destiny, Green, Black, Ochre, Magenta

Major Equipment:
Cloudbase, SPV, Angel Interceptors, SSC, SPJ

Guest Voice Cast:

Professor Gabriel Carney	**Gary Files**
Conrad Olafson	**Gary Files**
Guard 1	**Martin King**
Guard 2	**Gary Files**

31. ATTACK ON CLOUDBASE

Written by **Tony Barwick**
Directed by **Ken Turner**

'You don't understand, Colonel. He's really dead – permanent, final, absolutely dead!'

Symphony Angel is completing a patrol when her Interceptor's engine suddenly explodes. Reporting that she has apparently come under enemy fire, Symphony loses control of the aircraft and is forced to eject. Landing in the desert, she collapses and passes out...

As Spectrum forces are mobilized to search for Symphony, the Mysterons warn that Cloudbase is their next objective. All personnel are placed on red alert and the base is sealed from all external contact. Destiny is recalled to Cloudbase and Captain Blue is furious when he learns that the aerial search for Symphony has been abandoned. He confronts Colonel White, who explains that Spectrum ground forces have taken over the search. Blue requests permission to join the search parties, admitting to Colonel White that he is in love with Symphony, but the Colonel denies his request.

Night falls and Captain Magenta picks up a large, fast-moving trace on the radar. The UFO takes up a position hovering 25 miles from Cloudbase so Rhapsody is sent to investigate. She finds a flat, circular space vehicle which she estimates to be some 200 feet across. Colonel White instructs her to return to Cloudbase but her Angel Interceptor suddenly comes under fire from the spacecraft and Rhapsody is blown out of the sky. Colonel White realizes that the Mysterons themselves have come to Earth to annihilate Cloudbase!

Cloudbase is moved to a remote uninhabited area in the Himalayas so that no civilians will be hurt when the Mysterons attack. Colonel White briefs his officers, taking Scarlet on one side to tell him that, if they ever get out of this alive, he must have his hair cut. A waiting game begins, testing the nerve of the Spectrum personnel. Then Magenta reports more Mysteron craft approaching, so many that he cannot count them all. Scarlet volunteers to take on the spacecraft in an Angel Interceptor, and Colonel White lets him go despite Destiny's protests. Scarlet closes in for the attack but his Interceptor is hit and he is forced to return to Cloudbase, where he makes an emergency landing on the flight deck. Scarlet is rushed to the Sick Bay as the Mysteron craft close in and begin firing on the base. The Sick Bay is hit and Dr Fawn is killed as he attempts to revive Scarlet. Posing as Dr Fawn's assistant, Captain Black reports that Scarlet is finally dead, with no hope of recovery!

Magenta continues his attempts to count all of the Mysteron craft but he is killed when another Mysteron strike destroys the Radar Room. The Control Room is also hit and Green is caught in the blast. As Cloudbase begins to fall out of the sky, Blue and Colonel White are the only officers left alive. Blue is too badly injured to escape and the Colonel announces that he intends to go down with his command. As he gives a final salute, Cloudbase spins towards the Earth...

Recovering consciousness, Symphony is delighted to find that she has been rescued by Scarlet and Blue and that the attack on Cloudbase was all a horrible dream induced by the heat of the desert sun.

Notes

In his original script for this episode, Tony Barwick introduced a new Spectrum agent, Lieutenant Sienna. However, rather than go to the expense of making a new Spectrum uniform, the producers simply replaced Sienna with Captain Magenta.

This is the second of only two episodes in which all fourteen regular characters appear, the other being *Flight to Atlantica*. It is also the only episode in which no other characters appear apart from the fourteen regulars.

Original UK Broadcast:
    5.00 p.m., Tuesday 7 May 1968 (ATV Midlands)

Original Broadcast Episode Number: 31

First UK Network Broadcast:
    6.00 p.m., Friday 13 May 1994 (BBC2)

Regular Cast:
    Scarlet, Blue, White, Destiny, Symphony, Green, Black,
    Ochre, Rhapsody, Melody, Harmony, Grey, Magenta, Fawn

Major Equipment:
    Cloudbase, Angel Interceptors, Mysteron Spacecraft

It is never explained what actually happened to Symphony's Angel Interceptor at the start of the episode. Since the Mysteron attack on Cloudbase was part of Symphony's nightmare, what was the noise she heard just before her aircraft's tail exploded and what caused the explosion?

32. THE INQUISITION

Written by **Tony Barwick**
Directed by **Ken Turner**

'All you have to do is prove who you are.'

At the end of an off-duty meal at the Markham Arms with Captain Scarlet, Captain Blue complains of feeling strange after drinking his coffee. Scarlet goes to fetch their coats, but when he returns to their table, Blue has disappeared. Shortly after, the Mysterons issue a warning that one of the members of Spectrum will betray the whole organization.

Blue recovers consciousness in the Cloudbase Control Room, where he finds a stranger sitting at Colonel White's desk. The man introduces himself as Colgan of Spectrum Intelligence, explaining that Blue has been missing for three months and must now prove his identity by revealing the

Spectrum cipher codes. Reluctant to disclose such top-security information, Blue instead details one of Spectrum's first assignments, in which he and Scarlet saved London from being destroyed by a Mysteron-controlled atomic device. This report is insufficient proof for Colgan, but Blue still refuses to reveal the secret Spectrum codes. Colgan invites him to talk about the lunar mission to Crater 101, but afterwards the man is still not convinced that Blue is who he claims to be, as the Crater 101 mission was fully reported in the press and on television.

Blue decides that he can prove his identity by telling Colgan of the Mysteron attempt to assassinate the delegates of the International Air Conference, an incident that has never been released to the press. He does do, but Colgan persists in his demands for the cipher codes and Blue begins to smell a rat. He tries to leave the Control Room but the exit is blocked by another man armed with a gun and a syringe full of XK4, the ultimate truth drug. Blue escapes by smashing through the window at the end of the observation tube and is surprised to find himself outside a fake Cloudbase Control Room constructed inside a warehouse. Blue leaves the building just as Scarlet arrives in an SPV, having finally managed to locate him. Scarlet confirms that Colgan and his colleague are Mysteron agents before destroying the warehouse with the SPV cannon.

Notes

This is the only episode in which Colonel White does not appear. It is also the only episode in which we do not see the real Cloudbase. *The Inquisition* is CAPTAIN SCARLET's flashback episode and the bulk of the show is made up of lengthy excerpts from *Big Ben Strikes Again*, *Crater 101* and *The Trap* – so lengthy, in fact, that only eleven minutes of new footage was filmed.

Colgan is portrayed by the puppet that originally appeared in the series as the Supreme Commander in *Point 783*, making one last appearance in CAPTAIN SCARLET before being groomed for his regular role as Sam Loover in JOE 90.

The Inquisition was postponed from the end of the first UK network broadcast run on BBC2 in 1993–4 and did not receive its first UK television network transmission until the following September, at the start of a repeat BBC2 run of the series.

Original UK Broadcast:
5.00 p.m., Tuesday 14 May 1968 (ATV Midlands)

Original Broadcast Episode Number: 32

First UK Network Broadcast:
6.00 p.m., Friday 9 September 1994 (BBC2)

Regular Cast:
Scarlet, Blue, Symphony, Green, Black

Major Equipment:
SPV, SPV A75, Jet-Pack, Transporter, Moonmobile 4, Lunar Tractor, Lunar Tank, CB29 Rocket, Magnacopter

Guest Voice Cast:

Colgan	**David Healy**
Waiter	**Gary Files**
Macey	**Charles Tingwell**
1st Policeman	**Martin King**
2nd Policeman	**Paul Maxwell**
3rd Policeman	**Jeremy Wilkin**
4th Policeman	**Charles Tingwell**
Linda Nolan	**Sylvia Anderson**
Frazer	**David Healy**
Shroeder	**Jeremy Wilkin**
Commodore Goddard	**David Healy**
Holt	**Gary Files**

When Captain Blue finally makes his escape from the fake Cloudbase by smashing through the window at the end of the observation tube, the arm of a puppeteer is visible in two separate shots hurling the puppet through the glass.

ADVENTURES IN MERCHANDISING 4

While Captain Scarlet and the Mysterons was still in production at the Century 21 Studios in Slough, the staff of Century 21 Merchandising Ltd at Century 21 House in St Martin's Lane, London, prepared to launch the series to the British public with the biggest TV character merchandising promotional campaign that had, at that time, ever been seen in the UK. A careful study of the company's experience with the promotion and merchandising of Fireball XL5, Stingray and Thunderbirds enabled Derek Cook, general manager of Century 21 Merchandising, and his merchandising manager, Richard Culley, to develop a campaign which would incorporate all the facets of character merchandising: toys, games, comics, books and records. Their approach to the promotion of Captain Scarlet and the Mysterons pioneered character merchandising in the UK, developing the concepts of coordinated merchandise styling, sales support materials and personality promotions that were to become standard marketing practices in this field over the next thirty years.

All merchandise licensees were issued with a merchandising specification sheet which illustrated the Captain Scarlet and the Mysterons logo, the Spectrum personnel and vehicles. This sheet enabled toy designers and packaging illustrators to create products that closely matched what viewers would see on television and packaging that coordinated with other manufacturers' products. One of the contractual agreements in all merchandising licences was that Century 21 would have final approval of all products, and representatives were sent to the source of production, from Liverpool to Kowloon, to vet the items as they came off the production line.

To assist with in-store promotion of the full range of Captain Scarlet merchandise, 6,589 retail toy shops and department stores in the UK were issued with a special dealer mailing kit which incorporated the specification sheet, a six-page leaflet with information about the property listing the names of all licensees, illustrations of dealer advertisements and an order slip to purchase the print blocks, three 36-inch-long window streamers and a window pennant announcing 'Captain Scarlet's in Town!' Store managers were encouraged to place large orders for certain lines of merchandise, with the chance to win bottles of specially produced Captain Scarlet pink champagne.

Throughout October and into November 1967, the company also organized a six-week 'personality' tour of more than 1,000 sites in the ATV Midlands (Birmingham) and London television areas, from toy shops, department stores and cinemas to schools, playgrounds and shopping centres. This involved a pair of models dressed in the appropriate Spectrum uniforms – Spectrum Captain and Angel pilot – arriving at each tour site in a Mini Moke emblazoned with the Spectrum motif to hand out leaflets, pennants and window stickers.

Cook and Culley deliberately limited the number of merchandise licences available to manufacturers, issuing them only to those with a proven track record so as to ensure that all Captain Scarlet products maintained a high standard. None the less, Century 21 Merchandising still authorized over sixty licences to manufacture Captain Scarlet products. Pedigree Toys, then enjoying the immense success of their recently launched Sindy doll, broke new ground with a 12-inch jointed Captain Scarlet action doll at a time when dolls for boys were almost unheard of (Palitoy's Action Man had only recently appeared on the market). John Waddington Ltd produced

a CAPTAIN SCARLET board game and a series of four jigsaws featuring photographs from the television series. Airfix manufactured a 7-inch-long model kit of the Angel Interceptor, while Rovex Industries Ltd released battery-powered Patrol Car Scalextric-style racing sets under their Tri-ang Toys label. Craft Master produced three painting-by-numbers sets, Berwicks issued wipe-off colouring cards and a stencil set, and Scalecraft manufactured a set of five three-dimensional painting kits.

There were balloons from Lewis Knight and Co., Plasticine from Harbutt's Plasticine Ltd, die-cast metal cap pistols from Lone Star Products, kites from Bowman Jenkins, Spectrum badges from Plastoid Ltd, bubble-gum cards from Anglo Confectionery, sweet cigarettes from Barratt and Co. and colour transfers from Tower Press, among many other items of CAPTAIN SCARLET merchandise that appeared in shops in the autumn of 1967. However, the most popular products by far were Dinky Toys' range of die-cast vehicles, the Spectrum Patrol Car, Maximum Security Vehicle and Spectrum Pursuit Vehicle. Sales of the latter far outstripped the competition and the SPV became Dinky's biggest-selling toy of all time.

The other arms of the Century 21 Organization produced their own lines of CAPTAIN SCARLET merchandise, also marketing 'The Angels' as a separate range of products for girls with their own distinctive logo. Century 21 Toys produced a set of plastic friction-drive Patrol Car, SPV and Angel aircraft toys, Captain Scarlet playsuits, dart guns, ball puzzles, cap guns, key chains, wallets, water pistols, Angel beauty sets, jewellery sets, pendants and sling bags. Century 21 Publishing released two storybooks, two painting books, three doll-dressing books, a pair of make-a-model books, two sticker fun books, two puzzle books and various hardback annuals, in addition to joint ventures with Armada Books (a trio of original novels published in paperback) and City Magazines (CAPTAIN SCARLET comic strips in *TV Century 21*, *Lady Penelope*, *Solo* and *TV Tornado* comics). And in association with Pye Records, Century 21 Records released five original CAPTAIN SCARLET audio productions as part of their range of Century 21 mini-albums.

1967 CAPTAIN SCARLET merchandise including the Pedigree action doll, a range of books from Century 21 Publishing and the Century 21 Toys plastic friction-drive SPV.

THE MINI-ALBUMS

Between September 1965 and September 1967, Century 21 Records achieved considerable success when they issued thirty 7-inch vinyl EP records aimed at the then burgeoning children's market. Collectively known as Century 21 mini-albums, these records were primarily spin-offs from the various popular Gerry Anderson television series. The first release was a FIREBALL XL5 record, followed by three STINGRAY EPs, nineteen THUNDERBIRDS EPs and four EPs of themes and incidental music tracks. Although several EPs were released that presented recordings of other children's television properties licensed by Century 21, such as the Daleks from the BBC's DOCTOR WHO, Topo Gigio and Tingha and Tucker, it was the Anderson-based mini-albums that were the best-sellers.

Of the twenty-three Gerry Anderson story EPs released to that date, sixteen were simply edited recordings from the soundtracks of THUNDERBIRDS television episodes with additional narration (in character) by the series' voice artists. Although 'Into Action with Troy Tempest' incorporated situations and dialogue from a pair of STINGRAY television episodes to create a new interactive adventure (listeners were encouraged to play the roles of the lead characters at various points), the remaining seven records were straight dramatizations that presented either entirely new audio adventures or background information in the form of a guided tour of the featured secret organization. Once again, the original television voice artists re-created their puppet roles for complete authenticity.

To coincide with the television launch of CAPTAIN SCARLET AND THE MYSTERONS in September 1967, Century 21 Records released five CAPTAIN SCARLET story EPs. The first of these, 'Introducing Captain Scarlet', essentially retold the story of the series' initial episode, *The Mysterons*, using audio clips from the programme, but unlike the earlier THUNDERBIRDS TV adaptations, the narrative came in the form of a newly recorded dramatic framing sequence which added much background to the TV episode and the series as a whole.

The script of this first CAPTAIN SCARLET EP was written by Angus P. Allan, then script editor of Century 21 Publishing's *TV Century 21* comic. Allan had a very close connection with the Gerry Anderson productions for many years, penning the THUNDERBIRDS storybook *The Target* for World Distributors and the *Thunderbirds Are Go* film novelization for Armada Books in addition to his *TV Century 21* chores. He later scripted the SPACE: 1999 strip in *Look-in* magazine, as well as both writing and producing four SPACE: 1999 annuals for World Distributors. Allan scripted two further CAPTAIN SCARLET mini-albums ('Captain Scarlet and the Mysterons' and 'Captain Scarlet of Spectrum'), while the other two ('Captain Scarlet is Indestructible' and 'Captain Scarlet Versus Captain Black') were written by his *TV Century 21* associate Richard O'Neill. All five records were produced by Denis Skelton, who had previously produced the last two THUNDERBIRDS mini-albums, 'One Move and You're Dead' (MA 128) and 'Thirty Minutes After Noon' (MA 129).

With an average running time of twenty-one minutes (the established length of the Century 21 mini-albums), each of the four original CAPTAIN SCARLET stories presented on these records was about the same length as the individual television episodes. Indeed, with many of the original voice cast employed to reprise their roles, music composed by Barry Gray and sound effects from the series, these stories played very much as additional CAPTAIN SCARLET episodes, albeit audio only.

The very last Century 21 mini-album was a music collection entitled 'TV Themes from Gerry Anderson's Captain Scarlet' (MA 136), although this record actually featured only two pieces of CAPTAIN SCARLET music: Barry Gray's commercial release recordings of the title theme and 'The Mysterons Theme'. Both tracks appeared on the 1981 PRT 10-inch LP *No Strings Attached*, which was later released on CD by Castle Communications in 1990 (CLACD 204) and then remastered and re-released in 1999 on Castle Music's Cinephile label in association with Fanderson (CINCD 011). The other tracks on 'TV Themes from Gerry Anderson's Captain Scarlet' were incidental pieces from THUNDERBIRDS and cover versions of the themes from THE MONKEES and MAN IN A SUITCASE television series arranged by Barry Gray.

'INTRODUCING CAPTAIN SCARLET'
Written by **Angus P. Allan**

The World Security Council has convened a meeting to look into the circumstances surrounding the death of Spectrum agent Captain Scarlet and to investigate the reasons for his earlier inexplicable behaviour. Colonel White opens the investigation by explaining to the assembled delegates that the reports they will see and hear are based on videotape recordings made at the time of the action. The delegates watch a video recording of Spectrum's first contact with the Mysterons in which Captain Black mistakes a Mysteron sensor device for a weapon and opens fire on the complex. Colonel White reveals that radio contact with the MEV was cut off at that point and there was no further contact until the exploration craft returned to Glenn Field with only Captain Black aboard. Black disappeared before he could be questioned and a clear transmission from the Mysterons was received all over the world, threatening vengeance for the unprovoked attack on their complex and warning that the assassination of the World President would be their first act of retaliation.

The delegates watch more video footage, which shows how Captains Scarlet and Brown apparently escaped unhurt from an accident in their Saloon Car, and how Brown later appeared to have smuggled a bomb into the Maximum Security Building in an attempt to kill the World President. Colonel White goes on to relate how Captain Scarlet kidnapped the World President and flew to London. He then hands the conference over to Captain Blue, who continues the story, detailing his pursuit of Scarlet to the London Car-Vu and the gun battle which ended with Scarlet falling to his death from the sky park.

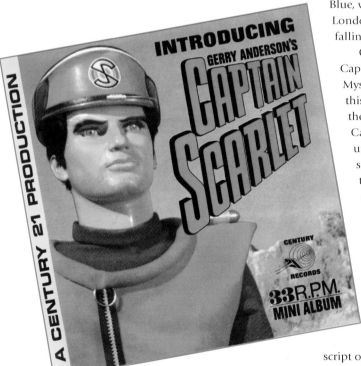

Colonel White explains to the assembled delegates that Captains Black, Brown and Scarlet were all taken over by the Mysterons, but their problem now is to find out how and, once this is ascertained, decide on a method of combat. Suddenly, the conference is interrupted by Dr Fawn, who reveals that Captain Scarlet is alive after his fall of 800 feet! As unbelievable as it seems, Scarlet's wounds are healing and somehow the Mysterons' power over him has been broken by the fall. Dr Fawn believes that, with the aid of a specially designed computer, Captain Scarlet can be brought back under Spectrum control. The Colonel realizes that the new Captain Scarlet could be Spectrum's greatest weapon in fighting the Mysterons.

Notes

This story takes place just before the last scene of *The Mysterons* television episode (Colonel White briefing the Spectrum officers and Angels) and reintroduces one of the abandoned concepts from the original shooting script of that episode: the reconstructed Captain Scarlet returning to his former Spectrum loyalties with the aid of a specially designed computer.

The only voice artists involved in the recording of this mini-album were Ed Bishop, Donald Gray and Jeremy Wilkin; the other actors are heard just in audio sequences from *The Mysterons* television episode. Dr Fawn is therefore performed by Jeremy Wilkin rather than by his television voice artist, Charles Tingwell. Ed Bishop's voice for the Conference Chairman is no different from that of Captain Blue, which occasionally causes some confusion as to which character is supposed to be speaking.

Colonel White clearly states that the Zero X expedition to Mars took place 'last October', which conflicts with the continuity established in the television episodes. The record ends with the original version of the series' end title music as heard on the first fourteen episodes of the television series.

Originally released as Century 21 mini-album MA 131, 'Introducing Captain Scarlet' was re-released by PolyGram in 1993 on side one of the audio cassette collection *Captain Scarlet and the Mysterons – Volume 1* (Cat. No. 518 185–4).

VOICE CAST			
Captain Blue	**Ed Bishop**	Rhapsody Angel	**Liz Morgan**
Colonel White	**Donald Gray**	Harmony Angel	**Liz Morgan**
Dr Fawn	**Jeremy Wilkin**	Captain Black (Mysteron)	**Donald Gray**
Conference Chairman	**Ed Bishop**	Captain Black (Original)	**Jeremy Wilkin**
General	**Jeremy Wilkin**	Voice of the Mysterons	**Donald Gray**
Conference Guard	**Jeremy Wilkin**	World President	**Paul Maxwell**
FROM ORIGINAL TV RECORDING		Captain Brown	**Charles Tingwell**
Captain Scarlet	**Francis Matthews**	Lieutenant Dean	**Charles Tingwell**
Lieutenant Green	**Cy Grant**	Radio Voice	**Jeremy Wilkin**
Destiny Angel	**Liz Morgan**	Helicopter A42 Pilot	**Charles Tingwell**

'CAPTAIN SCARLET AND THE MYSTERONS'
Written by **Angus P. Allan**

Cloudbase receives the latest Mysteron threat, which warns of the destruction of the Atlantic Airport at Boston, the world's most widely used terminal, with tens of thousands of passengers an hour. Shortly after, the atomic-powered World Air Force jet Goliath collides with a fighter plane and crashes, but it is immediately reconstructed by the Mysterons. When the Spectrum Investigation Room then reports a complete break in communications with Goliath, Colonel White dispatches the Angels to locate and track it. Destiny and Rhapsody soon spot the jet and try to make radio contact, but when there is no response the Angels are ordered to attack. Unfortunately, Goliath's special prototype forcefield defence deflects the Angel Interceptor missiles.

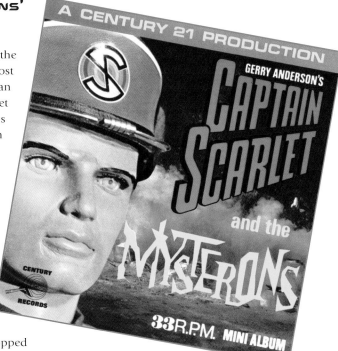

Colonel White realizes that the Mysterons intend to crash Goliath on Atlantic Airport and Captain Scarlet agrees that the aircraft has to be destroyed in the air. He suggests putting a man on board the plane, an engineer specialist who knows the controls and layout of the Goliath. As flesh and blood would not react to the forcefield, a man could be dropped from above by parachute so that the parachute became wrapped around Goliath's tailplane, enabling the man to climb the cords to the aircraft. The Colonel points out that the stresses would cause the volunteer engineer to black out, so Scarlet's solution is that the drop could be two-man – with himself as the other man!

At Atlantic Airport, Captains Scarlet and Blue meet Goliath's top design man, Dr Haggerty, and the trio set off in a Starstriker fighter. Scarlet and Dr Haggerty are to exit the craft on a single parachute with the doctor lashed to Scarlet, who will be wearing the harness. Meanwhile, Destiny has overflown Goliath and reports that the flight deck is empty and the plane is entirely unmanned. The Starstriker takes up position directly above Goliath and Scarlet and Dr Haggerty eject. They pass through Goliath's forcefield, the parachute successfully catches on the tailplane and the pair gain access to the jet.

On the flight deck, the controls fail to respond to Dr Haggerty's instructions and the engines still function even when the electrical systems are cut off. Dr Haggerty suggests that they blast apart the atomic reactors, which means the whole plane will vanish in dust, but it will take them with it. Captain Scarlet tells Dr Haggerty to get a parachute on, but the doctor argues and Scarlet is forced to knock him out, strap a parachute on him and push him out of the plane. He then contacts Cloudbase to report that he intends to destroy the aircraft and Colonel White orders the Angels to peel off so as to avoid the explosion. Scarlet is successful and the World Air Force plane is destroyed in a massive fireball.

Later, the World President contacts Colonel White to offer his condolences for the death of

Colonel White and Captain Scarlet in the Amber Room.

Destiny and Rhapsody arrive in the Control Room wearing mufti.

Spectrum's most valiant officer, but Colonel White is certain that, although the centre of an atomic explosion is something that even Captain Scarlet has never experienced before, he will show up again in one piece.

Notes

As Paul Maxwell was not available to reprise his role as the World President from the television series, the character was performed here by Francis Matthews. Matthews also played the World President on the fourth mini-album, 'Captain Scarlet of Spectrum'.

Due to a typing error in the script, Colonel White learns of the break in communications with Goliath and describes it as 'a typical *Spectrum* take-over pattern' instead of 'a typical *Mysteron* take-over pattern'.

Originally released as Century 21 mini-album MA 132, 'Captain Scarlet and the Mysterons' was also released on side two of the 1967 Marble Arch LP *Gerry Anderson Presents Thunderbirds and Captain Scarlet* (HMA 227), remixed in electronically created stereo. It was then re-released the following year on side two of the Marble Arch LP *Gerry Anderson Presents TV Favourites – Volume 2* (MAL 771). In 1993, the story was released by PolyGram on side four of the audio cassette collection *Stingray and Captain Scarlet* (Cat. No. 518 466–4).

VOICE CAST			
Captain Scarlet	**Francis Matthews**	Dr Haggerty	**Jeremy Wilkin**
Captain Blue	**Ed Bishop**	Captain Hogan	**Jeremy Wilkin**
Colonel White	**Donald Gray**	Co-pilot Vic	**Jeremy Wilkin**
Rhapsody Angel	**Liz Morgan**	Spectrum Investigation Room	**Ed Bishop**
Destiny Angel	**Liz Morgan**	Cloudbase Deck Controller	**Jeremy Wilkin**
Lieutenant Green	**Cy Grant**	Airport Security 1	**Donald Gray**
Voice of the Mysterons	**Donald Gray**	Airport Security 2	**Liz Morgan**
World President	**Francis Matthews**	Atlantic Airport	**Liz Morgan**

'CAPTAIN SCARLET IS INDESTRUCTIBLE'
Written by **Richard O'Neill**

As instruments for the Salzburg Symphony Orchestra are being unloaded at Shannon Airport in Ireland, one of the baggage handlers accidentally steps on a violin case, smashing the instrument inside. The Mysterons reconstruct the violin and then issue a warning of their next act of retaliation: the destruction of the World Cultural Council. Thirty minutes later, the orchestra begins a rehearsal in the village hall at Ballyglass and as the string section begins to play the violin explodes, killing all the musicians.

On Cloudbase, Colonel White briefs Captain Blue on the explosion at Ballyglass, revealing that the village is only 2 miles from the Athlone Entertainments Complex, where the World Cultural Congress is to open that night. If the explosion had not destroyed the orchestra prematurely, it would have wiped out the Council at a gala concert. Captain Blue is dispatched to Athlone, while Captain Scarlet and Rhapsody are assigned to escort Dr Brodski, head of the World Cultural Council, who does not believe in the existence of the Mysterons. The trio leave immediately to collect Dr Brodski's luggage from her hotel, but when they get there, Dr Brodski insists on having a shower and changing her clothes. Captain Black introduces a quick-acting poison into her shower water and Dr Brodski is killed, only to be reconstructed into the service of the Mysterons.

Black tells Dr Brodski that she is to trigger a bomb at the concert hall that will destroy the Athlone Entertainments Complex. The charge has already been planted, but she must wait until all the members of the WCC are present. Scarlet spots Black slipping out of the hotel and tries to follow him, while Rhapsody sets off for Athlone with Dr Brodski, but when Scarlet loses the Mysteron agent, he returns to the hotel to check Dr Brodski's room. There he finds her body and realizes that the woman Rhapsody is now escorting is a Mysteron agent. Scarlet meets Captain Blue at the Athlone Entertainments Complex and the pair begin to search the funfair, but Dr Brodski has managed to lose Rhapsody, injecting her with an anaesthetic during a ride on the Ghost Train. Scarlet suddenly feels faint and realizes that Dr Brodski must be nearby. Blue spots her and follows her on to the Big Dipper, but Dr Brodski jumps from her car while Blue's view is obscured.

As the Angels overfly the complex, Scarlet trails the Mysteron agent to the concert hall, where members of the WCC are assembling. Quickly clearing the hall by firing his gun into the air, Scarlet implores Dr Brodski to give herself up, but she is determined to carry out the Mysteron threat – as soon as she triggers the explosive charge, the whole complex will go sky high! With no time to search the hall for the bomb, Scarlet contacts Destiny and orders her to destroy the building. Destiny opens fire and the hall is completely obliterated, but Captain Blue suddenly realizes that Scarlet must have relayed his orders while still inside the building. As he approaches the ruins of the concert hall, he wonders if Captain Scarlet could have survived the blast...

Notes

Captain Blue's reaction to Captain Scarlet's apparent death implies that he has not previously witnessed his colleague's ability to survive this kind of devastating explosion. If so, this must be a very early story.

The record ends with the original recording of the series' end title music as heard on the first fourteen episodes of the television series.

Originally released as Century 21 mini-album MA 133, 'Captain Scarlet is Indestructible' was re-released by PolyGram in 1993 on side three of the audio cassette collection *Captain Scarlet and the Mysterons – Volume 1* (Cat. No. 518 185–4).

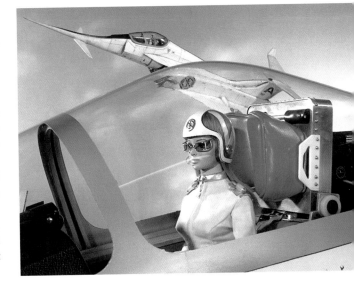

Rhapsody Angel at the controls of her Angel Interceptor.

VOICE CAST			
Captain Scarlet	**Francis Matthews**	Dr Brodski	**Liz Morgan**
Captain Blue	**Ed Bishop**	Orchestra Leader	**Jeremy Wilkin**
Colonel White	**Donald Gray**	Baggage Handler 1	**Francis Matthews**
Rhapsody Angel	**Liz Morgan**	Baggage Handler 2	**Jeremy Wilkin**
Destiny Angel	**Liz Morgan**	Hotel Clerk	**Jeremy Wilkin**
Lieutenant Green	**Cy Grant**	Panicking Woman	**Liz Morgan**
Captain Black	**Donald Gray**	Panicking Man	**Jeremy Wilkin**
Voice of the Mysterons	**Donald Gray**	Airport Tannoy	**Liz Morgan**

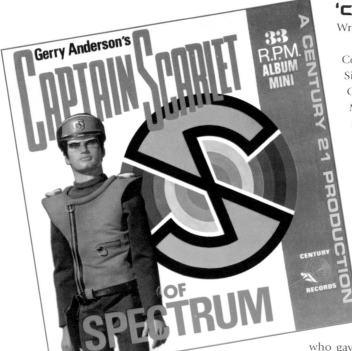

Gerry Anderson's
CAPTAIN SCARLET
33 R.P.M. ALBUM MINI
A CENTURY 21 PRODUCTION
CENTURY RECORDS
OF SPECTRUM

'CAPTAIN SCARLET OF SPECTRUM'

*Written by **Angus P. Allan***

Colonel White and Lieutenant Green fly to a rocket base in Siberia to attend the pre-launch security conference for Probe Omega, an unmanned space probe which will explore the Mexican Hat galaxy. As they near the base, a navigational satellite which will guide Omega on its journey is about to be launched, but Lieutenant Green is informed by the controller of Sub-Station 2 that the satellite's launch has been delayed, so they are given permission to land. Suddenly, he spots ignition vapour at the base of the satellite rocket and their Spectrum Transporter goes out of control when it is caught in the blast wave as the rocket launches.

The two men eject at low altitude as the Transporter crashes, but fortunately their landing is cushioned by snow. The Lieutenant is uninjured, but the Colonel suffers fractures and mild concussion, so he is taken to the base medical centre. Project director Professor Volochek arrives with the news that the controller of Sub-Station 2 has been found murdered and Green realizes that the man who gave him permission to land was a Mysteron agent deliberately attempting to kill the Spectrum officers.

Cloudbase receives notice of the Mysterons' next act of retaliation, which threatens the destruction of the Moon. As Deputy Commander, Captain Blue is in charge of Cloudbase in Colonel White's absence. He speculates that the attempt on the lives of Colonel White and Lieutenant Green was made with the object of reconstructing them as Mysteron agents, to become the Mysterons' means of aiming the Probe Omega rocket directly at the Moon. The Angels escort Captain Scarlet to the Siberian rocket base, where Volochek reveals that there are only two people who could alter the course settings on the Probe Omega rocket without arousing suspicion: the senior technicians, Banda and Corrigan. Scarlet is introduced to both and, with his Mysteron sixth sense, he is able to determine that neither has been replaced by a Mysteron agent. With the final course settings due to be made in just half an hour's time, both technicians are kept under constant surveillance, but the blast-off course is plotted and set on the nose cone without incident.

Spectrum Saloon Car on patrol at an Outer Space Defence System base.

Scarlet and Professor Volochek visit Colonel White in the medical centre and he tells Scarlet to contact the World Government to try and persuade them to cancel the Probe Omega launch, but even the World President refuses Scarlet's request without more tangible evidence. Suddenly, the Colonel and Lieutenant Green realize that if a Mysteron agent were to gain access to Sub-Station 2, he could alter the orbit of the navigational satellite to a position where its signals would draw Probe Omega into a collision course with the Moon!

Captain Scarlet races to Sub-Station 2 and discovers Captain Black tampering with vital controls, but Black tells him that the satellite is already in position. Scarlet forces Black to step backwards into the main terminals, where he is electrocuted, shorting out the systems and cancelling the influence of the satellite. Probe

Omega is launched as planned, but without the navigational satellite it goes wildly off course and crashes on Mars.

Notes

It almost seems a shame that this was not the final CAPTAIN SCARLET mini-album, as minor adjustments to the last few pages of the script would have offered a most satisfactory conclusion to the saga, with Captain Black's death by electrocution and the destruction of the Mysteron complex by Probe Omega. However, with Captain Black's reported escape from Sub-Station 2 and uncertainty over the fate of the Mysteron complex, the ending is left open for further adventures.

Originally released as Century 21 mini-album MA 134, 'Captain Scarlet of Spectrum' was re-released by PolyGram in 1993 on side two of the audio cassette collection *Captain Scarlet and the Mysterons – Volume 1* (Cat. No. 518 185–4).

VOICE CAST			
Captain Scarlet	**Francis Matthews**	Dr Lavelle	**Liz Morgan**
Captain Blue	**Ed Bishop**	Corrigan	**Jeremy Wilkin**
Colonel White	**Donald Gray**	Dominique Banda	**Liz Morgan**
Lieutenant Green	**Cy Grant**	Sub-Station 2 Controller 1	**Francis Matthews**
Captain Black	**Donald Gray**	Sub-Station 2 Controller 2	**Ed Bishop**
Voice of the Mysterons	**Donald Gray**	Siberia Base Control	**Jeremy Wilkin**
World President	**Francis Matthews**	Cloudbase Radio Room	**Francis Matthews**
Professor Volochek	**Jeremy Wilkin**	Cloudbase Control	**Jeremy Wilkin**

'CAPTAIN SCARLET VERSUS CAPTAIN BLACK'

Written by **Richard O'Neill**

Captain Blue and Captain Magenta trail a Mysteron agent along the Cornish coast, trapping him on a cliff edge. Captain Magenta is operating a new electro-ray rifle which Spectrum scientists claim will be effective on Mysteronized subjects. He has a clear shot at the Mysteron agent and, as the rifle beam hits, the man falls from the cliff edge. Returning to their SPV, Blue reports that the electro-ray rifle has proved effective in the field. It will become standard equipment in all patrol and pursuit vehicles from now on.

The Mysterons call on Captain Black to explain the failure of his agent in Cornwall, ordering him to obtain one of the electro-ray rifles as a new tool in the Mysterons' campaign against Earth. Black visits a farm in north Devon and steals an SPV equipped with one of the rifles, but Lieutenant Green uses the video tracker to pinpoint his position in the middle of Bodmin, Cornwall.

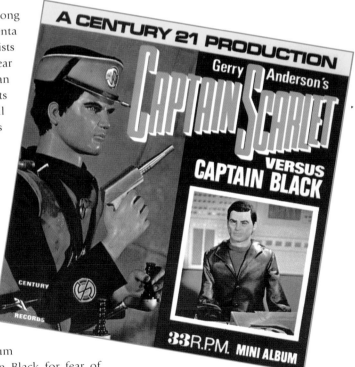

Captains Scarlet and Blue are assigned to pursue Black, as the new rifle offers a chance to dispose of the Mysteron agent once and for all. However, Black is fully aware that Spectrum is on his tail and lures two children, Betty and Timmy, inside the SPV as protection. With the children held hostage, the Spectrum officers will be unable to take any action against Captain Black for fear of harming them.

As Scarlet and Blue close in on Black's stolen SPV, they come to a police roadblock, where they learn that Captain Black has kidnapped the children. They trail him to Truro, where Blue spots the SPV parked in a warehouse, but there is no sign of Black. Suspecting a trap, Scarlet tells Blue to create a diversion while he uses a jet-pack to access the warehouse from the roof. Scarlet

The Angels target Captain Black's stolen SPV.

bursts into the warehouse through a skylight, but Black grabs hold of Betty and warns Scarlet that he will kill the girl unless he stays where he is. He tells Scarlet to drop his rifle, aiming his own rifle at Scarlet at point blank range, but Timmy attacks Black from behind, forcing him to drop his rifle, and Scarlet throws both rifles out through the skylight. However, Captain Black still holds Betty hostage and forces Captain Scarlet to hand over the jet-pack, but Scarlet then launches himself at Black, freeing Betty and grabbing hold of the Mysteron agent as he uses the jet-pack to fly out through the skylight.

As Black tries to shake him off, Scarlet contacts Captain Blue and urges him to shoot Black down with one of the electro-ray rifles, but Black destroys Scarlet's radio to prevent any further communication. Blue is reluctant to open fire on Black, for fear of hitting Scarlet, so he borrows an old motor cycle to trail Scarlet and Black along a cliff road as they head for the open sea. Once the pair are over water, Blue takes careful aim and opens fire, destroying the jet-pack so that the two struggling men fall into the sea. Blue takes a launch out to sea and soon finds Captain Scarlet's body, but there is no sign of Captain Black.

Captain Scarlet dons a jet-pack to access the warehouse.

Notes

The subtext of this story warns children not to accept lifts from strangers. This was a topic of great public concern at the time and short public information films which warned of the dangers of such folly were regularly screened during children's television programmes.

Voice artist Gary Files was not available to reprise his television role as Captain Magenta, so the character is voiced here by Jeremy Wilkin. It would probably have made more sense just to exchange Captain Magenta for Captain Ochre in the script, as Wilkin voiced Ochre in the TV episodes.

After post-production work on the story was completed, the final running time was discovered to be well under the requisite twenty-one minutes, so someone had the bright idea of increasingly slowing down the soundtrack in the second half to stretch out the length. This had the effect of deepening all the voices to such an extent that by the end Ed Bishop is unrecognizable as Captain Blue. The soundtrack speed could have been corrected for the PolyGram audio cassette release in 1993, but instead the tape was issued with the fault intact.

Originally released as Century 21 mini-album MA 135, 'Captain Scarlet Versus Captain Black' was re-released the following year on side two of the Marble Arch LP *Gerry Anderson Presents TV Favourites – Volume 1* (MAL 770), and then released by PolyGram in 1993 on side four of the audio cassette collection *Captain Scarlet and the Mysterons – Volume 1* (Cat. No. 518 185–4).

VOICE CAST			
Captain Scarlet	**Francis Matthews**	Betty Pengenny	**Melody Kaye**
Captain Blue	**Ed Bishop**	Robert	**Ronnie Caryl**
Colonel White	**Donald Gray**	Timmy	**William Burleigh**
Lieutenant Green	**Cy Grant**	Mrs Pengenny	**Liz Morgan**
Captain Magenta	**Jeremy Wilkin**	Farmer	**Jeremy Wilkin**
Captain Black	**Donald Gray**	Policeman	**Jeremy Wilkin**
Voice of the Mysterons	**Donald Gray**	Skipper	**Jeremy Wilkin**

THE COMICS

In the same week that the series premiered on British television, CAPTAIN SCARLET AND THE MYSTERONS also made its comic-strip debut in issue 141 of *TV Century 21*, the best-selling boys' weekly comic published by City Magazines Ltd in association with Century 21 Publishing. However, the CAPTAIN SCARLET concept had been slowly introduced to readers over the previous four months with tantalizing news reports of Captain Black's mission to Mars.

Edited by former Supermarionation series scriptwriter Alan Fennell, *TV Century 21* was launched in January 1965 as a quality weekly comic that featured strip stories based on the various Gerry Anderson programmes. Presenting artwork by some of British comics' most talented artists, backed by superior print production, *TV Century 21* had become Britain's top-selling comic within weeks of its launch. Initially featuring strips based on SUPERCAR, FIREBALL XL5 and STINGRAY, over the next two years the comic also introduced readers to THUNDERBIRDS, as well as the crew of *Zero X* in a spin-off strip from the *Thunderbirds Are Go* feature film.

Styled as a newspaper of the future, *TV Century 21* presented mock newspaper stories on its front cover that previewed the contents of the strips inside, so regular readers were puzzled by the headline which appeared on the cover of issue 125 (dated 3 June 1967): 'Captain Black Heads Expedition'. The mystery began to unravel three months later with the publication of issue 137 (2 September 1967), which reported the loss of Captain Black's Mars expedition and queried which organization Captain Black belonged to, pointing out the unfamiliar badge on his hat in the accompanying photo (actually a picture of Captain Grey). A separate news item on the cover of that issue reported a sighting of a mysterious floating aircraft carrier over Nice, France, together with an artist's impression of the craft.

Two issues later, readers were introduced to the new Spectrum organization via an 'official press release' from the World Government as page three of issue 139 (16 September 1967) printed the first pictures of the Angel aircraft and several members of Spectrum. An ongoing original strip, *Front Page*, which was illustrated by John M. Burns, followed the dangerous investigations of *TV Century 21* reporter Pete Tracker and his photographer, Lens. In this particular issue, their plane narrowly missed a collision with an SPJ piloted by Colonel White and, tailing the SPJ to Glenn Field, they suddenly found themselves in the flight path of Zero X on its return to Earth.

TV Century 21, issue 140 (23 September 1967).

Left: A panel of artwork by Ron Embleton from TV Century 21, *issue 144 (21 October 1967).*

The following issue (140, dated 23 September 1967) featured the Spectrum logo and a photo of Cloudbase on the cover, accompanying the headline 'Spectrum is Green'. More Spectrum secrets were revealed inside, while in the *Front Page* strip Tracker and Lens survived their collision with Zero X, but Captain Black was able to slip away in the confusion. Colonel White granted Tracker an interview in which he revealed details of the Spectrum organization that were published in issue 140 of *TV Century 21*.

With the readers' curiosity suitably whetted, the CAPTAIN SCARLET strip made a triumphant debut on the double-page colour centre spread of issue 141, with glorious artwork by Ron Embleton. Regarded as the definitive CAPTAIN SCARLET artist for the ten paintings he provided for the closing titles of the television series, Ronald Sydney Embleton was perhaps best known at the time for his work on the *Wulf the Britain* strip, which graced the cover of *Express Weekly* from 1956 to 1961. However, Embleton was a highly prolific artist whose naturalistic style with its subtly textured colours had appeared in *Comic Cuts*, *Mickey Mouse Weekly*, *TV Express* and *Eagle*, among many other comics of the 1950s and early 1960s.

He joined the artists on *TV Century 21* direct from *Eagle* to illustrate the STINGRAY strip in the first seventy-one issues (barring four issues in which the strip was illustrated by his younger brother, Gerry), but his work was very much in demand elsewhere and apart from occasional strips in summer specials and annuals, Embleton was absent from *TV Century 21* until his return with CAPTAIN SCARLET fifteen months later.

Embleton illustrated forty pages of the CAPTAIN SCARLET strip comprising three stories across seventeen issues of *TV Century 21*, taking the strip through its transition from the centre spread to the first four pages of each issue. From issue 155 (6 January 1968) the mock newspaper front covers were dropped in favour of the first page of the CAPTAIN SCARLET strip.

Artwork by Ron Embleton from TV Century 21, *issue 155 (6 January 1968), above, and issue 143 (14 October 1967), below.*

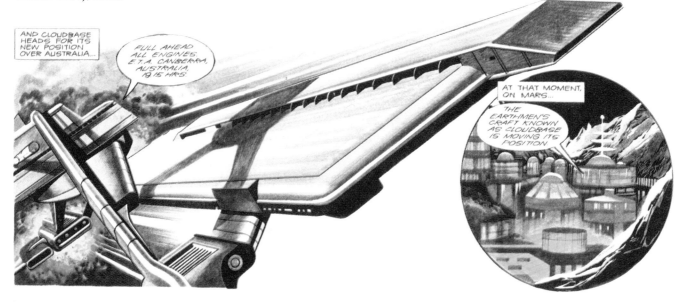

1. WE WILL DESTROY UNITY CITY

Written by **Angus P. Allan**

Art by **Ron Embleton**

Published in *TV Century 21*, issues 141–149
(30 September–25 November 1967)

The Mysterons threaten to destroy the World Government headquarters at Unity City. As the Angel flight leaves Cloudbase, Harmony is shot down by an aircraft piloted by Captain Black. She ejects to safety but her Angel Interceptor is reconstructed by the Mysterons and heads for Cloudbase. Captain Scarlet rams the craft with his SPJ, totally destroying it but in the process sustaining considerable injuries.

His shattered body is recovered from the sea and taken to Sick Bay, where it is placed in a hermetically sealed recovery unit. Colonel White realizes that the Mysterons intend to crash a Mysteronized Cloudbase on to Unity City, so he moves the Spectrum headquarters to a new position over Australia. But en route Cloudbase passes through a cloud of nerve gas sprayed into the carrier's path by Captain Black, so when Scarlet recovers, he finds that everyone else is unconscious.

Captain Black arrives and Scarlet tackles him in the flight control room, but the automatic pilot fuses and Cloudbase lurches out of control. Scarlet manages to get the carrier back under control before pursuing Black, jumping aboard his jet as he makes his escape, but Black ejects and Scarlet is trapped inside as it crashes into the sea off the Fijian Islands. Local natives rescue Scarlet's body and give him a warrior's funeral in a blazing pyre, but he recovers and is hailed as a god. Black has been watching from nearby and tries to kill Scarlet, telling the natives that the Captain is an evil spirit. The natives stake both men out on the beach as prey for land crabs.

Back on Cloudbase, the nerve gas wears off and everyone regains consciousness. Shortly after, Lieutenant Green receives a call for help from Captain Black, who has managed to activate his cap microphone. Destiny arrives to rescue Scarlet and Black, and they are soon joined by Melody and Harmony, but the Mysterons activate Captain Black's audio-field, emitting a high-frequency sound wave that knocks out the four Spectrum agents.

Taking Scarlet, Black escapes into the sea and calls for assistance from a Mysteron agent who has infiltrated the WASP base Marineville. In Stingray, this agent ferries Black and Scarlet to a coastal rocket base, where they board a probe rocket bound for Alpha Centauri. A Mysteron agent at the base programmes the rocket on a course for Mars, where the Mysterons plan to bring Captain Scarlet back under their control. Colonel White contacts the WSP and a trio of Fireball spacecraft pursue the probe rocket. Fireball XL2 destroys the rocket and the crew recover Scarlet's body from space, but the Mysterons reconstruct the rocket and Captain Black makes his escape.

TV Century 21, issue 141 (30 September 1967), above, and issue 143 (14 October 1967), below.

REPRINT HISTORY

TV Action + Countdown, issues 63–70 (Polystyle Publications, 29 April–17 June 1972)

Action 21, issues 1–7 (Engale Marketing, July 1988–July 1989)

Captain Scarlet and the Mysterons, issues 1–7
(Fleetway Editions, 23 October 1993–28 January 1994)

Captain Scarlet and the Mysterons: Indestructible (Ravette Books, 1993)

2. WE WILL DESTROY THE OBSERVATORY NETWORK

Written by **Angus P. Allan**

Art by **Ron Embleton**

Published in *TV Century 21*, issues 150–154 (2–30 December 1967)

Dr Balatta of the Mount Kilimanjaro observatory is killed in a climbing accident and reconstructed by the Mysterons, who then issue a warning of their intention to destroy the Earth Observatory Network. Colonel White assigns his officers to different observatories on the network and Captain Scarlet is dispatched to Mount Kilimanjaro. He collects a Spectrum Helicopter in Mombasa, unaware that it has been booby-trapped by Captain Black, and as he flies over the Tanzanian border the helicopter explodes. Scarlet ejects at low altitude and soon recovers from the impact. Colonel White dispatches Lieutenant Tan in an SPV to pick him up, but Black sets a trap for Tan and gains control of the SPV. He attempts to run Scarlet down and then causes an elephant stampede, but Scarlet survives both attempts on his life and makes his way to the observatory. Black sets charges which will destroy the observatory when the telescope is rotated through 160 degrees, but Scarlet prevents the rotation of the telescope and pursues Black as he escapes in the SPV. Harmony opens fire on the vehicle, destroying it, but Black escapes with a jet-pack.

TV Century 21, issue 152 (16 December 1967).

REPRINT HISTORY

TV Action + Countdown, issues 78–82 (Polystyle Publications, 12 August–9 September 1972; part 5 redrawn by Martin Asbury)

Action 21, issues 8–10 (Engale Marketing, August–October 1989; parts 1–3 only)

Captain Scarlet and the Mysterons, issues 7–10 (Fleetway Editions, 28 January–11 March 1994)

Captain Scarlet and the Mysterons: Indestructible (Ravette Books, 1993)

3. WE SHALL MAKE EARTH A PLANET OF SILENCE

Written by **Angus P. Allan**

Art by **Ron Embleton**

Published in *TV21*, issues 155–157 (6–20 January 1968)

When Communications Satellite 4 breaks down, Colonel White sends Professor Gallen to effect repairs, unaware that he is a Mysteron agent. Cloudbase receives a Mysteron threat to 'make Earth a planet of silence' and Captain Scarlet realizes that Satellite 4 is in the hands of the Mysterons. He dispatches the Angels to destroy the satellite, but Gallen broadcasts an ultra-high-frequency signal which sends the Angel Interceptors spinning out of control and shatters all the Cloudbase viewing ports, sucking oxygen from the craft. While the Colonel and Lieutenant Green hand out oxygen masks, Scarlet manages to pilot Cloudbase into the radio-resistant ionosphere, but without radio communications Spectrum can neither warn Earth nor use radio-controlled missiles to destroy the satellite. Scarlet sets off in an Angel Interceptor, ejecting from the jet when the instruments are knocked out by the ultra-sonic wave. Using a jet-pack, he gains access to the satellite and guns down Professor Gallen, but the Mysterons still control the satellite and set it plunging into Earth's atmosphere. Scarlet escapes as the satellite burns up and explodes, and his body is recovered from the sea by Kremer, a wealthy businessman. Captain Black arranges for Scarlet to be buried at sea in a lead coffin, but the chains snap as the coffin is being lifted overboard and it smashes through the deck of Kremer's cruiser into the engine room, detonating the boat's atomic reactor. The coffin sinks to the sea bed, but Scarlet forces his way out and escapes to the surface.

The retitled TV21, issue 155 (6 January 1968), with cover art by Ron Embleton.

REPRINT HISTORY

Captain Scarlet and the Mysterons, issues 1–3 (Fleetway Editions, 23 October–20 November 1993)

Captain Scarlet and the Mysterons: Spectrum is Green (Ravette Books, 1993)

Apart from the CAPTAIN SCARLET strip in *TV Century 21*, Embleton also provided the box artwork for Anglo Confectionery's CAPTAIN SCARLET AND THE MYSTERONS bubble-gum cards and painted the spectacular artwork that appeared as a jigsaw on the back of the cards. This artwork was also published as a poster that was available by mail order direct from Anglo.

After leaving *TV Century 21*, Embleton maintained occasional connections to the Gerry Anderson programmes, providing artwork for the jigsaws that appeared on the backs of Anglo's sets of JOE 90 and UFO bubble-gum cards, both of which were also issued as posters. He illustrated articles for *Look and Learn* and *World of Wonder* magazines, the *Daily Mirror Book for Boys* and a number of Ladybird Books' children's educational hardbacks, but for the last fifteen years of his life Embleton was fully employed illustrating adult comic-strip stories for *Penthouse* magazine. He died in February 1988, aged fifty-seven.

His replacement on the *TV21* CAPTAIN SCARLET strip was Mike Noble, a former advertising artist who began his prolific comics career in the 1950s on *Robin*, a comic for very young children. He went on to illustrate *Life with Sally* in *Woman* magazine, *The Lone Ranger* in *Express Weekly* and *Range Rider*, *Beetle Bailey* and *Popeye* in *TV Comic*, before he was hired by his ex-*TV Comic* colleague Alan Fennell to work on the FIREBALL XL5 strip in *TV Century 21* from issue 6 (27 February 1965).

From this point on, Noble never looked back. His run on FIREBALL XL5 continued until issue 108 (11 February 1967), with only two four-week holiday breaks during the whole two-year period. He then developed the comic's *Zero X* strip with Angus Allan and began a forty-nine-week uninterrupted run on the strip with issue 105 (21 January 1967), before switching to the CAPTAIN SCARLET strip with issue 158 (27 January 1968). Although his work occasionally alternated with that of other artists such as Keith Watson, Don Harley and Frank Bellamy, Noble illustrated the CAPTAIN SCARLET strip up to issue 196 (19 October 1968) and then returned to *Zero X* until the strip was cancelled at issue 241 (30 August 1969).

Mike Noble retains fond memories of his work on *TV Century 21*. 'The way it worked was that I would get a call from my agent, Billy Cooper, who would say that *TV21* wanted me to do a new strip – CAPTAIN SCARLET, for example. He would say, "Watch the telly when it's on, see what you think and we'll get some stills down to you." I was sent a lovely book for *Zero X* which showed how it all fitted together, but I was never invited to the studios to see the models and puppets – I think that would have been a great help really. Invariably, I would be sent a script outlining the story and what should appear in each frame and I was then just told, "Get on with it – you're the artist!" *Zero X* was a bit of a worry for me for a while, because it came apart and bits flew off, but I got it right in the end.

'I was also involved in drawing cutaway blueprints for the vehicles, which were similar to drawings that I had done during my National Service days with the Regimental Drawing Office at the Royal Tank Regiment in North Yorkshire, where I drew the insides of tanks and other equipment for manuals and that sort of thing. With the CAPTAIN SCARLET vehicles, I just made up the interiors, because you never really saw any internal workings in the shows themselves, so I just tried to make things look interesting and dramatic.

'With CAPTAIN SCARLET, I became aware just by looking at the vehicles that this was a far more realistic programme, both vehicle and technology-wise, than those that had gone before. The

Spectacular artwork by Mike Noble from the cover of TV21, issue 162 (24 February 1968).

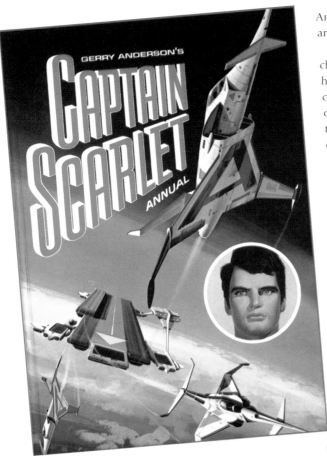

Angel jets and Spectrum vehicles weren't too far off real things like armoured cars and stuff like that.'

Noble's dynamic but realistic style and talent for capturing character likenesses earned him a reputation as British comics' most hard-working, reliable and durable illustrator of television-based comic strips. After the Gerry Anderson programmes were phased out of *TV21* (as it was by now titled), Noble worked for a time on the comic's STAR TREK strip before moving to *Look-in*, a new comic edited by Alan Fennell featuring a range of ITV television series. Noble's art appeared regularly in *Look-in* over the next fifteen years, illustrating strips based on TIMESLIP, FREEWHEELERS, FOLLYFOOT, THE ADVENTURES OF BLACK BEAUTY, THE TOMORROW PEOPLE, THE FAMOUS FIVE, MAN FROM ATLANTIS, WORZEL GUMMIDGE, INTO THE LABYRINTH, STAR FLEET and ROBIN OF SHERWOOD, among others. He also renewed his acquaintance with the Gerry Anderson programmes when he replaced John M. Burns on the comic's SPACE: 1999 strip in 1976.

Comic strips based on CAPTAIN SCARLET AND THE MYSTERONS also appeared in *TV Century 21*'s companion comics *Lady Penelope* and *Solo*, in both cases well in advance of the television series' premiere broadcast. Spectrum's élite group of female pilots appeared first in *The Angels*, a strip illustrated by Jon Davis which made its debut in issue 53 (21 January 1967) of *Lady Penelope*, only weeks after filming began on the television series. Here, readers were introduced to the five pilots in their pre-Spectrum days, gathered together by a mysterious benefactor to undertake secret missions in state-of-the-art fighter planes (unmarked Angel Interceptors) under the cover of an aerial display team. In issue 84 (26 August 1967), the Angels finally met Colonel White, who explained that they had been undergoing training to join the Spectrum organization. At this point, other characters from the television series were introduced and the strip began to follow the CAPTAIN SCARLET format.

CAPTAIN SCARLET *annuals for 1967, above, and 1968, below.*

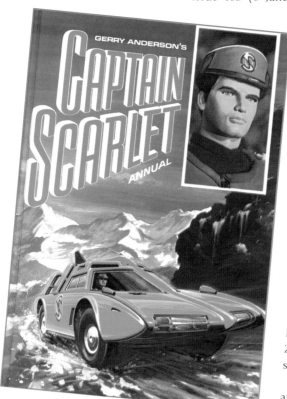

Issue 103 (6 January 1968) of *Lady Penelope* introduced readers to *The Spectrum* in a humorous strip drawn by Tom Kerr which featured the fictional Monkees-style antics of the pop band who had performed the television series' end titles song. *The Angels* continued for a further thirty-six weeks, until it was dropped at issue 120 (4 May 1968) and the comic was revamped as *Penelope*.

Solo comic introduced readers to the concept of the Mysterons in *The Mark of the Mysterons*, a strip set in the present day which debuted in issue 19 (17 June 1967). The previous issue had included a feature article warning readers of this threat from space and the new strip, illustrated by Don Harley, continued in this vein, following the exploits of reporter John Marsh as he investigated reports of Mysteron activity in 1967. Of course, this strip turned out to be only loosely based on the television series and, in fact, directly contradicted the series' presentation of the Mysterons as peaceful beings prior to their contact with Captain Black.

In mid-September, *Solo* merged with *TV Tornado* and *The Mark of the Mysterons* was revamped as *The Mysterons*, taking the concept into the twenty-first century with the title characters intent on conquering other planets to form an empire. Apart from a brief reference to the destruction of the Mysteron complex on Mars in the opening instalment, the Mysterons' power of retro-metabolism and occasional appearances by the Zero X MEV, there was no real connection to the television series and the strip was dropped after issue 58 (17 February 1968) of *TV Tornado*.

Just before Christmas each year from 1965 to 1969, City Magazines and Century 21 Publishing produced a series of hardback annuals tied in to the various Century 21 comics and Gerry Anderson programmes. Robust, large-format, ninety-two-page coffee-table-style books, these were packed with comic strips, text stories, feature articles and colour photos. For 1967, the regular *TV Century 21*, THUNDERBIRDS and *Lady Penelope* annuals were joined by the first CAPTAIN SCARLET annual. This introduced readers to the whole CAPTAIN SCARLET concept, with full biographies of the characters, a detailed tour of Cloudbase, cutaway spreads of the vehicles and features on the Mysterons and the formation of Spectrum. The text and strip stories also introduced a graphic form of lettering for the voice of the Mysterons which became the standard presentation of the Mysteron threats in all of the annual strips and text stories over the next three years.

CAPTAIN SCARLET did not appear in the regular *TV21* annual until the following year and, although *The Angels* were billed on the back cover of the 1967 *Lady Penelope* annual, they did not appear inside. However, the emphasis was very much on CAPTAIN SCARLET in both the 1968 and 1969 *TV21* annuals and the standard of the strip artwork in the latter was particularly good, with no fewer than three strips from the highly stylized pen of Ron Turner, a pulp science-fiction cover artist who was best known for his *Rick Random* strip in *Super Detective Library*. Turner joined the roster of *TV Century 21* artists as illustrator of *The Daleks*, a strip based on the popular villains of the BBC's DOCTOR WHO series, but he went on to draw several STINGRAY and THUNDERBIRDS strips in various *TV Century 21* specials. Turner also contributed to the 1968 CAPTAIN SCARLET annual and the following year's combination CAPTAIN SCARLET and THUNDERBIRDS annual, which was the last from Century 21 Publishing.

Dropped from *TV21* after issue 242 (6 September 1969), CAPTAIN SCARLET AND THE MYSTERONS resurfaced as a comic strip in issue 1 (20 February 1971) of Polystyle's *Countdown*, the brainchild of former *TV Century 21* art editor Dennis Hooper, which featured strips of the Gerry Anderson Supermarionation programmes alongside strips based on DOCTOR WHO and Anderson's new live-action series UFO. Unfortunately, the CAPTAIN SCARLET strip, like *Countdown* itself, was relatively short-lived and after the initial five-part story drawn by Jon Cooper, it only appeared in selected issues as self-contained six-page stories. However, these were generally well written and imaginative stories with notable artistic contributions by Brian Lewis, Martin Asbury and Malcolm Stokes.

'Funnel of Flame', drawn by Lewis in issue 35 (16 October 1971), proved to be the last original CAPTAIN SCARLET strip for twenty-two years: reprints of Ron Embleton's first two *TV Century 21* strips appeared when *Countdown* was remodelled as *TV Action + Countdown*, but no new CAPTAIN SCARLET strips were commissioned before the comic finally folded with issue 132 (25 August 1973).

TV21 annuals for 1968, above, and 1969, left, with the CAPTAIN SCARLET/ THUNDERBIRDS *annual for 1969 below.*

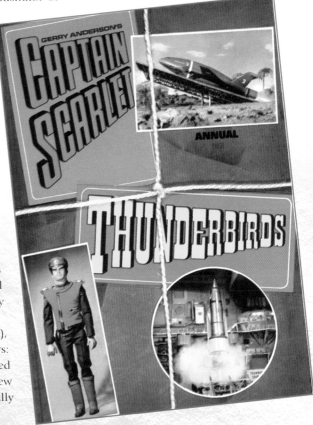

THE NOVELS

Delighted with the success of a series of original novels based on the previous Gerry Anderson programmes, STINGRAY and THUNDERBIRDS, Armada Books (a division of May Fair Books) were happy to work again with Century 21 Publishing to publish original novels based on CAPTAIN SCARLET. As before, they turned to the highly prolific British writer John William Jennison, who had shown his ability to quickly grasp the concepts and story potential of the earlier Supermarionation series in two STINGRAY novels and six THUNDERBIRDS novels.

The author of more than 100 novels for different UK paperback publishers from the 1940s to the early 1960s, Jennison primarily wrote Westerns and thriller novels, although he was capable of working in a variety of different genres. He made his debut as a science-fiction author in 1951 with *Conquerors of Venus*, using the pen name Edgar Rees Kennedy, one of at least forty pseudonyms that he employed during his career. Other works were credited to Neil Charles, Gill Hunt, King Lang and Matthew C. Bradford, although Jennison was perhaps best known as John Theydon, a name that he first used in 1946.

Jennison's first contact with the various Gerry Anderson productions came in 1965, when he was asked by World Distributors to write a SUPERCAR storybook, *Supercar on the Black Diamond Trail*. He followed this with a pair of STINGRAY storybooks, *Danger in the Deep* and *The Deadly Alliance*, before penning the first of his eleven paperback adventures for Armada as John Theydon. After *Stingray* and *Stingray and the Monster*, Jennison went on to write four THUNDERBIRDS novels for Armada, *Thunderbirds*, *Calling Thunderbirds*, *Thunderbirds: Ring of Fire* and *Lady Penelope: The Albanian Affair*, while at the same time maintaining his links with World Distributors, for whom he wrote a pair of hardback THUNDERBIRDS novels, *Operation Asteroids* and *Lost World*, under his real name.

When it came to the CAPTAIN SCARLET novels, Jennison was keen to go beyond the boundaries of what it

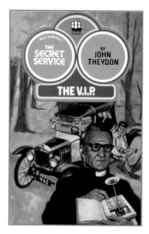

Some of John Jennison's other novels based on the Gerry Anderson productions: Stingray; Thunderbirds; Thunderbirds: Ring of Fire; Thunderbirds: Lost World; Lady Penelope: The Albanian Affair; The Secret Service: The V.I.P.

was possible to show in the television episodes. Although he was careful not to break from the established format, he constructed devious plans for the Mysterons, always showing them one step ahead of Spectrum and often leading the Spectrum officers on wild-goose chases or tricking them into unwittingly assisting their operations. He was also careful to follow the television series' lead and not talk down to the target audience – perceived as older children and young teenagers – and the result was a trilogy of exciting and accessible novels which made entertaining if undemanding reading in the pulp science-fiction tradition for adults as well as for children.

Unfortunately, Jennison was not available to pen either of Armada's two novels based on the next Gerry Anderson series, JOE 90. He did return to write *The Destroyer* and *The VIP*, a pair of novels based on the last Supermarionation programme, THE SECRET SERVICE, but these were both lacklustre affairs and well below the standard of his work on the CAPTAIN SCARLET and THUNDERBIRDS novels.

CAPTAIN SCARLET AND THE MYSTERONS

Written by **John Theydon (John W. Jennison)**
Published 1967 by Armada Books (paperback, 128 pages), illustrated by Chris Higham
Reprinted October 1989 as *Captain Scarlet 1: Captain Scarlet and the Mysterons* by Titan Books

Professor Arnold Deitz, President of the World Weather Control Organization, clashes with Professor Kurt Standahl at the launching of Deitz's weather control satellites at Mount Kenya. Professor Standahl, who has developed his own weather control system, believes that Deitz's satellite network is a primitive solution that will fail and is more likely to aggravate weather conditions. The four satellites, Alpha, Beta, Gamma and Omega, are launched and take up their respective orbits, but Omega inexplicably disintegrates and is reconstructed by the Mysterons. Shortly after, Cloudbase receives warning of a Mysteron threat to cause worldwide havoc by upsetting climatic conditions within forty-eight hours.

Standahl is trailed by Captain Black to his secret laboratory in Norway. There, Black introduces himself as a reporter and persuades the scientist to demonstrate his Dahl beam weather control system by causing a thunderstorm of incredible intensity centred on London. On leave in the city, Captain Scarlet and Rhapsody find themselves in deep water as the deluge sweeps London, breaking the banks of the Thames and flooding the city. His demonstration at an end, Standahl suddenly realizes what he has done, but it is too late – he is shot down by Captain Black and reconstructed in the service of the Mysterons, along with the Dahl beam projector and the Professor's laboratory. Under Mysteron control, the Dahl beam creates a hurricane of tremendous force that sweeps through the Bahamas and devastates Florida.

Suspecting that the Mysteronized Omega satellite may be to blame, Captains Scarlet and Blue embark on a dangerous mission in space aboard WSP cruiser XL19 in an attempt to force Omega into the sun, unaware that the ship's mechanic, Greg Waterman, is a Mysteron agent. Scarlet boards the satellite with Waterman, but the mechanic traps him in the engine room, activates Omega's motors and sends the satellite racing out of control towards the sun. Captain Blue chases after the satellite and manages to rescue Scarlet just before Omega explodes. However, the destruction of the satellite makes no difference to the weather conditions on Earth, and the Spectrum officers realize that they have been led on a wild-goose chase by Professor Standahl.

Scarlet trails Standahl to San José but he is captured by Captain Black, who attempts to kill him by binding him to the circuits of a power station. Rescued by a local woman, Scarlet requisitions an SPV and races after Standahl and Black, but the two Mysteron agents elude him by taking to the air in a private jet. The Angels pick up the trail and follow the jet to Norway, where Rhapsody is able to pinpoint the source of the Dahl beam as a shaft on a small plateau, but she is caught in a blizzard and smashes into a cliff. Rhapsody ejects to safety, only to be captured by Professor Standahl. Captain Scarlet ejects from an SPJ over the plateau and penetrates Standahl's laboratory. There, he frees Rhapsody, but the pair learn that the Professor has set the Dahl beam to transmit impulses into the atmosphere that will create havoc with the weather for a century. In a final race against time, Scarlet pursues Standahl to recover his master key and disconnect the Dahl beam before a time fuse programmed into the computer destroys the laboratory.

Notes

This is a very promising start to Armada's range of CAPTAIN SCARLET novels, an exciting, intelligent story with a variety of locations and situations that keep the plot moving. The regular cast are all very much in character, apart from the fact that everyone, including Colonel White, is rather too keen to call the Angels 'honey', which comes across as a bit demeaning.

Chronologically, this story must be set after the television episode *Spectrum Strikes Back*, as Spectrum reveals the Mysteron Gun and Mysteron Detector to the world's press. Theydon draws on the unified Anderson series continuity established in the CAPTAIN SCARLET promotional notes and the pages of *TV Century 21* with the introduction of Fireball XL19 and the officers of the World Space Patrol from the earlier Supermarionation series FIREBALL XL5.

The World Weather Control Organization's satellite Omega is launched from Mount Kenya.

CAPTAIN SCARLET AND THE SILENT SABOTEUR

Written by **John Theydon** (John W. Jennison)

Published 1967 by Armada Books (paperback, 128 pages), illustrated by Chris Higham

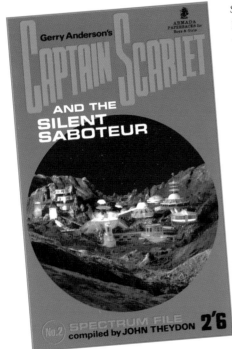

Suspecting Mysteron intervention, Captains Scarlet and Blue are assigned to attend the launching of Oceanus X, an exploratory submarine equipped with a stealth device which renders it undetectable by any known scanning system. The launch goes according to plan but two hours later, the Oceanus disappears and the crew are found dead, killed by intense radiation. Oceanographer Jacques Berlein is also reported missing and Scarlet believes that he has engineered the theft of the submarine.

Then Spectrum receives the latest Mysteron threat, which promises the devastation of Earth's greatest nation within seven days. A few hours later, a thermic power station near Sydney explodes, killing hundreds of people and destroying miles of the Australian coastline. Colonel White is contacted by Berlein, who reveals that he is tracking the Oceanus by means of a device that he had previously attached to the hull. Scarlet and Blue link up with Berlein and they track the submarine heading for Rio de Janeiro, but before they can intercept it the thermic power station outside Rio explodes. In the ruins of the power station, the Spectrum officers meet the Brazilian power controller, Señhor d'Oliviera, who explains that the operation of the thermic power network: energy waves being beamed to the two destroyed sub-stations from the mother station in the Nevada Desert has been automatically split between the four remaining sub-stations in Copenhagen, Cape Town, Nanking and Bombay. Scarlet detects that the station's resident director, Vasco, is a Mysteron agent, but is badly injured as he and Blue try to apprehend him.

Berlein contacts Spectrum again to report that he has developed a super detector to track Oceanus, but when he leaves his laboratory in the Swiss Alps to meet Scarlet at Berne Airport, he finds that his car has been sabotaged by Captain Black. He crashes on the mountain roads and is reconstructed as a Mysteron agent. Collecting Scarlet from the airport, Berlein attempts to kill him by deliberately driving his car over a precipice, but Scarlet is thrown out and climbs to safety. Evading Berlein's robot guardian Alphonse, he gains access to the laboratory and finds the super detector, which shows Oceanus apparently heading for Bombay. Black attempts to kill Scarlet with a Mysteron gun, but the beam of high-voltage electricity starts a fire which destroys the laboratory and Black escapes.

Scarlet flies to Bombay, where he is led into a trap by a Mysteron agent who seals him in a lead-lined tomb on Elephanta Island. Fortunately, Captain Blue follows his trail to the island and frees him just as his air runs out. Captain Black is spotted in Nanking and Colonel White realizes that the sub-station there is the Mysterons' next target. Scarlet and Blue arrive in Nanking and are detained by another Mysteron agent in the guise of a police commandant. Finally evading the police, they requisition an SPV and make their way to the thermic station, but they are too late: Black has already planted a detonation device in the reaction chamber which is activated by Oceanus when the submarine comes within range.

World Navy stealth submarine Oceanus X, under the control of the Mysterons.

With three sub-stations destroyed, if a fourth goes down, an overload of thermic power will cause a chain reaction beneath the Earth which will devastate North America. Recognizing that the sub-stations are being targeted in alphabetical order (Australia, Brazil and then China), Colonel White deduces that the last target will be the Copenhagen sub-station in Denmark. He alerts the World Navy and their forces destroy Oceanus in the Bering Strait, but the Mysterons put an alternative plan into operation. Scarlet and Blue race to the Nevada mother station and are just in time to prevent a Mysteron agent from tampering with controls that would increase the station's energy output and overload the three remaining sub-stations.

Notes

Without question the best of the three CAPTAIN SCARLET novels, *Captain Scarlet and the Silent Saboteur* is inventive and action-packed, with numerous location changes and plot twists that keep readers on the edge of their seats to the very last page. The destruction of the Oceanus is a bit disappointing as it is simply reported by a third party, but all of the main characters are true to their television counterparts – and no one calls the Angels 'honey'!

THE ANGELS AND THE CREEPING ENEMY

Written by **John Theydon (John W. Jennison)**
Published 1968 by Armada Books (paperback, 128 pages), illustrated by Chris Higham

While on leave in Florida, Melody spots Captain Black and follows him to a biological laboratory on an island in Lake Talachu owned by Dr Sneddon. There, she confronts Black but is unable to prevent him from killing Dr Sneddon and stealing Culture XO, a deadly bacteria that could kill millions. Shortly after, Cloudbase receives the Mysterons' latest threat, the destruction of vital sources of food supplies within forty-eight hours.

Dr Sneddon's assistant, Dr Grove, contacts Colonel White to inform him that, before he died, Sneddon scratched some letters on the floor which may have some significance: X-XO-RCKHO. Then, Captain Black is spotted in North Africa, en route to the World Food Organization's Sahara Project control centre at Kufra, and the Colonel realizes that he intends to contaminate the water in the subterranean lakes there, water that is pumped to the surface to irrigate a vast area of the desert which has become one of the largest corn producers in the world. He dispatches Harmony, Destiny and Symphony to Kufra with Captains Scarlet and Blue following close behind in an SPJ. Arriving at the control centre, the Angels find that Captain Black has already made his way down into the subterranean caverns. Following him, the three pilots pursue Black along the chain of lakes in a power launch. Meanwhile, Colonel White has learned that Dr Sneddon's cryptic message points to Dr R. C. Kholchak, a Russian bacteriologist who may know how to destroy Culture XO. Rhapsody is sent to Ecuador to find Dr Kholchak, who is conducting field research in the Amazon jungle, out of radio contact.

Harmony, Destiny and Symphony close in on Captain Black, but he turns the tables on them and the three girls are captured. Black's boat has been damaged so he takes the Angels' launch, leaving them tied up on the shore of the lake as the water level rises, menaced by a strange subterranean sea creature. They are rescued by Scarlet and Blue, who have followed them into the caverns, but they are unable to prevent Captain Black from contaminating the main lake.

Accompanied by Juan Alvarez, a young police captain, Rhapsody sets out to locate Dr Kholchak in the jungle, but Alvarez is killed by a Mysteron agent and reconstructed into the Mysterons' service. As they travel up river by power launch, Alvarez makes an attempt on Rhapsody's life. They fight but during the struggle they both fall overboard and Alvarez is eaten by piranhas. Rhapsody makes it to the river bank, where she is captured by a native jungle Indian. He takes her to his village and there she finds Dr Kholchak, who has befriended the Indians. He explains that the Indians will not harm her as they look upon her as a goddess because of the colour of her hair. The doctor is able to supply a formula which will destroy Culture XO and soon Lieutenant Viridian arrives in an SPV to take Rhapsody back to Cloudbase. But after they leave, the Indians turn on Dr Kholchak, killing him in the belief that he has allowed a jungle monster to devour their goddess. Dr Kholchak is reconstructed as a Mysteron agent.

All traces of Culture XO are eliminated with Dr Kholchak's formula, but a week later Cloudbase receives a report from western Canada that 200 acres of wheat have vanished overnight. Symphony is sent to investigate and discovers that the Mysteron Dr Kholchak has released an even more deadly threat than Culture XO: a rapidly growing lichen that eats everything in its path. All five Angels are ordered to attack the creeping menace with atomic missiles, but this only stimulates the lichen's growth. The situation seems hopeless until Harmony lands her aircraft near the edge of the lichen tide to rescue a young girl and notices the lichen flowing around a salt pan instead of through it. The lichen is destroyed by common salt and the Mysterons' plans are foiled again.

Notes

Although the focus of the story is fragmented to allow each of the five Angels a share of the limelight, *The Angels and the Creeping Enemy* is none the less an exciting and successful conclusion to Armada's CAPTAIN SCARLET range, with several very atmospheric scenes - particularly the Angels' pursuit of Captain Black along the chain of underground lakes at Kufra. Once again, the author presents numerous plot twists and changes of location which spin out the action to the very last page.

In the Amber Room, Destiny, Symphony and Rhapsody discuss the threat of Culture XO.

BEYOND CAPTAIN SCARLET 5

THE END OF AN ERA

Towards the end of October 1967, while principal photography was being completed on the last few episodes of CAPTAIN SCARLET AND THE MYSTERONS, the design department and puppet workshop at the Century 21 Studios were gearing up to start filming on the next Supermarionation series, JOE 90. This was something of a departure from the established Gerry Anderson series format, following the adventures of a nine-year-old boy, Joe McClaine, who becomes the most special agent of the World Intelligence Network. His father, Professor Ian 'Mac' McClaine, has developed a special computer, the BIG RAT (Brain Impulse Galvanascope Record And Transfer), which records the brain patterns of experts and transfers their knowledge to little Joe, enabling him to undertake dangerous assignments for WIN without arousing the suspicion of hostile authorities.

Anderson recalls how the idea for JOE 90 developed: 'I read somewhere that the human brain is controlled by electrical impulses and how thoughts are stored electronically. I started toying with the story potential of a process that would allow the recording of brain patterns and transferring them to another brain. I was really likening it to magnetic recording, where material could be stored or transferred to another tape.'

Set in the early years of the twenty-first century, the presentation of Joe's world in design and technology terms was much less advanced than had previously been seen in STINGRAY, THUNDERBIRDS and CAPTAIN SCARLET AND THE MYSTERONS. The emphasis of the series was much more on character than hardware, and the stories were more in the spy thriller genre than science fiction. As Anderson explains, 'The show majored on its characters, which I thought were all very good. The puppets had become so lifelike, I now strongly believed that they could carry the action without the usual massive assistance from futuristic hardware.'

Seated in the Rat Trap, Joe McClaine prepares to receive the brain patterns of a Russian MiG 242 pilot in the JOE 90 episode The Most Special Agent.

None the less, there were fantastical elements to the series that appealed to the audience who had grown up with the earlier Anderson series: Professor McClaine's incredible Jet-Air Car, with the ability to travel on land, in the air and on water, the BIG RAT computer and the Rat Trap, a spinning spherical cage used to channel the brain patterns into Joe's mind, as well as appearances by various super-aircraft, tanks, trains and submarines on an episode-by-episode basis.

Very few new puppets were created specifically for JOE 90. Although the puppets of Joe, his father and their housekeeper, Mrs Harris, were made especially for the series, the two other

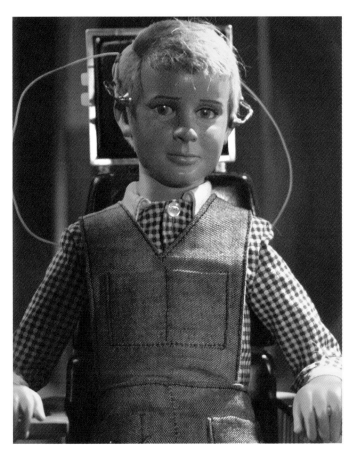

main characters, WIN agents Sam Loover and Shane Weston, were both revamp puppets that had previously appeared as guest characters in CAPTAIN SCARLET – the Sam Loover puppet most notably as the Lunar Controller in *Lunarville 7*, as President Roberts in *The Launching* and as Colgan in *The Inquisition*, and the Shane Weston puppet as Dr Kurnitz in *Dangerous Rendezvous*. In both cases, a new set of heads with a variety of expressions was created for JOE 90, based on the original 'expressionless' sculpts of the puppets' heads, and in addition the Shane Weston puppet was rewigged, its original blond locks replaced by dark brown hair.

Once filming on CAPTAIN SCARLET was completed, the puppets of the main characters were added to the pool of revamp puppets and so a number of the familiar CAPTAIN SCARLET faces reappeared as different characters in JOE 90. Colonel White took three major guest roles, as Sam Loover's father, Dr Willie Loover, in *Relative Danger*, Sir George Harris in *Trial at Sea*, and the corrupt businessman Ralph Clayton in *See You Down There*. Two Lieutenant Green puppets appeared side by side in *King for a Day* as twin palace guards. Destiny Angel was an air hostess in the same episode and also appeared as a concert guest in *International Concerto*. Symphony Angel portrayed a stewardess in *Operation McClaine* and various background characters in *International Concerto*, *Double Agent* and *Colonel McClaine*. Rhapsody Angel turned up as a nurse in *Operation McClaine* and a hospital visitor in *Relative Danger*.

Captain Ochre was seen as Dr Loover's colleague Banning in *Relative Danger*, a guard in *The Professional*, WIN agents in *Attack of the Tiger* and *Mission X-41*, the villainous high priest in *Child of the Sun God*, and a truck driver in *Viva Cordova*. Captain Grey was a helijet pilot in *Colonel McClaine*, Lieutenant Burns in *The Race*, Hawkins in *Mission X-41* and various background characters in *International Concerto* and *Viva Cordova*. Captain Magenta appeared in a string of roles as soldiers or guards in *Big Fish*, *The Fortress* and *The Race*, as well as an engineer in *Test Flight*. Dr Fawn made a notable appearance as Fearless Foley in *Attack of the Tiger* but was also seen in minor roles in *Big Fish*, *The Fortress*, *The Professional*, *Trial at Sea* and as two separate characters in *Viva Cordova*. The villain of the latter episode, General Valdes, was portrayed by

JOE 90

(episodes listed in official ITC recommended broadcast order)

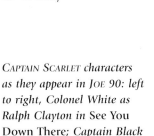

CAPTAIN SCARLET characters as they appear in JOE 90: left to right, Colonel White as Ralph Clayton in See You Down There; *Captain Black as General Valdes in* Viva Cordova; *Captain Ochre as Agent 26 in* Attack of the Tiger.

Professor McClaine's Jet-Air Car outside his cottage at Culver Bay, Dorset, in JOE 90.

An Angel Interceptor from CAPTAIN SCARLET re-dressed as a MiG 242 fighter plane in the JOE 90 episode The Most Special Agent.

Captain Black and his political opponent Juan Cordova was the World President, also seen as Dr Sherman in *Operation McClaine*, Colonel Henderson in *Business Holiday*, the Canadian prime minister in *Breakout* and Brad Johnson in *Test Flight*. He also appeared in minor roles in *International Concerto* and *Child of the Sun God*.

Filming on JOE 90 began on Monday 13 November 1967, just weeks after principal photography was completed on CAPTAIN SCARLET's final episode, and continued until mid-August 1968. As had largely been the case with CAPTAIN SCARLET, Gerry Anderson was less hands-on in his role as producer on JOE 90 than he had been on his earlier Supermarionation programmes. During production of JOE 90, he was initially supervising post-production on the *Thunderbird 6* feature film and then became closely involved with Century 21's major live-action feature film *Doppelgänger*. This was a stylish and thought-provoking science-fiction thriller about a manned mission to a planet on the far side of the sun, ultimately revealed to be a mirror-image duplicate of Earth. With principal photography shot from July to October 1968, *Doppelgänger* progressed through the design and planning stages of pre-production throughout much of JOE 90's production period, so Anderson entrusted the role of producer on the Supermarionation series to David Lane.

Lane remembers, 'I was asked to take over as producer on JOE 90 because after directing the two THUNDERBIRDS feature films, I had an understanding of every aspect of production on those shows. Lew Grade was only prepared for Gerry to go off and do these movies if the other side, the television series side of things, kept running successfully. Gerry thought that I was the obvious person to run the shop for him.

'JOE 90 was a great little programme. I was responsible for looking at the scripts, the effects, the puppets – the whole thing really. I was doing what Gerry had done on the earlier programmes but I think I took on too much myself and I didn't delegate well. I wanted to do it all myself and that was a mistake. Having said that, I'm really proud of JOE 90. I wanted to get back to the traditional themes of STINGRAY and THUNDERBIRDS, with a little bit of humour along with the action. I liked the idea of it all being a sort of family thing and I also liked the puppets themselves more than the ones in CAPTAIN SCARLET. They had more character and were a bit of a move back to the earlier characters. The Spectrum puppets were all sort of "pretty boys", everyone was good-looking and all the Angels were very sexy and beautiful, but in JOE 90 we had old-lady housekeepers and that sort thing, which I personally thought was much better.'

Unfortunately, JOE 90 failed to emulate the success of its predecessors, and this, together with Anderson's increasing desire to dispense with puppets altogether and move into live-action television production, spelled the beginning of the end for Supermarionation. The final series, THE SECRET SERVICE, began pre-production in late summer 1968, adding to the frenzy of activity at the Century 21 Studios. Set in the present day, THE SECRET SERVICE developed the espionage theme of JOE 90 with another unlikely secret agent – a parish priest. The series also expanded on Anderson's ideas of modelling the puppets' facial features on those of recognized actors who would then provide the puppets' voices, as suggested in the planning stages of CAPTAIN SCARLET.

Anderson was working on *Doppelgänger* at Pinewood Studios when he bumped into popular raconteur, entertainer and comedy actor Stanley Unwin, best known for his own nonsensical language, Unwinese. Unwin was taking a break from post-synching dialogue on *Chitty Chitty Bang Bang* (1968) when Anderson proposed the idea of creating a puppet television series that would feature him as the lead character. Anderson recalls, 'I have always enjoyed Stanley's work and find him very amusing. As far as I was concerned, Stanley came first and then the idea had to accommodate him. It wasn't that the show called for someone who could speak gobbledegook, it was a question of how we could fit him into the storyline.'

For THE SECRET SERVICE, Unwin became Father Stanley Unwin, operative of BISHOP (British Intelligence Service Headquarters Operation Priest), an unlikely secret agent who owns the Minimiser, a miniaturization device concealed in a Bible. He uses this device to shrink his assistant, Matthew Harding, to puppet size, thus enabling them to infiltrate areas that are inaccessible to other British Intelligence agents. Faced with opposition from those in authority, Father Unwin spouts gobbledegook to confuse the situation.

Mary Turner sculpted a puppet for the BISHOP agent that bore an uncanny resemblance to its real-life counterpart, and Unwin not only voiced the character but also appeared in person in live-action footage shot on location. This provided the programme-makers with the perfect solution to the problem of getting the puppets to walk convincingly, and the present-day setting for the series enabled a second unit team to go on location with Unwin to film inserts of the character driving his car (an antique Model T Ford named Gabriel) around the countryside, arriving at his destination, alighting from the car, walking to the door and going inside.

Ken Turner was assigned to organize and direct these live-action sequences. 'What became apparent quite soon into the production of the series was that we had to

Puppeteer Christine Glanville operates the Shane Weston puppet on the set of the character's WIN HQ office for a scene in JOE 90.

Left below: Filming an under-control Joe McClaine puppet for JOE 90.

Director Ken Turner prepares a scene for the JOE 90 *episode* Operation McClaine.

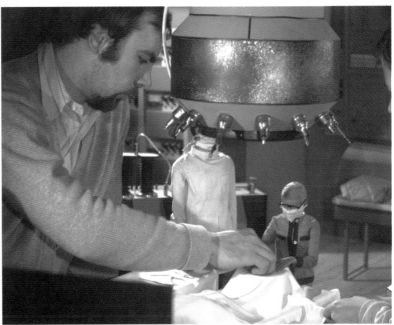

THE SECRET SERVICE

(episodes listed in official ITC
recommended broadcast order)

*Top right: Mrs Appleby
brings Father Unwin and
Matthew Harding a lunch of
raw carrots (THE SECRET
SERVICE – The Cure).*

*Bottom left: Father Stanley
Unwin, agent of BISHOP
(THE SECRET SERVICE –
Hole in One).*

*Bottom right: Father Unwin
tinkers with Gabriel, his
Model T Ford (THE SECRET
SERVICE – Errand of Mercy).*

totally rethink the order in which we filmed material. On THUNDERBIRDS, CAPTAIN SCARLET and JOE 90, all the puppet stuff was done first and if any live-action inserts or exteriors were needed, they would be shot later to fit in with what had been done on the puppet stages. With THE SECRET SERVICE that was the wrong way to do it – somebody had to shoot the location stuff first and then hand it over to the director so that he could fit his puppet stuff to match. It seemed a bit back to front to us at first, but with that programme it was what worked out the best. You had to think about the script and where you would be cutting to a puppet shot, or to a close-up of Stanley, or to a car shooting down a country lane. It was a very complicated little programme, in actual fact, because of all the elements involved: the puppets, the live-action and, of course, the model stuff that Derek's boys would be doing.'

Two other new puppets were sculpted for THE SECRET SERVICE to portray Unwin's British Intelligence superior, The Bishop, and Unwin's housekeeper, Mrs Appleby, a puppet which Christine Glanville based on her own mother. BISHOP agent Matthew Harding had originally been seen as Dr Mitchell in the CAPTAIN SCARLET episode *Treble Cross* and had gone on to play a variety of roles in JOE 90, most notably Constable Lewis in *The Unorthodox Shepherd*. For THE SECRET SERVICE, a new set of heads with different expressions was created for the Matthew character, and his formerly grey hair was replaced with a blond wig.

The last of THE SECRET SERVICE's regular characters was BISHOP agent Blake, but even a change of hair colour and a pair of glasses could not disguise the fact that the puppet chosen to portray him was none other than Captain Scarlet himself. The character appeared in four episodes, *A Question of Miracles*, *Last Train to Bufflers Halt*, *The Deadly Whisper* and *The Cure*. Rather better disguised was Captain Blue, who turned up with brown hair as Professor Graham in *Recall to Service* and, later on, as the ill-fated tool-maker Joe in *May-day, May-day!*

Other CAPTAIN SCARLET puppets reappeared in THE SECRET SERVICE. Colonel White became desalination plant controller Brooks in *A Question of Miracles* and the villainous Sir Humphrey Burton in *To Catch a Spy*. Captain Ochre appeared in no fewer than six episodes, most notably as John Masden in *The Feathered Spies* and Burrows in *The Cure*, but also in lesser roles in *A Case for the Bishop*, *To Catch a Spy*, *Last Train to Bufflers Halt* and *The Deadly Whisper*. Captain Grey

turned up again as the desalination plant designer Tom Williams in *A Question of Miracles*, Colonel Blair in *Recall to Service*, the villainous Brother Thomas in *School for Spies* and a pilot in *May-day, May-day!* Captain Magenta appeared as various background characters in *A Case for the Bishop*, *A Question of Miracles*, *Hole in One* and *More Haste Less Speed*. Dr Fawn appeared as British Intelligence agent Saunders in *A Case for the Bishop* and *To Catch a Spy*, and once again Captain Black portrayed a villain, Kroner, in *The Deadly Whisper*.

Unfortunately, the series did not go down too well with Lew Grade. In December 1968, Anderson screened the first episode, *A Case for the Bishop*, for him and as soon as Father Unwin began to talk in Unwinese, Grade stopped the screening and told Anderson that he was cancelling the series, claiming that viewers in America would not be able to understand what Unwin was saying. 'The point that no one was supposed to understand Father Unwin seemed to have escaped him,' explains Anderson. 'As far as Lew was concerned, it was a mistake so that was the end of that.' Only thirteen episodes of THE SECRET SERVICE were made.

At the time, Anderson was not entirely unhappy with Grade's decision, for the cancellation of THE SECRET SERVICE was tempered by the news that Grade wanted him to make a live-action science-fiction series. While *Doppelgänger* was still in post-production, and with the last few episodes of THE SECRET SERVICE being filmed, Gerry and Sylvia Anderson began work on UFO, a twenty-six episode series with a budget of £2,500,000, nearly as much as the cost of THUNDERBIRDS and CAPTAIN SCARLET AND THE MYSTERONS combined. The two puppet soundstages at Slough were to be transformed into visual effects stages, giving Derek Meddings and his team three entire stages on which to construct much larger model sets than had previously been possible. The rest of the production team would be relocated at the MGM British Studios in Borehamwood in preparation to begin principal photography on UFO there on Monday 28 April 1969.

The Century 21 puppet stages closed their doors on Friday 24 January 1969 with the completion of filming on THE SECRET SERVICE. As puppeteer Rowena White recalls, 'It was very sad when it all packed up. I found a note recently in an old diary for that day – "Last day. All had champagne...Cried." And that about sums it up, I suppose.' The Supermarionation era had come to an end.

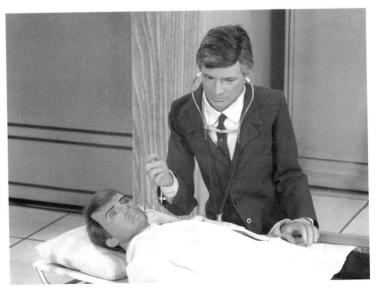

Top left: Captain Scarlet appears as BISHOP agent Blake in THE SECRET SERVICE *episode* A Question of Miracles.

*Top right: Undercover at Port Trennick desalination plant, Blake prepares to swallow a capsule supplied by the Bishop (*THE SECRET SERVICE *– A Question of Miracles).*

Right: The World President from CAPTAIN SCARLET *appears as a doctor who attends to the apparently dying agent Blake (Captain Scarlet) at the Port Trennick desalination plant (*THE SECRET SERVICE *– A Question of Miracles).*

The cover of TV World magazine for the week of CAPTAIN SCARLET's *first UK transmission.*

ATV MIDLANDS SCHEDULE
Friday, 29 September 1967

4.45	TINGHA AND TUCKER CLUB
5.00	HOW
5.25	CAPTAIN SCARLET AND THE MYSTERONS — The Mysterons
5.55	NEWS
6.05	MIDLANDS NEWS
6.15	ATV TODAY
6.35	CROSSROADS
7.00	SPORTSWEEK
7.30	THE PRISONER — Arrival
8.30	BAKER'S HALF DOZEN — Crimewave
9.00	INHERITANCE — Murder
10.00	NEWS AT TEN
10.30	THE UNTOUCHABLES — The Maggie Storm Story
11.25	CHIEF OFFICER
11.40	ALL OUR YESTERDAYS
12.08	EPILOGUE

BACK FROM THE DEAD

The closure of the Century 21 puppet studios was still some fifteen months in the future when CAPTAIN SCARLET AND THE MYSTERONS was unveiled to the British viewing public for the first time. Although the first episode had already received an unscheduled premiere five months earlier as a late-night test transmission in the London area (Saturday 29 April 1967), CAPTAIN SCARLET AND THE MYSTERONS made its formal debut on British television in the ATV Midlands region of the ITV network at 5.25 p.m. on Friday 29 September 1967. The series was screened in the ATV London area from the following Sunday 1 October 1967, and began to appear in other ITV regions shortly afterwards – Granada on Thursday 5 October, Anglia on Friday 20 October, and Southern, Westward and Channel on Sunday 22 October – although some regions held the series back until early 1968.

Viewer response was generally very positive, with ratings increasing in the ATV Midlands region alone from 450,000 for the opening episode to 1,100,000 by midway through the series. Indeed, the programme made such an impact on the general public that the producers of ATV's popular Saturday-evening live game show THE GOLDEN SHOT decided to devote their Christmas special edition to CAPTAIN SCARLET. Hosted by Bob Monkhouse, THE GOLDEN SHOT consisted of a series of shooting games in which viewers at home would, by telephone, direct a blindfolded marksman to fire a crossbow at illuminated apples fixed to illustrated backgrounds. For the CAPTAIN SCARLET edition, each of the target boards featured painted scenes from the series – the Mysteron complex, Angel Interceptors, Spectrum Helicopter and the Angels leaving the Amber Room on their injector seats. CAPTAIN SCARLET himself was the star guest (referred to as the 'Golden Partner'), with the puppet seen sitting at Colonel White's desk while Francis Matthews provided the voice off-camera. A musical interlude was provided by The Spectrum, who sang their latest hit, 'Headin' for a Heatwave', and hostesses Anne Aston and Carol Dilworth appeared in Angel uniforms. The programme was broadcast live in the ATV London region at 8.35 p.m. on Saturday 23 December 1967 and then shown next day at 1.05 p.m. in the ATV Midlands region. Sadly, all archive recordings of this programme were wiped some years ago.

Also seen on commercial television in the UK at this time were a trio of CAPTAIN SCARLET advertisements made for product licensees Kellogg's and Lyons Maid by Century 21 using the studio puppets on the original puppet sets. The first two of these, advertising Kellogg's Sugar Smacks cereal, were directed by Ken Turner. In one, Captain Scarlet, Colonel White, Destiny, Symphony and Harmony advocated the energizing benefits of eating Sugar Smacks, revealing that 'all Spectrum agents eat Kellogg's Sugar Smacks for breakfast', while in the other, Captain Scarlet was seen driving an SPV and announcing a new offer from Sugar Smacks: a series of six metal badges to be found in cereal packs. The third commercial, for Lyons Maid's new Orbit ice lolly, told how the Mysterons had taken control of the Post Office Tower and thrown the European communications network into confusion. Captain Scarlet

launched Orbit (the big ice cream on a stick) and the ice lolly flew around the wobbling Post Office Tower, stabilizing it and restoring communications.

Overseas, CAPTAIN SCARLET AND THE MYSTERONS was seen in more than forty countries, with syndicated television screenings in North America, Canada, Australia, New Zealand and Japan in 1968. An extensive promotional tour of Japan was announced in the press, accompanied by pictures of British Overseas Airways Corporation stewardess Marjorie Harris posing with the Captain Scarlet, Captain Blue, Colonel White and Destiny puppets. Similarly, to assist promotions in New Zealand, Miss World contestant Pamela McLeod (Miss New Zealand) was photographed on the Cloudbase lounge set with the Captain Scarlet, Captain Blue and Symphony puppets when she visited the Century 21 Studios.

The initial UK broadcast of the series came to an end on Tuesday 14 May 1968 in the ATV Midlands region, but, much like Scarlet himself, CAPTAIN SCARLET AND THE MYSTERONS has proved indestructible to British television audiences, returning again and again over the last thirty years. In the ATV Midlands region alone, the series was repeated in its entirety three times through to September 1973 and with ITV colour transmissions having begun on 15 November 1969, CAPTAIN SCARLET was seen for the first time in colour during the initial ATV Midlands repeat run from 27 December 1969 to 1 August 1970. A fourth and final repeat screening by ATV Midlands ran from 1 January 1974, but not all of the episodes were shown. Viewers in other regions were lucky to see episodes at all: in the Yorkshire Television region, for example, there were no repeats of CAPTAIN SCARLET until the series was purchased by the whole ITV network for a new screening in 1985–6.

UFO made its debut on ATV Midlands at 8.00 p.m. on Wednesday 16 September 1970. Starring Ed Bishop, George Sewell and Michael Billington, the series was seen by some critics as a live-action remake of CAPTAIN SCARLET AND THE MYSTERONS, with its concept of a secret organization battling to protect the Earth from extraterrestrial Aliens. However, the similarity between the two programmes really ends there.

The Aliens in UFO are humanoid members of a dying race from Alpha Centauri who come to Earth initially in search of a convenient supply of body parts that they can use in transplant surgery. Later on, their motives change as they require complete host bodies in which to supplant their consciousness. SHADO (Supreme Headquarters Alien Defence Organization) is established specifically to combat this Alien threat, and exists in total secrecy from the general public, who are blissfully ignorant of the menace from space. Certainly SHADO has an array of futuristic vehicles with which to defend Earth and the Aliens occasionally take control of ordinary people to do their bidding, but none of the SHADO operatives is indestructible and the Aliens' *modus operandi* has nothing to do with resurrecting the dead.

SHADO Interceptors, housed in craters on the Moon in UFO.

Opposite page: BOAC stewardess Marjorie Harris with CAPTAIN SCARLET puppets en route to Japan.

Bottom left: Ed Bishop as Commander Ed Straker and George Sewell as Colonel Alec Freeman in the UFO episode E.S.P.

SHADO Mobiles search a Canadian forest for an Alien spacecraft in the UFO episode Computer Affair.

Top left: The Hawkwing, atmospheric interceptor aircraft piloted by Kate Kestrel and Hawkeye (TERRAHAWKS).

Middle: Zelda's space fleet, based on the surface of Mars (TERRAHAWKS).

Above: The Battlehawk transporter craft mounted by the Terrahawk mobile command centre (TERRAHAWKS).

A better case for a CAPTAIN SCARLET remake could be levelled at Gerry Anderson's 1983 series TERRAHAWKS, made in association with London Weekend Television. Filmed at Bray Studios from January 1983 to August 1984, TERRAHAWKS was a return to puppetry for Anderson after fourteen years, apart from an unsuccessful television pilot THE INVESTIGATOR, made on location in Malta in 1972 with a pair of CAPTAIN SCARLET-style puppets, and ALIEN ATTACK, a commercial for Jif dessert toppings made in 1977 with the INVESTIGATOR puppets. However, rather than using string puppets again, TERRAHAWKS employed a sophisticated form of glove puppet with radio-controlled eyes in a process which became known as Supermacromation.

Set in the year 2020, TERRAHAWKS follows the adventures of an élite fighting force as they defend the Earth against alien androids based on Mars. Much like the Mysterons, these androids are not indigenous to the Red Planet. Led by the witch-queen Zelda, the androids had journeyed from the planet Guk in Alpha Centauri, where they had overthrown their oppressive humanoid creators and now sought vengeance on all human life for their crimes against the defenceless machines that they had created. In response to Zelda's initial attack on a NASA research station on Mars, the UN High Command devised and established a small, dedicated team called the Terrahawks, based at the secret Hawknest headquarters in South America and equipped with a fleet of sophisticated vehicles to defend the planet from Zelda's forces.

The commander of the Terrahawks is Dr Tiger Ninestein, one of nine clones of Professor Gerhard Stein created in 1973 and placed in different parts of the world to grow up under a cloak of secrecy. After a distinguished military career in which he established himself as a superb military tactician and a tough, relentless fighter, Ninestein was persuaded to mastermind the creation of the Terrahawks Earth Defence Squadron and to become its first commander. Every twenty-four hours, he plugs into his personal Data Dump to store his total knowledge, memories and experience so that in the event of his death his brain patterns can be transferred to one of the other Stein clones.

This process occurred in the third episode of the series, *Gold*, in which the original Tiger Ninestein, seen in the two previous episodes, is killed by a booby trap. A second clone is brought to Hawknest, receives Ninestein's brain patterns and becomes the new Tiger Ninestein, who commands the Terrahawks for the remaining episodes. (Unfortunately, the impact of killing off the hero early in the series and replacing him with an exact duplicate, as the producers originally intended, was lost in the original broadcasts when *Gold* was held back and screened as the final episode.)

The similarities of format will not be lost on CAPTAIN

SCARLET viewers: an alien intelligence that has settled on Mars wages a war of vengeance on the people of Earth; an élite World Government-authorized security force with the most advanced weaponry and equipment at its disposal defends the planet; the leading operative of this security force is killed by the aliens and replaced by a duplicate with the knowledge and experience of the original man. Tiger Ninestein even shared a measure of Captain Scarlet's indestructibility given that he could be killed and 'resurrected' at least another seven times, while some of Zelda's incredible powers had similarities with those of the Mysterons, such as the ability to control and transfer matter, and to create android duplicates of innocent humans. However, whereas there was little humour in CAPTAIN SCARLET, TERRAHAWKS thrived on it, being more overtly comedic in execution than any Gerry Anderson series since SUPERCAR.

Enormously popular on its initial run, TERRAHAWKS was regularly watched by more than 5 million viewers during its first season. The series premiered in most regions on the ITV network on Sunday 8 October 1983 and the thirty-nine episodes were broadcast as three seasons of thirteen episodes over the next three years.

Members of the TERRAHAWKS puppet cast: left to right, Terrahawks commander Dr Tiger Ninestein; Captain Mary Falconer; Captain Kate Kestrel; Zelda, Imperial Queen of the planet Guk.

Japanese video release of the CAPTAIN SCARLET compilation TV movie Revenge of the Mysterons from Mars.

Meanwhile, in America, Robert Mandell, the Vice-President of Creative Services at ITC's New York office, had been supervising the production of a series of feature-length Gerry Anderson presentations. These were created by splicing together similarly themed television episodes with the intention of reintroducing American viewers to the Anderson shows and, it was hoped, paving the way for renewed syndication sales of the complete series. Packaged under the banner of 'Super Space Theater', these TV movies were then sold to pay-cable and syndicated stations for afternoon family programming.

Working closely with *Starlog* magazine correspondent (and keen Anderson fan) David Hirsch, Mandell developed two CAPTAIN SCARLET features: REVENGE OF THE MYSTERONS FROM MARS (a compilation of *Shadow of Fear, Lunarville 7, Crater 101* and *Dangerous Rendezvous*) and CAPTAIN SCARLET VERSUS THE MYSTERONS (*The Mysterons, Winged Assassin, Seek and Destroy* and *Attack on Cloudbase*). Both films abandoned the existing opening title sequence in favour of a new video-animated title sequence, overlaid garish video-generated laser-beam effects in place of missile launches and cut some two minutes from each of the episodes to bring the total combined running time to ninety-five minutes (the maximum length for a two-hour commercial slot on American television). REVENGE OF THE MYSTERONS FROM MARS remained generally faithful to the original material, but CAPTAIN SCARLET VERSUS THE MYSTERONS incorporated an additional sequence featuring a hideous video-generated pyramid with a voice-over which suggested that the events of *Attack on Cloudbase* had actually taken place rather than being a dream.

Abhorred by the series' fans, these two films ultimately had a beneficial effect in two respects. First, they gave American viewers the opportunity to see at least some episodes of a television series that had not been shown there since the late 1960s. Second, their UK home video release by Channel 5 Video in 1986 was so successful that the company was encouraged to issue the remaining twenty-four episodes in their original uncut format. This was some consolation for viewers who had

Fleetway's Captain Scarlet and the Mysterons *comic, issue 6 (1 January 1994), with cover illustration by Mike Noble.*

failed to make their own video recordings of the episodes during the final ITV network screening in 1985–6 and would otherwise have had to wait for CAPTAIN SCARLET's next UK television appearance seven years later.

Hard on the heels of THUNDERBIRDS and STINGRAY, both of which had been successfully relaunched by the BBC in the previous two years, CAPTAIN SCARLET AND THE MYSTERONS made a triumphant return to British screens at 6.00 p.m. on Friday 1 October 1993 with its first ever network broadcast (all parts of the country receiving the same episode simultaneously) on BBC2. Screened on the BBC's 'minority interest' channel, the opening episode (*The Mysterons*) attracted an audience of over 4 million viewers, ranking third in the BBC2 ratings chart for that week and beating that week's episode of STAR TREK by more than half a million viewers.

The series' return received a great deal of enthusiastic press coverage in the weeks leading up to the relaunch as reports of the BBC's new autumn season line-up were spearheaded by the twenty-six-year-old programme. Unexpected additional attention focused on the series' political correctness (or perceived lack of it) when criticism was aimed at the use of the names White and Black to represent the good and bad characters respectively. The programme had been targeted by the anti-racism lobby to illustrate their objection to the everyday use of the word 'black' to convey evil or villainy, arguing that when the same word is used to describe skin colour, young people become confused and equate ethnic difference with wrongdoing. Unfortunately, they made a terrible mistake by choosing CAPTAIN SCARLET to make their point, since Captain Black, the villain, is white while all of the ethnic characters, Lieutenant Green, Melody Angel and Harmony Angel, are on the side of good. The media's attempt to brand the series as racist and politically incorrect backfired and left the people involved in the campaign with egg on their faces when Gerry Anderson pointed out that CAPTAIN SCARLET AND THE MYSTERONS had been one of the first children's television series to feature ethnic characters in major heroic roles. As a series which provided positive role models for children of ethnic origin, CAPTAIN SCARLET should have been lauded by the anti-racism lobby rather than ridiculed.

The bad press didn't deter viewers and as Christmas 1993 approached, the country was gripped by SCARLET fever as the shops were flooded with new CAPTAIN SCARLET merchandise. Boxtree Books, Ravette Books and Hodder & Stoughton all added new CAPTAIN SCARLET books to their existing ranges of THUNDERBIRDS and STINGRAY books, Wesco launched a talking CAPTAIN SCARLET alarm clock, King International produced a set of five CAPTAIN SCARLET jigsaws, and Fleetway Editions published a *Captain Scarlet and the Mysterons* fortnightly comic which reprinted classic *Captain Scarlet* and *Zero X* comic strips from *TV Century 21* alongside brand-new strips written by Alan Fennell and Graeme Bassett, with art by Barrie Mitchell, Mike White and John Cooper.

Other CAPTAIN SCARLET merchandise followed: LCD games and walkie-talkies; socks, vests, briefs, boxer shorts, sweat tops, jogging pants, pyjamas and slippers; bubble bath, shaped soaps and toothbrushes; bowls, plates, napkins, tablecloths, mugs, cups and sports bottles; toffee popcorn, chocolate mini-rolls, cakes, yoghurt and fromage frais; stickers, badges and fridge magnets; balloons, birthday cards, gift wrap and gift tags; playing cards, board games and playsuits; duvet covers, valences, sheets, pillowcases and curtains, as well as Christmas crackers, pasta shapes and wellington boots!

The runaway success story of the 1993 CAPTAIN SCARLET Christmas was that of the newly formed Vivid Imaginations company, which had been established by a group of former Matchbox employees. On 25 September 1993, they launched a range of CAPTAIN SCARLET action toys which comprised a set of action figures, die-cast vehicles, a 12-inch Captain Scarlet jointed doll, and a Cloudbase playset in scale to the die-cast vehicles. Within ten weeks, the company had sold over £10 million worth of CAPTAIN SCARLET toys and the Cloudbase playset became the toy that every kid wanted for Christmas that year, equalling the sales of Matchbox's THUNDERBIRDS Tracy Island playset in 1992. The following year, the company went on to produce Angel Interceptor and SPV playsets in scale to their action figures, a 12-inch Captain Black doll and additional action figures, all of which sold in greater numbers than anyone at Vivid Imaginations might have expected, and launched the company on its way to becoming one of the UK's most successful toy manufacturers.

Vivid Imaginations' 1993 Captain Scarlet Spectrum Command Team set, a boxed set of the company's die-cast SSC, SPV, SPJ and Angel Interceptor toys.

Vivid Imaginations' managing director Nick Austin recalls, 'CAPTAIN SCARLET was an amazing property with which to kick-start the business because the range was designed and manufactured in eight months, crashing the normal lead-times by four months. We had no choice but to do that because the BBC planned to air the show from September 1993. The consequences of missing that in-store date would have been catastrophic, as most of the company's working capital was tied up in the project. It was undoubtedly the biggest commercial risk that we have ever taken, yet at the time we all felt very comfortable with it as we knew that the collectors and kids would devour the product in the same way that they had done with THUNDERBIRDS the year before.'

Six years later, Gerry Anderson was commissioned by Carlton International Media, the new owners of the seven Supermarionation television series, to look into the possibility of re-creating the Supermarionation titles for a twenty-first-century television audience. CAPTAIN SCARLET was selected for trials of an innovative process of computer-graphic imaging similar to that currently being used on major motion pictures. Produced at the London-based Moving Picture Company, the resulting four-minute test film, *Captain Scarlet and the Return of the*

SPV Mark II production design illustration by Steven Begg for Gerry Anderson's **Captain Scarlet and the Return of the Mysterons** CGI test film.

Above and opposite: scenes from Gerry Anderson's **Captain Scarlet and the Return of the Mysterons** *CGI test film.*

Mysterons, re-created the appearance of the original puppet characters but was rendered entirely with computer animation, which enabled them to run, jump and fight with fluid movements for the first time.

Miniature busts of the heads of Captain Scarlet, Captain Black and Captain Blue were sculpted by Mackinnon and Saunders, who had created the puppets for Anderson's stop-motion animated children's series LAVENDER CASTLE. The busts were then cyber-scanned to create computer models of the three main characters that retained the likenesses of the original series puppets. Mime actors Andrew Dawson (Captain Scarlet), Rob Thirtle (Captain Black) and Wayne Forester (Captain Blue) performed the action sequences required for the characters with sensors attached at key points all over their bodies so that their movements could be recorded digitally and transferred to three 3D computer-generated figures using sophisticated motion-capture technology.

Original series voice artists Francis Matthews and Ed Bishop reprised their roles as Captain Scarlet and Captain Blue respectively, while Gary Martin replaced the late Donald Gray to provide vocals for Captain Black and the voice of the Mysterons. All three voice artists were fitted with sensors which recorded their facial movements while performing the dialogue and this information was imposed on the computer-generated character heads so as to match the dialogue to realistic facial expressions.

Visual effects supervisor Steven Begg subtly revamped the original designs of the Spectrum Saloon Car (renamed the Spectrum Patrol Car), Spectrum Pursuit Vehicle and Angel Interceptor to give them the appearance of having been modified with new technology. These vehicles were computer-modelled and textured with Maya 3D software and then animated to fulfil the requirements of the script.

A complete adventure in itself, the *Captain Scarlet and the Return of the Mysterons* test film takes place a few years after the end of the original Supermarionation series and sets the scene for a renewal of the Mysterons' war of nerves with Spectrum.

CAPTAIN SCARLET
End Titles Song
Lyrics by Barry Gray

Captain Scarlet!
He's the one who knows
The Mysteron game
And things they plan.

Captain Scarlet!
To his Martian foes,
A dangerous name,
A superman.

They crash him
And his body may burn,
They smash him,
But they know he'll return
To live again.

Captain Scarlet!
As the Angels are flying
Wing to wing
Into the scene,
Spectrum is Green!

Captain Scarlet!
Though the Mysterons plan to
*   conquer the Earth,*
This indestructible man will show
*   what he's worth.*

Captain Scarlet!
Indestructible Captain Scarlet!

CAPTAIN SCARLET AND THE RETURN OF THE MYSTERONS
Written and directed by **Gerry Anderson and John Needham**

The Cloudbase control room has been refitted with upgraded computers and communications equipment and Captains Scarlet and Blue, returning to Spectrum after a long absence, are admiring the new set-up when Captain Black arrives. He reminds them that he is no longer under the control of the Mysterons and has been cleared for access by the computer. However, after Scarlet leaves for an important meeting, Black is revealed to be still acting as a Mysteron agent when he knocks Blue down and takes control of his mind.

Driving at breakneck speed along a mountain road in one of Spectrum's new SPVs, Captain Scarlet pursues Captains Black and Blue, who are heading for the atomic power station at Drontenon in a new Spectrum Patrol Car filled with explosives. As the SPC crosses a bridge which spans a deep ravine, Black ejects an explosive device which destroys the bridge once the SPC has reached the other side. Scarlet activates rocket booster motors and the SPV flies across the ravine, landing on the other side with only yards to spare and careering out of control ahead of the SPC. Scarlet ejects from the SPV, jumping out on to the road, rolling over into a firing position to shoot at the tyres of the fast-approaching SPC. The car skids out of control towards the edge of the ravine, hitting a boulder at the roadside, and the impact throws Blue out just

before the car plunges over the edge into the ravine. The explosives aboard detonate on impact.

As Captain Blue shakes off Captain Black's control over him, Captain Scarlet helps him to his feet. On the floor of the ravine, Black rises from the wreckage of the SPC, while above Scarlet realizes that this is just the beginning...

VOICE CAST			
Captain Scarlet	**Francis Matthews**	Destiny Angel	**Leone Connery**
Captain Blue	**Ed Bishop**	Voice of the Mysterons	**Gary Martin**
Captain Black	**Gary Martin**		

Part of the Vivid Imaginations 2001 range of CAPTAIN SCARLET *toys: top, Spectrum Saloon Car, Spectrum Helicopter and Angel Interceptor; bottom, Spectrum Cloudbase Playset.*

The full test film was screened in public for the first time to a packed auditorium of some 400 Gerry Anderson fans at Fanderson's *Century 21* convention in Allesley, Coventry, on 7 October 2000, and then again in front of a more general audience as part of a lecture delivered by Anderson at the Culham Science Centre in Abingdon, Oxfordshire, on 21 March 2001. On both occasions, the film was very enthusiastically received by the audience, but Anderson stressed that, while he would dearly love to be able to make a full new series of CAPTAIN SCARLET using the CGI techniques employed in the test film, the processes involved would be expensive and time-consuming, requiring a very significant financial commitment.

Thirty-four years after it first appeared, CAPTAIN SCARLET AND THE MYSTERONS returned again to British television in September 2001, this time in a spectacular new digital transfer prepared by BBC Resources. Painstakingly cleaned and colour-corrected, the new digital remastering improved the audiovisual quality of each of the thirty-two episodes beyond all expectations and it was no exaggeration when Carlton International Media announced that 'CAPTAIN SCARLET has never looked or sounded better!' Once again, the BBC2 screening was accompanied by a completely new range of merchandise, including a boxed set of the entire series on DVD, books, calendars, computer games and a new range of talking vehicle toys and dolls from Vivid Imaginations.

Although the series tends to live in the shadow of THUNDERBIRDS, CAPTAIN SCARLET AND THE MYSTERONS has illustrated time and again that it is still one of the best-loved and most fondly remembered children's television programmes of the 1960s, and remains just as popular with the British public as ever before. Seen by many as the pinnacle of Gerry Anderson's achievements in Supermarionation, CAPTAIN SCARLET has proved its longevity and durability in a way that is matched by few other British television series of its era, and will continue to delight new generations of children well into the twenty-first century.

INDEX

Also available from
Carlton Books:

Supermarionation Cross-Sections
1 84222 4 11 5 £14.99

Captain Scarlet Annual 2002
1 84222 404 2 £6.99

Captain Scarlet Sticker Book
1 84222 403 9 £3.99

**Thunderbirds International
Rescue Annual 2002**
1 84222 375 5 £6.99

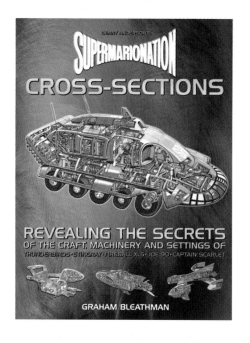

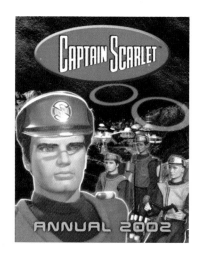

Also available from Carlton Video:

Captain Scarlet VHS Volume 1
(episodes 1-4) Sept 2001

Captain Scarlet VHS Volume 2
(episodes 5-18) Sept 2001

Captain Scarlet VHS Volume 3
(episodes 9-12) Nov 2001

Captain Scarlet VHS Volume 4
(episodes 13-16) Nov 2001

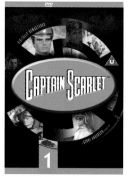

Captain Scarlet DVD Box set –
Complete Series Sept 2001

Captain Scarlet VHS Box Set –
Complete Series Sept 2001

Captain Scarlet DVD Volume 1
(episodes 1-6) Sept 2001

Captain Scarlet DVD Volume 2
(episodes 7-12) Sept 2001

Captain Scarlet VHS Volume 5 (episodes 17-20) Jan 2002

Captain Scarlet VHS Volume 6 (episodes 21-24) Jan 2002

Captain Scarlet VHS Volume7 (episodes 25-28) March 2002

Captain Scarlet VHS Volume 8 (episodes 29-32) March 2002

Captain Scarlet DVD Volume 3 (episodes 13-18)
Sept 2001

Captain Scarlet DVD Volume 4 (episodes 19-24)
Sept 2001

Captain Scarlet DVD Volume 5 (episodes 25-31)
Sept 2001